How Open Is
the U.S. Economy?

How Open Is
the U.S. Economy?

Edited by
R.W. Hafer
Federal Reserve Bank
of St. Louis

Lexington Books
D.C. Heath and Company/Lexington, Massachusetts/Toronto

Library of Congress Cataloging-in-Publication Data
How open is the U.S. economy?

  Papers presented at the Federal Reserve Bank of
St. Louis's Tenth Annual Economic Conference, Oct. 12–13,
1985.
  Includes index.
  1. United States—Economic policy—1971–1981—
Congresses. 2. United States—Economic conditions—
1971–1981—Congresses. I. Hafer, R.W. (Rik W.)
II. Federal Reserve Bank of St. Louis. Economic
Conference (10th : 1985 : St. Louis, Mo.)
HC106.7.H72   1986   338.973   86–45063
ISBN 0–669–13086–9 (alk. paper)

Published simultaneously in Canada
Printed in the United States of America
Casebound International Standard Book Number: 0–669–13086–9
Library of Congress Catalog Card Number: 86–45063

The paper used in this publication meets the minimum requirements of
American National Standard for Information Sciences—Permanence of
Paper for Printed Library Materials, ANSI Z39.48–1984.

86 87 88 89 90 8 7 6 5 4 3 2 1

Contents

Part III.   Policy Responses to Increased Openness

Figures

Tables

Preface

The papers and comments presented at the Federal Reserve Bank of St. Louis's Tenth Annual Economic Conference are contained in this book. The topic of this conference, held on October 12–13, 1985, was "How Open Is the U.S. Economy?"

Recent events suggest the need to reassess previously held ideas about the insulation of the U.S. economy from external events. The appreciation of the U.S. dollar and that appreciation's subsequent effects on various sectors of the U.S. economy have shown that the world has become a much more open marketplace. Competition for goods and services comes from domestic and increasingly from foreign challengers. Not only are producers affected, but labor also is cognizant of the foreign competition for its services. Indeed, the wave of protectionist sentiment in the United States is but one outward manifestation of this changing environment.

The changing nature of the world economy and the role of the United States also are evident in the policymakers' growing recognition of foreign influences. Failure to achieve expected domestic policy goals may stem from the fact that policy actions no longer influence only the U.S. economy, but have both direct and indirect effects on other economies as adjustments in exchange rates, foreign prices, and financial yields. Indeed, calls for coordinated policy actions, exemplified by the Group of Five (G-5) announcement, increase the awareness among policymakers that their actions must be considered in a context broader than the domestic economy alone.

This book is divided into three parts. Part I provides a background on the increasing openness of the economy and an analysis of the effects of such openness. The chapters in part II explore the macroeconomic effects of this integration, and part III deals with policy reactions to increased openness.

In "The United States as an Open Economy," Richard N. Cooper examines the reasons, effects, and implications of an increasingly open U.S. economy. He notes that a major factor explaining increased foreign interaction is technological advances in communications and transportation. As lower transactions costs are realized, the volume of transactions correspondingly rises. Because of this, there is evidence of a loss of insulation of the economy to external events, such as the OPEC oil price shocks of the 1970s. More recently, Cooper notes, increased openness has broadened the base of competition that domestic firms must face, thus influencing wage and price developments in some sectors. Cooper comments that greater interdependence allows foreign events to impact the domestic economy, but also that domestic events have results much faster in the rest of the world. These factors may influence not only domestic policy multipliers, but also the usefulness of policy recommendations once followed under a more closed economy.

Peter B. Kenen provides a different view of economic integration in his comments on Cooper's chapter. He notes that in contrast to financial markets, goods markets may well have become less integrated among developed countries. Rather, a greater integration has taken place between developed and less-developed countries, as the former become increasingly dependent on the latter's raw materials. Much of Kenen's discussion focuses on the effects of floating exchange rates on the conduct of domestic policy. He notes that many formal models' predictions of the change from fixed to floating rates have not adequately captured the importance of increased capital mobility. While Kenen generally agrees with Cooper's assessment of the failure of these models to predict what actually occurred, he does not find Cooper's argument about the impact of foreign interest rates on domestic U.S. money demand convincing. Kenen also raises some questions with regard to the dominance of the United States in world monetary affairs, a position argued by Cooper.

Jeffrey A. Frankel examines the contention that "the U.S. economy has become so open financially as to be characterized by perfect capital mobility." In his chapter, "International Capital Mobility and Crowding-out in the U.S. Economy: Imperfect Integration of Financial Markets or of Goods Markets?," he investigates this belief by reconsidering the observation of Feldstein and Horioka that investment rates and national savings rates are highly correlated, implying low capital mobility. Based on U.S. data for a variety of periods and using several econometric techniques, Frankel's evidence corroborates the argument that "international capital mobility does not fully prevent exogenous changes in the government budget or in private saving from crowding out domestic investment." More important, Frankel finds that among the several definitions of perfect capital mobility, the failure of real interest parity automatically explains the findings of crowding-out. Thus, he concludes that crowding-out takes place not because of imperfect integration of financial markets, but because of imperfect integration of goods markets.

In his comments on Frankel's chapter, Frederic S. Mishkin argues that the evidence from the Feldstein-Horioka test is not convincing. The reason is model misspecification, with Mishkin questioning the notion of the investment rate modeled as a function of the savings rate. He also notes that the most relevant evidence for the question of capital mobility concerns the tests of real rate equality. Mishkin argues, however, that other evidence indicates that complete crowding-out does not occur, as Frankel's results may suggest. Thus, Mishkin maintains that, among other things, international capital lessens the negative effects of large budget deficits on the domestic economy, and that supply-side policies aimed at stimulating private savings to increase domestic capital formation may, based on the evidence, be less than successful.

John Kuszczak and John D. Murray use vector autoregressive (VAR) procedures to investigate the relationship of the domestic economy to foreign influences in their chapter, "A VAR Analysis of Economic Interdependence: Canada, the United States, and the Rest of the World." Through their extensive empirical analysis, the authors find that U.S. variables are affected by international variables to a greater extent than many would think. An example is the sensitivity of domestic money demand to movements in foreign interest rates and in exchange rates. An important finding in their work is that the shift from a fixed exchange rate regime to a flexible exchange rate regime does not statistically influence the time series properties of the variables studied. This finding, along with other results reported in their chapter, lead Kuszczak and Murray to state that "international economic interdependence need not preclude independent policy action by small open economies."

Georg Rich's comments on the chapter by Kuszczak and Murray focuses on the difficulty of interpreting the VAR evidence in terms of policy recommendations. As Rich notes, the astructural nature of VAR models may generate misleading policy signals to the monetary authority. Indeed, this problem of interpreting the empirical evidence is recognized by Kuszczak and Murray in their discussion of the finding that the Canadian money supply is quite sensitive to changes in U.S. interest rates. While the empirical finding may reflect the existence of currency substitution, the economic cause of the empirical relationship is obscured in the VAR framework.

Rich also comments that the diversity of economic experience and institutional makeup argues against the broad application of the conclusions reached by Kuszczak and Murray. In their chapter, they test the relationship between the United States and a composite of industrial countries. Rich disagrees with such a procedure for the basis of policy recommendation, by noting the disparity between the authors' conclusions and those reached by Genberg and Swoboda in a similar paper focused on the response by Swiss economic variables to changes in foreign macroeconomic variables. Such case-by-case studies, Rich notes, may be necessary to understand existing economic relationships and to provide a firm foundation for the implementation of policy decisions.

An increasing net capital inflow "has become the outstanding failure of U.S. macroeconomic performance in the 1980s." The effects of this imbalance are the subject of the chapter "Implications of the U.S. Net Capital Inflow," by Benjamin M. Friedman. He notes that the massive inflow of capital from abroad has been a key factor in equilibrating savings and investments in the United States despite large federal government deficits. Friedman argues that financial activity will shift away from capital formation as the increased foreign ownership of U.S. financial assets increases the "expected return premium on long-term debt." The policy implications Friedman derives are that easing monetary policy would reduce the capital inflow and, therefore, stimulate capital formation. In terms of fiscal policy, he argues that a similar outcome would arise from a tightening of fiscal policy, most notably through a reduction of large federal budget deficits.

John Huizinga agrees with the general thrust of Friedman's chapter, namely, that the recent transformation in the United States to net debtor status may have far-reaching effects on our economic well-being and future policy decisions. Huizinga notes, however, that two important considerations of the recent capital inflows have been slighted. The first aspect is the fact that more of the capital inflow has been "bank reported" than that associated with foreign net purchases of U.S. Treasury obligations. This suggests that domestic policies to influence the confidence of foreign investors increasingly may focus on the U.S. banking system.

Another aspect of the recent capital inflow is its possible effect on domestic inflation policy. Because most U.S. liabilities are nominal and denominated in U.S. dollars, creation of unexpected inflation would reduce the real value of the indebtedness to foreign holders. As Huizinga notes, "the incentive to inflate away our foreign debt might well be one of the more important consequences of continued capital inflows for U.S. economic policy."

Huizinga also raises some doubts regarding the usefulness of Friedman's empirical evidence on the appropriate policy to curtail the inflow of capital. Friedman's evidence argues for increased money growth and decreased government expenditures, or for increased tax collections. Huizinga argues that the reliability of these results as the basis for macroeconomic policy are questionable not only on the grounds of the endogeneity of the policy variables — a concern shared by Friedman — but also because of the uncertainty surrounding the stability of these estimates during the sample period used and in the future as policy regimes change.

The effect on policy of increased openness is the subject of Jacob A. Frenkel's chapter, "International Interdependence and the Constraints on Macroeconomic Policies." Focusing primarily on monetary policy, Frenkel shows that the combination of a more open economy and a flexible exchange rate regime quickens the effects of monetary changes on prices and wages. Moreover, he argues that using a policy guide such as purchasing power parity serves to keep domestic price and exchange rate behavior in perspective. That is, domestic policies to influence the domestic price level will also affect the exchange rate. Thus, Frenkel suggests that the monetary authority's main consideration should be the achievement of price stability and that by reducing the variability of monetary expansion, the monetary authority can positively contribute to reducing costly exchange rate fluctuations. With regard to policy in the current environment, Frenkel argues that "it makes no sense to agree just on real exchange rate targets without accompanying such an arrangement with a similar agreement about other targets for macroeconomic policies including, of course, fiscal policies."

William Poole's discussion of Frenkel's chapter focuses on several issues. For example, he argues that policy coordination between monetary and fiscal authorities fails if one party is unable or unwilling to "set its policy instruments appropriately." In light of recent developments, trading off monetary policy for fiscal policy—that is, changing money growth to offset budget deficits—may exacerbate one set of policy errors with another. Poole agrees with Frenkel that, as a long-run proposition, the exchange rate system does not have a great influence on policy opportunities. The existing regime does, however, influence the short-term adjustment process among the different sectors. This effect, he suggests, may arise from the changing character of certain sectors, changing them from ones in which prices are determined in auction markets to ones in which changes are discrete.

Unless there is a move toward greater international monetary policy coordination, sharp exchange rate fluctuations are inevitable. This is the focus of Ronald I. McKinnon's chapter "The Dollar Exchange Rate and International Monetary Cooperation." The basis for this position is the fact that under a floating exchange rate regime, governments are not required to follow common monetary policies, a condition that generally characterizes a fixed exchange rate regime. Because of this, investors seeking the best investment must continually guess which of the many fiat currencies to hold. Thus, in such a world, McKinnon argues, large swings in exchange rates will occur because the speculative forces that would restore equilibrium to the exchange rate market are weakened in a world of nonaligned national monetary policies. These exchange rate fluctuations give rise to protectionist pressures that supporters argue will protect domestic industry and insulate domestic prices. To avoid this chain of events, McKinnon argues that a stable international monetary system is required to assure free trade of goods and services. In his analysis, the main participants of such a new order would be the Federal Reserve, the Bank of Japan, and the Bundesbank. To achieve exchange rate stability, McKinnon suggests that these three monetary authorities establish a four-point program that, among other things, coordinates their domestic monetary policies along with explicit intervention in markets to achieve certain target exchange rates.

Roger E. Brinner is in general agreement with McKinnon's hypothesis that the exchange rate could be stabilized through coordinated intervention and policy actions by central banks. In contrast to McKinnon's analysis, however, Brinner argues that such a coordination of monetary policies during the early 1980s likely would have led to faster price-level increases than those which actually occurred. Based on simulations from the DRI econometric model, Brinner finds that if the United States had followed McKinnon's preferred combination of stimulative fiscal and monetary policies, U.S. inflation would have increased, unless Europe and Japan had chosen to engineer severe economic recessions. Even in this scenario, Brinner argues that the United States still would have faced a real appreciation of the dollar, thus leading to the same basis for protectionist pressures that such a policy is theoretically designed to avert.

Acknowledgments

Many people in the Research and Public Information Department of the Federal Reserve Bank of St. Louis contributed to the success of the conference on which this book is based. Foremost is Sandy Batten, who was instrumental in formulating the topic areas of the conference as well as arranging for the participation of several contributors. I also would like to thank Dan Brennan, Melissa Daubach, Linda Moser, and Carol Steimel for their assistance in running the conference and producing this book.

Part I
Integration of the
U.S. Economy

1
The United States as an Open Economy

Richard N. Cooper

I t is widely recognized that the United States has become more integrated into the world economy than it was, say, twenty-five years ago. For reasons that I hope to make clear, the United States is also more heavily integrated into the world economy than it was in the 1920s, the last period of great foreign investment, or in the 1890s as well, although in certain respects the United States was very open to foreign events a hundred years ago and indeed felt them, as when the Baring collapse in London set off the U.S. bank panic of 1890.

The Facts of Greater Openness of the U.S. Economy

It has become commonplace to cite certain measures of openness today. For instance, 40 percent of U.S. cropland and one-sixth of workers in the manufacturing sector are engaged in production for export. One-third of the loans of the largest banks are to overseas borrowers, and half of the profits of the largest U.S. corporations come from their investments abroad—at least in some years.

These figures, while suggestive, do not really capture the full impact of the openness of the U.S. economy. It is necessary to differentiate among different kinds of dependence that may develop on the rest of the world. In particular, a distinction must be made between "vulnerability" and "sensibility" to events elsewhere impinging on the U.S. economy. This distinction has been made much of by political scientists. Vulnerability concerns the real harm that can be done to the U.S. economy—and possibly to U.S. security—by the loss of access to foreign supplies or foreign markets. Sensitivity has to do with the frequency with which outside developments call for responsive adjustments within the U.S. economy, albeit perhaps at low real cost.

Some idea of the first type of dependence is given in table 1–1, which shows the high and growing dependence of the United States on foreign

Table 1–1

Net U.S. Imports of Key Materials as Shares of Apparent Consumption, 1960–83

	1960	1970	1980	1983
Manganese	89%	95%	98%	99%
Bauxite	74	88	94	96
Cobalt	66	98	93	96
Platinum Group	82	78	88	84
Chromium	85	89	91	77
Nickel	72	71	71	77
Potassium	—a	42	65	75
Tin	82	81	79	72
Zinc	46	54	60	66
Tungsten	32	50	53	39

Source: *Statistical Abstract of the United States.*
aNet exports.

sources of supply for a number of key materials, sudden loss of which would be serious for the economy and possibly for security. For this reason, the United States maintains strategic stockpiles of most of these products for use in event of war, which is the contingency most likely to lead to a serious cutoff of those commodities for which sources of supply are diverse. Gradual diminution of supply of such materials, as reflected in rising relative prices, would not be especially critical to the United States economy, as the technical possibilities exist for substituting away from them. Tin provides an example. Improved recovery techniques, tin-saving tinning processes, and wholesale substitution away from tinplate (especially in beverage vessels) have gradually reduced the use of tin in the U.S. economy.

The major import dependence of which all Americans have become aware concerns oil. Table 1–2 shows a growing dependence since 1960 on imports of energy supplies, and especially of oil, which increased through the late 1970s, after U.S. domestic production peaked and went into slow decline while U.S. consumption continued to grow with GNP. The U.S. economy experienced two major oil price shocks in the period 1973–80, and has built up a strategic petroleum reserve of nearly 500 million barrels (against a target of 750 million barrels) to deal with another future major shortfall, whether or not it is associated with war.

These commodities may appear to be special cases, and indeed they are in the degree of import dependence and their essentiality. But the growing openness of the U.S. economy is more general. As newspapers constantly remind people these days, over 20 percent of automobiles and steel consumed in the United States are imported, as are 17 percent of apparel by value (the more

Table 1–2
U.S. Energy and Petroleum, 1960–83
(quadrillion Btu)

	1960	1970	1980	1983[a]
Primary energy				
Domestic production	41.4	62.0	64.7	61.0
Exports	1.5	2.7	3.7	3.7
Consumption	43.7	66.4	75.9	70.5
Imports	4.2	8.4	16.0	11.9
(as a percentage of supply)	(9.3)	(12.2)	(20.1)	(16.9)
Petroleum and natural gas liquids				
Domestic production	16.4	22.9	20.6	20.5
Consumption	19.9	29.5	34.2	30.0
Imports	4.0	7.5	14.7	10.5
(as a percentage of consumption	(20.1)	(25.4)	(43.0)	(35.0)

Source: *Statistical Abstract of the United States.*
Note: One barrel of oil contains about 5.8 million Btu.
[a]Preliminary.

Table 1–3
U.S. Trade in Goods and Services as Shares of GNP, 1929–84

	Exports	*Imports*
1929	6.8%	5.7%
1940	5.4	3.6
1950	4.9	4.2
1960	5.5	4.6
1970	6.4	6.0
1980	12.9	12.0
1984	9.9	11.7

Source: Council of Economic Advisers, *Economic Report of the President,* and *Economic Indicators* (various issues).

frequently mentioned 33 percent refers to square yards), and by 1984, an impressive 75 percent of shoes.

Table 1–3 shows the trend of total foreign trade in goods and services relative to U.S. GNP since 1929. The ratio of trade to output fell in the 1930s, but has risen steadily since World War II; exports reached nearly 13 percent of GNP in 1980, before falling in recent years of world recession. Exports of merchandise grew from 9 percent of goods output in 1929 to

17 percent in 1979. Imports roughly tracked the path of exports until the past few years, when they grew sharply relative to exports.

But trade figures only partially capture the increased openness of the U.S. economy. It is necessary also to look at the ownership of production, at financial markets, and at the labor force.

Under the heading of assets, table 1–4 gives claims on the rest of the world by private residents of the United States (government claims are excluded here). Direct investment involves U.S. ownership of production facilities abroad, which rose from $12 billion in 1950 to $215 billion in 1980 when valued at acquisition cost; the current market valuation would be considerably higher. For purposes of comparison, U.S. nominal GNP grew by a factor of 9.2 between 1950 and 1980, so the book value of U.S. direct investment abroad grew about twice as fast as U.S. GNP, and even faster if the investment were valued at current prices.

Foreign direct investment in the United States, shown under liabilities in table 1–4, grew from $3.4 billion to $83 billion during this period, about one-third faster than U.S. direct investment abroad. By 1980, foreign owned firms accounted for 11 percent of depreciable assets, 7 percent of sales, and 6 percent of employment in all U.S. manufacturing. The foreign share of assets in manufacturing had increased by a factor of three since 1963.

As far as U.S. corporations were concerned, their majority-owned foreign affiliates accounted for 25 percent of their worldwide sales in 1977 (the year of a detailed census of U.S. investment overseas), and 21 percent for

Table 1–4
U.S. Private Claims on and Liabilities to Foreigners, 1950–80
($ billion)

	1950	1965	1980
U.S. private assets abroad	19.0	81	517
Direct investment	11.8	49	215
Claims by banks	1.3	12	204
Other nonbank claims	5.9	20	97
Bonds	3.2	10	43
Stocks	1.8	5	19
U.S. liabilities to foreigners[a]	17.6	59	501
Direct investment	3.4	9	83
Liabilities reported by banks	5.8	17	151
U.S. government securities	3.0	12	134
Other liabilities	5.4	21	132
Bonds (exc. U.S. govt.)	0.2	1	10
Stocks	2.9	15	65

Source: U.S. Department of Commerce, *Survey of Current Business* (various issues).
[a]Including foreign governments.

manufacturing firms alone. But U.S. firms had already invested heavily abroad by the mid-1960s, and the capital expenditure of U.S.-owned manufacturing firms overseas grew at roughly the same pace as their U.S. domestic capital expenditures from 1963–80, with foreign spending amounting in both years to about 21 percent of their worldwide capital spending. Since 1980, their capital spending overseas has declined relative to their capital spending in the U.S. economy.

In terms of funding, U.S. nonfinancial corporations in 1980 drew 13 percent of their total domestic funds from abroad, up from 5 percent in the mid-1960s, involving both repatriated earnings on their foreign investments plus new foreign investment in the United States.

A comparable story can be told for financial assets. Table 1–4 also shows the growth in U.S. financial claims on foreigners plus foreign financial claims on the United States from 1950 to 1980. Foreign financial claims on the United States have gone up over three times faster than U.S. GNP, and U.S. private financial claims on the rest of the world rose over four times more rapidly, from $7 billion to $301 billion, with the most rapid growth being claims by U.S. banks. Indeed, by the end of 1983, the 209 U.S. banks that do virtually all of the foreign bank lending had $357 billion in claims on foreigners, compared with $1,126 billion in total loans by all U.S. commercial banks.

Foreign banks operating in the United States accounted for 4.9 percent of bank assets and 9.5 percent of business loans in 1974; by 1983, they accounted for 14.6 percent of bank assets and 18.3 percent of business loans. Foreigners (including international organizations) held 16.3 percent of the U.S. government debt in the hands of the public at the end of 1983; this actually represented a decline from a peak of 24.8 percent in 1978, but it was still up sharply from 6.4 percent in 1970. Indeed, between 1970 and 1978, foreigners acquired no less than 40 percent of the increase in publicly held U.S. government debt.

Table 1–5 shows foreign ownership of selected categories of financial assets drawn from flow of funds statistics for 1966 and 1983. The figures suggest that foreign ownership of U.S. corporate and government securities more than trebled in relative importance between the mid-1960s and the present time.

What table 1–5 does not show is foreign ownership of U.S. currency, for this is unknown. But it is striking that of the roughly $169 billion in U.S. currency in circulation at the end of 1984, about $74 billion was in the form of $100 bills. Such bills represented 54 percent of the increase in currency in circulation between 1973 and 1984. Where are all these $100 bills? They show up only rarely in ordinary transactions. It is often alleged that this large denomination currency is tied up in the drug trade, but that can account for considerably less than half of the total.[1] I conjecture that over $20 billion in

Table 1–5
Foreign Ownership of U.S. Financial Assets, 1966 and 1983

	1966	1983	Total Value 1983 ($ trillion)
Corporate stocks	1.8%	4.5%	$2.2
Corporate and foreign bonds	1.5	7.9	0.6
U.S. government securities	3.8	14.1	1.2
Open market paper	2.4[a]	14.4	0.3

Source: Federal Reserve, *Flow of Funds.*
[a]Time and savings accounts.

U.S. currency, mostly $100 bills, is abroad. U.S. currency is the legal currency in Panama and Liberia, two small countries, but it is widely used for transactions in Argentina—where Argentinian estimates place U.S. currency in circulation at over $5 billion—and in Israel. It is also used extensively as a store of value throughout South America, the Arab countries, and indeed much of the rest of the world. The rapid growth of foreign holdings of $100 bills suggests that effective *M-1* growth in the United States has been overstated during the past ten years.

Foreigners evidently traded their asset holdings more rapidly than did the typical American resident. In 1983, foreigners purchased about $70 billion of U.S. corporate stock, representing about 7.5 percent of total gross stock purchases, compared with foreign ownership of less than 5 percent. This higher turnover rate is not new; foreigners accounted for 4.2 percent of gross purchases of U.S. corporate stock on all stock exchanges in 1963, compared with foreign ownership of less than 2 percent.

Population and the labor market also reflect an increased openness over the past quarter century. In 1980, there were 14.1 million foreign-born persons in the United States, 6 percent of the total population. The rate of legal immigration into the United States increased from 1.5 persons per 1,000 people in 1965 to 2.6 persons per 1,000 people in 1981, both figures remaining well below the record 10.4 persons per 1,000 during the period 1901–10. In addition to 597,000 legal immigrants in 1981, there were probably several hundred thousand illegal immigrants. Indeed it is probable that over 40 percent of annual increments to the labor force are now accounted for by immigrants.

Apart from immigrants, 11.8 million foreigners entered the United States in 1981, compared with only 1.1 million in 1960. Of the 11.8 million foreigners who entered, 1.1 million were on business, 272,000 were students, 65,000 were intracompany transfers of foreign personnel, and 81,000 were other traders or investors admitted to temporary residence (see table 1–6).

Table 1–6
Foreign Visitors to the United States, 1960–81
(thousands)

	1960	1970	1981
Immigrants admitted	265	373	597
Nonimmigrants admitted	1,141	4,432	11,757
Temporary visitors	779	3,345	10,651
For pleasure	n.a.	3,020	9,515
For business	n.a.	325	1,135
Treaty traders and investors	n.a.	19	81
Students	35	107	272
Intracompany transfers	n.a.	*a	65

Source: *Statistical Abstract of the United States: Historical Statistics from Colonial Times to 1970.*
a400 individuals.

Table 1–7
U.S. Travelers to Overseas Destinations, 1960–80
(thousands)

	1960	1970	1980
Total	1,634	5,260	8,163
To Europe and Mediterranean	832	2,829	3,934

Source: U.S. Department of Commerce, *Survey of Current Business* (various issues).

Travel by Americans has also increased sharply, as shown in table 1–7. In 1980, 8.2 million Americans traveled abroad (excluding Canada and Mexico), up from 1.6 million in 1960.

This quick survey of data gives some impression of the increased openness of the U.S. economy over the past decade or three, depending on availability of the data. Roughly speaking, it suggests a doubling of the relative importance of foreign ownership or activity in the "real" side of the U.S. economy, and a trebling of the relative importance of foreign ownership or activity of foreigners in the financial side of the U.S. economy. In both instances, however, foreign ownership or activity, while growing rapidly, remains relatively small; the U.S. economy still looks relatively closed on this profile. That appearance is deceptive, however, as will be made clear.

It is of interest to compare the United States today with the Federal Republic of Germany, a large economy thought to be very open. Indeed, exports of goods and services account for over 30 percent of German GNP, and the FRG is dependent on imports for about half of its energy supply, both counts suggesting considerably greater openness than the United States offers.

In financial markets, about 15 percent of German time deposits and money market paper are owned by foreigners, as are 8 percent of stocks and 4 percent of bonds. About 8 percent of long-term German bank loans are to foreigners. By these financial measures, the German economy is not markedly more open than the U.S. economy.

Before turning to the consequences and implications for policy of the increased openness of the U.S. economy, one should ask how it came about, and whether the tendency toward greater openness is likely to continue.

Reasons for Increased Openness

It is an oversimplification but nonetheless a basic truth to suggest that the increased openness of the U.S. economy, and indeed the greater openness of other countries along with the general growth of world economic interdependence, has occurred as a result of rapid technological developments in the fields of transportation and communication. The impact of these changes has been to reduce sharply the barriers to economic transactions imposed by geographic distance. These factors have been reinforced by reductions in tariff barriers to trade both in the United States and in the other major industrial countries. In 1900, the average U.S. tariff (weighted by import value) was 26 percent. By the 1950s, this had fallen to 7 percent; by 1980, it had fallen further to 3.5 percent. In 1900, it cost 25 cents per word to send a telegraphic message from New York to major European capitals. The cost was hardly more than this in 1985—26.5 cents per word to London and 30.5 cents per word to Paris. Corrected for the twelvefold increase in the consumer price index that took place between 1900 and 1985, telegraphic communication cost in the latter year only 8–9 percent of what it had cost in 1900.

The cost of international telephone messages fell even more sharply. A three-minute off-peak phone call between Washington and Frankfurt cost $12 in 1950, but only $2.76 in 1985, for a decline in real terms to only 5 percent of the cost 35 years earlier.

Comparable developments can be seen in the costs of air carriage. Table 1–8 shows the average revenue per passenger mile for U.S. domestic and international air traffic over the past fifty years. These figures represent the revenues from the service in question divided by the number of passenger miles traveled by paying passengers. The figures show a drop by two-thirds from 1940 to 1983 in the average fare for domestic travel, and a drop by five-sixths in the case of international travel. There was an even sharper decline for air freight. In 1983, international air freight cost an average of 37 cents per ton mile, about one-fourth in real terms of what it cost in 1950. (An aviation ton is a measure of volume, about 100 cubic feet.)

Of course, these average figures also reflect changes in the character of

Table 1–8
Average Revenue for Air Travel, 1930–83

| | Passengers | | | | International Freight | |
| | Domestic | | International | | | |
	Nominal[a]	1985 dollars[a]	Nominal[a]	1985 dollars[a]	Nominal[b]	1985 dollars[b]
1930	8.3	53.2	n.a.		n.a.	
1940	5.1	38.6	8.8	67.3	86[c]	533[c]
1950	5.6	24.6	7.3	32.1	36	158
1960	6.1	21.9	6.3	22.9	31	111
1970	6.0	16.5	5.0	13.8	21	56
1980	11.5	14.9	8.8	11.4	32	42
1983	12.1	13.0	9.8	10.5	32	34

Sources: Civil Aeronautics Board, *Reports to Congress,* various issues; Federal Aviation Administration, *Statistical Handbook of Aviation,* various issues; and calculations from *Statistical Abstract of the United States.*
[a]Cents per revenue passenger-mile.
[b]Cents per revenue ton-mile.
[c]1943.

international travel as regards both the length of the trip and the class of service. Table 1–9 attempts to correct for that by citing fares between fixed points during the peak season. The first transoceanic commercial flight (a seaplane via Hawaii, Guam, and Manila) was from San Francisco to Hong Kong in August 1937. It was followed by the first commercial trans-Atlantic flight, from New York to Southampton and Marseilles (by seaplane via Bermuda, the Azores, and Lisbon). The round-trip fare across the Pacific in 1937 was $1,710, or over $12,000 in 1985 purchasing power. The round-trip fare across the Atlantic two years later was $675, or over $5,000 in 1985 dollars. Fares are much more complicated today, with three classes of service, high-season and low-season fares, and excursion and advance-purchase fares. But if one takes high-season excursion or APEX fare as a point of comparison, the trans-Pacific fare today is only 8 percent of the 1937 fare in real terms, and the New York–London fare is only 12 percent of the 1939 fare in real terms. These comparisons neglect charter flights and People Express, which are cheaper still.

Lower fares are not the only improvements that have occurred. There have been dramatic reductions in the time required as well. The first trans-Atlantic cable was laid in 1867, making it possible for the first time to send a message between Europe and North America faster than a man could travel. Wireless made it possible to communicate with ships at sea and, later, with aircraft and spacecraft. The radio was still novel when the *Titanic* sank in

Table 1–9
Round-Trip Air Fares, 1937–85

		Current $	1985 $
Trans-Pacific			
August 1937	San Francisco–Hong Kong	1,710	12,725
August 1939	San Francisco–Hong Kong	1,368	10,523
May 1949	San Francisco or Los Angeles–Hong Kong	1,360.80	5,827
	San Francisco or Los Angeles–Tokyo	1,170	5,244
January 1964	Los Angeles–Tokyo	783	2,697
January 1973	Los Angeles–Tokyo	773.80[a]	1,860
August 1985	Los Angeles–Tokyo	930[b]	930
	San Francisco–Hong Kong	1,094[b]	1,094
Trans-Atlantic			
August 1939	New York–Southampton	675	5,192
	New York–Marseilles	675	5,192
May 1949	New York–London	630	2,824
	New York–Paris	666	2,985
January 1964	New York–London	302.30	1,041
	New York–Paris	391.80	1,350
January 1973	New York–London	332[c]	798
	New York–Paris	344[c]	827
August 1985	New York–London	645[b]	645
	New York–Paris	692[d]	692

[a]14–21-day excursion. Full economy fare L.A.–Tokyo was $911.40; New York–London, $461–499.70, depending on season; New York–Paris, $541.50.

[b]21-day advance purchase (APEX), high season. Full economy fare New York–London was $1,395; L.A.–Tokyo, $1,410.

[c]22–45-day peak period excursion. Peak period full economy fare New York–London was $626; New York–Paris, $676. Winter excursion rate New York–London was $233, and off-peak full economy, $456; New York–Paris, $243 and $480, respectively.

[d]Excursion high season, 14-day minimum stay. Full economy fare was $1,604.

1912. With modern practice, the 1,500 passengers who drowned would have been rescued. Unfortunately, the closest ship nearby had turned its radio receiver off before the *Titanic* sent its distress signal. But that signal permitted those in lifeboats to be rescued by a ship that traveled over fifty miles to the location of the disaster, a rescue that could not have occurred only five years before.

An English packet ship took five weeks to reach North America in the 1820s. By the 1870s, with steam vessels, steel hulls, and screw propellers, scheduled service between England and the United States took twelve days. By 1914, this had dropped to six days. Commercial air flights took about 18 hours in 1950, dropping to 8 hours with the introduction of commercial jet aircraft in 1958, and to 3.5 hours with the Concorde. Moreover, these improvements have occurred with a great saving of capital. A single Boeing 747 can move more people across the Atlantic in a season than the *Queen Mary* liner could.

The volume of transactions has responded to the reduction in costs. Table 1–6 has already shown that the number of foreigners visiting the United States grew from 1.1 million in 1960 to 11.8 million in 1981. By 1983, no less than one quarter of U.S. merchandise exports and nearly one-sixth of U.S. imports were moved by air, up from negligible amounts in 1950. Commercial overseas telegraph messages (excluding leased lines) originating in the United States rose only slowly from 23 million messages in 1950 to 32 million messages in 1970, and then declined to 20 million messages in 1980, although the length of the average message increased sharply. International telephone calls originating in the United States, in contrast, rose enormously, from 700,000 in 1950 to 23 million in 1970, to 200 million in 1980, and to 311 million in 1982. The reason is the increase in the number of transoceanic telephone cable systems from 1 in 1950 to 18 in 1982; communications satellites increased from 1 in 1965 to 6 in 1982; and international direct dialing was introduced in the 1970s.

Both as a cause and as a consequence of these developments, foreign transactions are becoming more like domestic transactions. The foreignness is going out of international trade and financial relations, not so much because Americans are becoming more skillful at dealing with foreigners, as because foreigners are becoming more skillful and more accustomed to dealing with Americans. English has become the predominant language of international commerce, and differences in conventions of doing business are diminishing. Direct conversation and face-to-face meetings have always been the most effective way to close a business deal, with confirmation in writing (or by Telex), and in this respect the barriers of geographic distance have been greatly eroded by technology. With the advent of the commercial jet, it is possible to travel to Europe overnight, have a five-hour meeting, and return to the United States in time for supper after reporting in at the office. A comparable trip can take place originating in Europe. Close managerial supervision can thus be maintained over vast distances, and the changing nature of the modern corporation reflects that fact.

What of the future? The technological pipeline suggests further reductions in the cost of air transport and long-distance communication for at least another ten to fifteen years. Digitalization of voice communication and the introduction of fiber optic cables will enormously increase the capacity and reduce the cost of transoceanic communication. It is not absurd to think that by the year 2000, a given message can be sent to Europe for less than 10 percent of what it now costs in real terms. Much more efficient aircraft are also on the drawing boards (on both these points, see Keatley, 1985). So the barriers of distance will continue to decline rapidly, unless blocked by government action.

Consequences of Greater Openness

The greater openness of the U.S. economy was dramatically made evident to the American public by the world oil price increases of 1974 and 1979–80. Nixon's attempt to insulate the American public from price increases by price controls was only half successful, since only half of U.S. oil consumption was produced domestically; the world price had to be paid for the other half. The American public also became aware of the openness, albeit on a smaller scale, with the fivefold increase in sugar prices in 1973–74 as a result of a world sugar shortage. By the same token the world grain shortage of 1972–73 was a bonanza to U.S. farmers although a cost to U.S. consumers. Less evident than these price shocks but nonetheless important were the benefits that flowed to American consumers following the leveling off of U.S. oil production and from the rapid growth of imports of oil supplied by increased OPEC output from 1968 to 1977.

More recently economists have seen confidence in the major U.S. banks shaken by their heavy exposure to foreign debt combined, since late 1982, with an inability of debtors to pay their obligations on schedule. There has been a noticeable deterioration in the value of bank shares, correlated with the extent of overseas debt.[2] Moreover, withdrawal of foreign funds from Continental Illinois, following difficulty with some of its domestic loans, greatly weakened that bank and led the Federal Reserve to lend it over $2 billion during a period of adjustment.

The openness of the U.S. economy has permitted a much sharper drop in U.S. inflation rates than otherwise would have occurred since 1981. This drop was facilitated by a sharp appreciation of the dollar relative to other foreign currencies, which in turn was due in large measure to tight monetary policy in the United States, followed by expansionist fiscal policy since late 1981. Import prices (as measured by their GNP deflator) declined by 14 percent between 1981 and the first quarter of 1985, compared with an increase ranging from 10 to 25 percent in the deflators for sectors of the economy that are not exposed to foreign trade, such as housing, defense spending, and most services. The rise in the dollar put competitive pressure on the entire tradable sector, both export industries and those that compete with imports. Indeed, a sectoral analysis of price movements in the period since 1980 shows a striking downward impact arising from increased foreign competition on those sectors that are exposed to such competition, compared with sectors that are not (see S. Marris, 1986, chapter 2).

Furthermore, increased foreign competition has put special pressure on those sectors (notably autos and steel) where U.S. wages had gotten out of line with the general wage level. The early practice of "give-backs" was concentrated in those sectors subject to heavy foreign competition or to deregulation, although by 1984–85, such wage adjustments had spread to other sectors as well, as employers were emboldened and unions were weakened by the increasingly competitive environment brought on partly by foreign trade, partly by deregulation, and partly by high unemployment (see D. Mitchell, 1985). Dornbusch and Fischer (1984) have estimated that a 10-percent average dollar appreciation lowers the consumption deflator by 2.1 percent, partly through its direct impact on prices of imports and import-competing goods, and partly indirectly through the exercise of wage restraint, with a mean lag of just under three quarters for the direct effect on prices and a lag of four quarters for the indirect effect through wages (see Dornbusch-Fischer, table 10).

The same forces have also helped to depress farm income. The stronger dollar has led to weaker dollar prices of all commodities sold into the world market, putting American farmers, whose debt is in dollars and whose costs have not declined proportionately, into a bind not unlike the developing countries that export primary products and whose debt is largely in dollars.

Another consequence of enlarged openness is to mitigate—indeed on some measures to eliminate entirely—the crowding out of private investment that many economists and others predicted would flow from the growth in the U.S. structural budget deficit since 1981. Instead, tight monetary and expansionist fiscal policies pulled foreign funds into the United States, to the historically unprecedented amount of 2.6 percent of GNP in 1984. The net inflow of funds kept U.S. interest rates lower than they otherwise would have been, and imports filled what otherwise would have been a real resource gap, although the appreciation of the currency probably also inhibited the recovery of U.S. domestic output.

Finally, world debt problems combined with weak economic performance elsewhere in the world have hurt badly those sectors of the U.S. economy—such as heavy construction machinery—that have become dependent on worldwide investment for their sales.

Implications of Increased Openness and Higher International Mobility

At the outset of this chapter I drew attention to the distinction between "vulnerability interdependence" and "sensititivity interdependence," a distinction made by and useful to political scientists. An analogous distinction should be made by economists, with a somewhat different orientation, between the openness of a national economy and the international mobility of goods, services, and factors of production. A country can be highly open, as demonstrated by Japan's dependence on imported energy, yet still have low responsiveness to the emergence of small incentives to move capital, goods, or labor across national boundaries. Many of the factors just discussed have led both to greater openness and to greater sensitivity of the U.S. economy to events abroad. Other developments, such as gradual resource exhaustion, have led to greater openness, but by the same token to less sensitivity because the substitution possibilities from domestic production have been reduced. Each has its own set of implications for private and public economic decision making.

Greater openness leads to a larger impact of disturbances to the economy emanating from abroad, such as the oil and the sugar shocks already mentioned. On the other hand, it also leads to greater dissipation of disturbances that are domestic in origin, as the rest of the world acts as a kind of sink into which surplus production can be poured, or a source from which excess demand can be supplied. This phenomenon was first noticed by Americans in 1959, when a steel strike closed down U.S. steel production for much of the year, but a surge of steel imports diminished substantially the impact of the strike on the U.S. economy. Growing imports of oil and other raw materials as U.S. resources have been depleted have already been mentioned in the same connection.

The more rapid dissipation of disturbances originating in the domestic economy also applies to changes in domestic macroeconomic policy. If Americans spend more on imports out of each additional dollar of income received, then fiscal actions designed to stimulate the U.S. economy by increasing after-tax income in the hands of Americans will leak abroad more rapidly, reducing the fiscal impact on the U.S. economy (but not in general reducing its global impact). In the early 1960s, economists generally assumed a fiscal multiplier for the United States in the range of 2–2.5; that is, every million-dollar increase in government spending would increase GNP by $2–2.5 million. More recently, the generally accepted multiplier is in the range of 1.5–2, even before allowing for the effects of flexible exchange rates, which are discussed later. The lower multiplier implies a smaller impact of a given fiscal policy action today than was the case some years ago.[3]

A similar story can be told for monetary policy. Under a system of fixed exchange rates, with integrated capital markets, any attempt by a country to deviate from the world norm in monetary policy will simply evoke large movements of capital. The money supply becomes endogenous as a result of the commitment to fix the exchange rate, and even short-run deviations from the world norm become impossible if a country's money market is merely a part of a larger world money market.

The United States stands out as a partial exception to this extreme loss of monetary autonomy. The United States is so large a part of the world economy, and the dollar is so widely used, that the United States can influence world monetary conditions to the point of determining them. For this reason, other countries must accept U.S. leadership in the monetary arena under a regime of fixed exchange rates. It was their ultimate unwillingness to accept U.S. leadership that led to the breakdown of the exchange rate features of the Bretton Woods system in 1970–73. First Canada, then Britain, then Europe and Japan set their currencies free from the dollar in order to restore some monetary autonomy. The result is the present system of flexible exchange rates. It is noteworthy, however, that most countries in fact still fix their currencies to something—to the U.S. dollar, to the French franc, to some combination of currencies, and in the case of the eight currencies in the European monetary system, to each other. Thus relatively few currencies literally float freely, but they happen to be important ones—including the U.S. dollar, the Canadian dollar, the Japanese yen, and the British pound.

Flexible rates have indeed restored some monetary autonomy, as table 1–10 indicates. The correlation in movements between British and U.S. short-term interest rates rose sharply from the pre–World War I period to the interwar period, when London and New York rates were widely considered to have been closely integrated. Differences between the interest rates dropped sharply, and rates tended to move together. The correlation dropped and the average difference increased during the post–World War II period, represented in table 1–10 by the years 1964–71. Both Britain and the United States maintained some restraints on outward capital movements

Table 1–10
Measures of New York–London Money Market Linkages: Short-Term Interest Rates, 1876–1984
(percentage points)

	Correlation Coefficient	Average Difference	Standard Deviation of Difference
1876–1914[a]	.45	2.17	1.21
1925–38[a]	.93	0.24	0.71
1964–71[b]	.79	1.33	0.72
1974–84[b]	.55	2.23	2.67
1974–84[c]	.99	.63	.60

Sources: Compiled from R. Dornbusch and S. Fischer, "The Open Economy: Implications for Monetary and Fiscal Policy," National Bureau of Economic Research Working Paper no. 1422, August 1984; and author's calculations.

[a]For 1876–1938, New York commercial paper rate and London private discount rate, monthly data from Morgenstern.

[b]For 1964–84, Treasury bill rates from International Financial Statistics, monthly averages.

[c]For 1974–84, 90-day Eurodollar deposit rate and U.S. CD rate, from DRI monthly averages.

during this period. Flexible exchange rates prevailed during the most recent decade, whereupon the correlation between British and U.S. interest rates dropped markedly and the average difference between them increased sharply. As expected, this was a function wholly of differences in the currency of denomination. The correlation between movements in interest rates on dollar-denominated claims in London and in New York was extremely high during this period, the average difference in interest rates was markedly lower than in the preceding decade, and the standard deviation of the difference was no greater than the difference itself. The coefficient of variation (the standard deviation of the difference divided by the mean difference) on dollar-denominated claims dropped to one-third of that prevailing between New York dollar securities and London pound-denominated claims during the period 1925–38. In comparing the average difference in interest rates in the 1925–38 period with the average difference in the most recent period, it is worth recalling that interest rates were very much lower in the former period, actually averaging below 1 percent during 1931–38, in contrast to short-term interest rates that ran from 5 to 16 percent in the most recent decade. So the average difference between interest rates as a fraction of the interest rates themselves was much smaller for dollar-denominated securities in the period 1974–84 than in 1925–38.

Flexible exchange rates have not only permitted greater national autonomy in the pursuit of monetary policy; they have also altered the way in which both monetary and fiscal policy work. Consider fiscal policy first, holding the money supply constant. An expansionist fiscal action will raise interest rates and induce a desire in foreigners to invest more in the country in question, while the attempted capital inflow will lead to an appreciation of the country's currency. That in turn will worsen the trade balance and hence weaken the influence of the expansionist fiscal action on the economy, an effect that augments the weakening that has already arisen from greater openness just noted. Taking these induced exchange rate effects of fiscal action into account may lead to a multiplier for the United States that is less than unity.[4]

Monetary policy used to operate on domestic economic activity primarily through two channels. Changes in monetary policy would raise or lower interest rates, and this in turn would discourage or encourage purchases for inventory, plant and equipment expenditure, and new housing construction. In addition, changes in monetary policy would alter the total wealth privately held through their influence on the prices of stocks and bonds; alterations in total wealth in turn affect current rates of spending in the same direction as the first effect. The second of these two effects was pervasive; the first was focused on interest-sensitive expenditures, most notably, in the United States, housing.

Under flexible exchange rates, a third impact of alterations in monetary policy must be allowed for: the impact on the exchange rate. Tighter monetary policy will lead to a currency appreciation, and that in turn will lead to substitution of foreign for domestic goods, thereby reducing the demand for domestic production. In this case, unlike the first two channels, total spending is not reduced, but spending on domestic output is reduced via substitution of foreign goods. This development is not necessarily undesirable. It spreads the impact of changes in monetary policy more widely throughout the economy, with smaller effects on particular sectors. But Americans are not yet accustomed to this effect of monetary action, and they identify increased foreign competition with particular actions or practices taken by foreign governments—often practices that have prevailed for many years and that they are inclined to call "unfair" because they differ from practices that prevail in the United States. There is no doubt some justification in some of the complaints along these lines. But most of the complaints should be directed, not at foreigners, but to the fiscal and monetary authorities of the United States, whose combined actions are in fact responsible for most of the increased foreign competition in the U.S. economy today—effects which, it should be recalled, were brought about deliberately as a way to combat inflation.

Adjustment to these new conditions and channels by which monetary policy works has lagged not only in American perception but also in U.S. laws and administrative practices. Under section 201 of the Trade Act of 1974, any firm can appeal for import relief if its industry has been substantially injured by an increase in imports. (The provision long prevailing in the U.S. law that the increase in imports must be due to tariff reductions negotiated by the United States was dropped in 1974.) Thus the United States currently faces the anomalous situation in which the Federal Reserve may tighten money to combat inflation, thereby appreciating the U.S. dollar relative to other currencies and encouraging greater import competition, thereby triggering legally justifiable complaints by U.S. industries and permitting temporary import protection in order to diminish the resulting injury. (The president has the authority to reject recommendations by the International Trade Commission for temporary import relief, but he must justify to Congress his reasons for doing so, and he can be overridden by Congress.) Thus under flexible exchange rates there exists an unintended impact on microeconomic policy arising from macroeconomic actions.

In summary, an open economy under flexible exchange rates behaves very differently from a relatively closed economy under fixed exchange rates. (1) Monetary contraction operates directly on the price level by appreciating the currency as well as indirectly by depressing aggregate demand, so that the short-run Phillips curve is steepened. (2) Fiscal expansion will be less inflationary for the same reason, namely higher interest rates will lead to appreciation of the currency in the short run, but by the same token a given fiscal action will stimulate aggregate output less. How the impact of movements in the exchange rate, and expected future movements in the rate, following either of these kinds of actions, will influence domestic investment, and hence aggregate demand and output, is still an unresolved but important empirical question.

Just as flexible exchange rates have altered the channels by which monetary measures influence the U.S. economy, they also have altered the nature of the transmission of policy actions to other countries. Tight money in the United States, which under fixed exchange rates would have led to tight money in other countries as well, is not necessarily contractionary for others under flexible exchange rates. While it can put upward pressure on foreign interest rates, it also leads to a depreciation of currencies seen from the perspective of other countries, and hence improves the international competitiveness of their products. So contractionary monetary policy in the United States may on balance be expansionary for other countries.

Increased openness of the U.S. economy also casts further doubt on the already weak rationale underlying the universally used demand for money equation $M/P = F(Y,r)$. The only argument in the equation that is not brought into question by greater openness is the interest rate, r. How is M to be defined when dollar-denominated bank accounts running several hundred billion dollars exist outside the United States, held by U.S. residents as well as nonresidents, when nonresidents hold substantial time deposits in the United States, and when even a substantial fraction—perhaps one-seventh—of U.S. currency is held abroad? Should the price level pertain to domestic output or domestic expenditure? That is, how much weight should be given to exchange rate movements? Does demand for money, however defined, depend on output, expenditure, or some combination of the two? Such questions can be ignored for a relatively closed economy. They should not be ignored for an open one.

The Implications of Greater Mobility

Higher international mobility has implications for all economic agents, especially for business firms. They can now think about marketing strategy not only in the home market, but in a worldwide market, as many do. They must worry about competition not only from domestic competitors, actual or potential, but also from foreign ones. Strategic decisions of oligopolist industries must be made on a global basis, not merely on a national basis, if the oligopolist position is to be preserved. This strategic thinking applies not only to product competition and marketing, but also to the location of production, since the combination of transport costs and actual or potential import barriers may exceed the disadvantages of buying or building and managing a plant at long distance. Labor unions too must take an international view if they want to preserve a superior relative position for their members.

But the same improved mobility that in today's world influences business investment and marketing decisions also makes business more sensitive and hence more responsive to differences in national policies with respect to regulation and to taxation. Higher mobility leads to a generalization of arbitrage—a tendency to equalize conditions worldwide. Outflows of technology and capital raise productivity and incomes abroad toward levels in the originating countries. Inflows of labor put downward pressure on wages in the country of immigration. Arbitrage also leads to convergence of national regulation and taxation. Tax havens, most notably Switzerland, have existed for many decades, permitting firms to run their international transactions through trading companies whose profits are taxed at much lower rates than they are taxed either in the country of production or in the country of final sale. Appropriate adjustment of intracorporate prices permits maximization of after-tax profits.

More recently regulatory havens have also sprung up: first Luxembourg in banking and security issues, then the Bahamas, Cayman, and other off-shore banking centers. As long as these havens remain relatively small, they co-exist with normal flows of trade and finance and with historic regulation and taxation. But when they exceed a certain size, they put pressure on the regulatory or tax environment everywhere. The growing use by U.S. corporations of the Netherlands Antilles for raising funds abroad on which interest payments were not subject to withholding tax at source (under the terms of a U.S.–Netherlands tax treaty) put such pressure on U.S. tax revenues from this source that the U.S. Treasury persuaded Congress in 1984 to remove the withholding tax altogether on interest payments to foreigners. France and Germany promptly followed suit, and Japan is actively discussing a similar change. The growth of nameplate banking facilities in Grand Cayman, the Bahamas, and Bermuda (whereby bank deposits could avoid the reserve requirements and interest rate limitations imposed on bank deposits in the United States) and disputes over state taxation of such activity, led in 1981 to the creation of international banking facilities (IBFs) in the United States. IBFs are generally exempt from these regulations subject to certain restrictions on the type of transactions that they can undertake.[5]

The responsiveness of internationally mobile firms has led some countries—and governmental jurisdictions within countries—to take advantage of this mobility by creating a favorable environment for these firms in order to generate local income and employment. Thus the cities and states within the United States compete with one another and with Canadian provinces for the location of major new factories. Not so long ago the province of Ontario and the state of Ohio were locked in a competition of favors for the location of a new automobile engine factory. Smaller countries such as Ireland and Singapore have also competed vigorously for internationally mobile firms by offering land and by creating an especially favorable tax or regulatory environment; and as already discussed, even the United States has responded to this competition in limited areas such as allowing international banking facilities, removing the withholding tax on interest payments to foreigners, and permitting states to compete for new firms through the flotation of tax-exempt development bonds.

Accommodation to this competitive environment in policy is only one response. The United States has also from time to time engaged in aggressive action to extend its regulatory or tax jurisdiction to residents in other countries. Thus the Securities and Exchange Commission (SEC) has served disclosure requirements on foreign firms whose securities are traded (without the approval of the firms) in the U.S. over-the-counter market. The United States government or courts have often subpoenaed information abroad pertaining to enforcement of U.S. tax or antitrust laws. And of course there was the recent celebrated conflict between the United States and several European countries over their ability to sell the Soviet Union gas turbines made abroad under U.S. license, in alleged violation of U.S. export control laws. This extraterritorial extension of U.S. laws has led in turn to blocking legislation by several other countries, including Britain, France, and Germany, whereby firms located in those countries, regardless of ownership, are prohibited from complying with government or court orders emanating from another country (meaning mainly the United States). Such laws of course put firms in a direct conflict of jurisdictions, whereby they cannot avoid violating the laws or injunctions of one country or another.[6] This kind of situation is obviously unsustainable in the long run, and it suggests the need for cooperation agreements between countries concerning the enforcement of regulations and taxation. Indeed, such agreements have been reached with Australia and Canada with respect to the collection of information pertaining to antitrust enforcement, and ad hoc cooperative arrangements have been established with Germany.[7] But the necessity for cooperation with other countries also implies a mutual accommodation of national policies into a common framework, and a corresponding loss of autonomy. The problem arises because of greater international mobility, and it will become more acute over time as international mobility increases even further due to technological improvements in travel and communication.

Notes

1. It is estimated that the U.S. drug trade runs about $110 billion a year. If one applies the average M1 velocity of 6.7 to the drug trade and assume that only $100 bills are used for transactions, that would account for only about one-fifth of the $100

bills in circulation. Even if transactions velocity were only half of what it is for M1 with respect to GNP, only $33 billion of the $100 bills would be accounted for.

2. According to calculations by S. Kyle (1985), by late 1983, the market value of bank shares suggested a discount of 22 percent on Latin American debt in each bank's portfolio.

3. Ideally, it would be possible to compare the multipliers estimated in the various large-scale macroeconomic models developed for the U.S. economy over the last thirty years. Unfortunately, such a comparison is badly marred by the often radically different treatment given to other dimensions of economic policy (especially monetary policy) and to the greater complexity of models permitted by modern computational facilities, giving rise to much more complex compositional effects in recent models than was the case in earlier ones. The model of project LINK shows modestly higher multipliers for the United States, Canada, and Germany in the early 1970s than for the early 1960s, but lower multipliers for Britain, France, and Japan. See Helliwell and Padmore, 1985.

4. In open economy macroeconomic models that have become fashionable, incorporating the portfolio balance approach to international capital movements, fiscal expansion with money held unchanged *must* lead on impact to an appreciation of the currency. (See, for example, Obstfeld, 1985.) But a more eclectic approach to modeling capital movements leads to the result that a country's exchange rate could go either up or down depending on the nature of interest-sensitive capital mobility and the response of domestic interest rates to expansionist action. Indeed the more complex macroeconomic models more often than not yield the result that fiscal expansion will lead to depreciation of the currency for countries other than the United States. Under these circumstances, of course, the fiscal multiplier is augmented rather than diminished.

5. For a description of the origin and early creation of IBFs, see Sydney Key, 1984.

6. Two recent tax cases involve Marc Rich (whose firm agreed to turn over certain documents to U.S. prosecutors, only to have them confiscated by Swiss authorities who charged that their delivery would violate Swiss secrecy laws) and the Italian firm of Gucci, which found itself charged with contempt of court by a U.S. court for not delivering documents which a Hong Kong court had enjoined it from delivering. See *International Herald Tribune,* August 17–18, 1985, pp. 9, 12. In a similar vein, squabbles over jurisdiction of liability with respect to the Union Carbide–Bhopal plant disaster will very likely continue for years.

7. On the international legal aspects of antitrust enforcement, see Atwood and Brewster, 1981. Of course, openness of the economy raises questions about the value of traditional antitrust criteria, such as concentration indexes. An open economy may have only one firm producing at home and still enjoy the advantages of competition due to actual or potential sales by foreign producers.

References

Atwood, James, and Kingman Brewster, Jr., *Antitrust and American Business Abroad,* 2nd edition, New York: McGraw-Hill (1981).

Dornbusch, Rudiger, and Stanley Fischer, "The Open Economy: Implications for Monetary and Fiscal Policy," National Bureau of Economic Research, Working Paper No. 1422 (August 1984).

Helliwell, John, and Timothy Padmore, "Empirical Studies of Macroeconomic Interdependence" in Ronald W. Jones and Peter B. Kenen (eds.), *Handbook in International Economics,* vol. 2, Amsterdam: Elsevier Science Publishers (1985).

Keohane, Robert O., and Joseph S. Nye, Jr., *Power and Interdependence: World Politics in Transition,* Boston: Little Brown (1977).

Keatley, Anne G., ed., *Technological Frontiers and Foreign Relations,* Washington: National Academy of Sciences (1985).

Key, Sydney, "International Banking Facilities as a Free Economic Zone," *Aussenwirtschaft* vol. 39, 1984, pp. 57–74.

Kyle, Steve, unpublished Ph.D. dissertation, Department of Economics, Harvard University (1985).

Marris, Stephen, *Deficits and the Dollar: The World Economy at Risk,* Washington: Institute for International Economics (1986).

Mitchell, Daniel B., "Shifting Norms in Wage Determination," *Brookings Papers on Economic Activity,* No. 2, 1985, pp. 575–99.

Morganstern, Oskar, *International Financial Transactions and Business Cycles,* Princeton, N.J.: Princeton University Press (1959).

Obstfeld, Maurice, "Floating Exchange Rates: Performance and Prospects," *Brookings Papers on Economic Activity,* No. 2, 1985, pp. 369–450.

Comments

Peter B. Kenen

L et me start with a rather long quotation. I have taken a few liberties with it to disguise its source temporarily.

[E]conomic interdependence among industrial countries has increased sharply in the last several decades, and this increase is likely to continue unless it is deliberately checked. . . .

The vast accumulation of capital and the international transmission of knowledge have reduced inter-country variation in comparative cost structure. . . . This narrowing of cost differences has been complemented by the reduction of transportation and communication costs and, since 1949, by the policy-guided reduction in tariffs and other artificial barriers to trade. . . .

[T]he psychological and institutional barriers to international capital movements among industrial countries [also] have eroded rapidly. . . . Capital tends increasingly to move in great volume from country to country in search of small yield differentials.

This greater economic interdependence has three consequences for national economic policy. First, it increases the number of "disturbances" with which national policy-makers must cope. Changes in incomes, prices, costs, and interest rates abroad are more rapidly transmitted into changes in the demand for domestic output or funds than they used to be, and these changes in turn affect domestic income, employment, prices, [and] interest rates. . . .

Second, the enlarged interactions among national economies will generally slow the speed with which traditional measures of economic policy take effect on the level of domestic employment, output, and interest rates, for each move will "spill over" into other economies and will evoke policy reactions there which will often weaken the influence of the measures initially instituted. . . .

Third, competition by one nation with another in the use of national policies can leave the community of nations worse off than it need be. Regulatory action or taxation may be thwarted by the prompt movement of regulated businesses beyond the jurisdiction of the regulating nations or by the shifting of profits through intracorporate pricing. . . .

In sum, as national economies become more closely integrated, national freedom to set national economic objectives and to pursue them effectively with national instruments of policy is increasingly circumscribed.

Who wrote this passage? When was it published? It comes from Richard Cooper, in the final chapter of his book *The Economics of Interdependence,* published in 1968.

I do not mean to chide Cooper for repeating himself. Some things have to be repeated, because economists can barely keep up with newly published work and cannot reach back to refresh their memories or, for that matter, to read what was written before they began to practice the trade. Furthermore, there are important differences between Cooper's earlier treatment of the subject and the excellent chapter he has written for this book. I will return to these differences shortly. First, two observations about his earlier treatment of the subject.

Cooper was right in predicting that integration would continue. In fact, it continues even now, and the deregulation of domestic financial markets that is going on today in several countries will probably carry the process further. During the past decade, however, there has probably been some significant *dis*integration of goods markets, as distinguished from financial markets, with the spreading use of quantitative trade barriers outside the GATT framework. Comparing the current situation with the one in 1968, I would guess that goods markets are less closely integrated, despite the Kennedy and Tokyo rounds of tariff cuts and the enlargement of the European Community. But integration has gone on in another direction. In his book, Cooper concentrated on relations among developed countries. In his chapter here, he calls attention to many ways in which their economies are now closely tied to those of the less-developed countries (LDCs): The increasing dependence of the United States on raw materials that come mainly from the LDCs, the impact of recession and austerity in the heavily indebted LDCs on the level of U.S. exports, and, most important right now, the complex set of relationships described as the debt problem.

In one important respect, economic thought has gone in an unexpected direction. Cooper wrote his book shortly before the breakdown of the Bretton Woods system, and he did not anticipate or advocate the shift to more flexible exchange rates that took place in its wake. That is one important contribution of his chapter. It examines the ways in which floating rates have altered the policy problem facing industrial countries, and I will say more about this issue. But something else is new. Cooper made a recommendation in 1968 that he has chosen to omit from his current chapter. He noted in 1968 that the increased interdependence forces policymakers to confront three alternatives:

1. to accept the integration and the consequential loss of national freedom, and to engage in the *joint* determination of economic objectives and policies;

2. to accept the integration but attempt to preserve as much national autonomy as possible by providing financial accommodation for prolonged
   payments deficits;
3. to reject the integration by deliberate imposition of barriers to the inte-
   grating forces, freedom of foreign trade and international capital movements.

In his view, governments were not ready in 1968 to adopt the first solution,
partly because they confused formal sovereignty with real freedom of action,
and they were not even ready for the second, because it involved substantial
confidence on the part of each government in the ability of the other governments to manage their policies. The third option he viewed as possibly win-
ning by default. He ended his book on the pessimistic note that "unhappily,
the principal contender to controlled use of restrictions is uncontrolled use
of restrictions," which seemed to be the direction in which the world was
moving late in the 1960s.

   If Cooper had written his book shortly after the breakdown of the
Bretton Woods system and the shift to more flexible exchange rates, he might
have been less pessimistic. Speaking for myself, because I cannot speak for
him, I was prepared to believe that floating rates could rehabilitate national
autonomy, not merely because central banks would be able to control
national money supplies but also because the effects of monetary and fiscal
policies would be bottled up to a greater extent, having more effect at home
and less effect abroad. And many of us thought that floating rates would have
important normative implications. Governments would not be constrained to
pursue external balance, and there would be less need for them to concern
themselves with the coordination of national policies, let alone the joint
determination of policies, which was the first option on Cooper's list in 1968.
At the very least, some economists expected that floating exchange rates
would reduce the temptation for governments to interfere with integration by
the uncontrolled use of controls and would surely reduce governments' need
to interfere by the controlled use of controls.

   In his chapter here, Cooper explains why those expectations were wrong.
Formal models had not caught up with the process of integration; they did
not pay enough attention to the consequences of capital mobility for the
modus operandi of monetary and fiscal policies. To be sure, Mundell (1963)
had brought some of those consequences to our attention, but economists
were inclined to regard them as footnotes to standard exchange rate theory
rather than basic revisions. They did not truly appreciate the chief consequence of capital mobility—that monetary and fiscal policies would function
in large measure by attracting or repelling capital flows, which would in turn
call forth balancing adjustments in trade flows, by way of the exchange rate,
and that the adjustments in trade flows would have first-order effects on
output and employment. They did not begin to understand that a floating
exchange rate could lead a life of its own, nurtured by expectations about

future policies and other events, and that price flexibility in the market for foreign exchange could combine with price stickiness in the markets for goods and labor to generate large changes in real exchange rates, which could in turn affect output and employment more or less independently of current policies.

Economists have revised their views, and so have governments. Indeed, governments may have come full circle with the recent decision by the Group of Five (G-5), that is, France, Germany, Japan, the United Kingdom, and the United States, to concern themselves with the behavior of exchange rates, to intervene in foreign exchange markets, and, by implication, to assess the compatibility of their national policies by reference to their impact on capital movements and exchange rates. Economists may therefore confront today a set of options not too different from the set that Cooper set before them in 1968: (1) the close coordination of national policies, leading in the limiting case to the joint determination of those policies; (2) the partial financing of imbalances, by way of intervention; and (3) the controlled use of controls to reduce integration and restore national autonomy.

I may be reading too much into the G-5 decision. I hope not. But I would like to have Cooper's view. Let me ask him directly, then, what options are available? Is it still possible to contemplate a selective use of controls to separate national capital markets? Or have markets passed a point of no return? Would an attempt at selective disintegration induce enough avoidance and evasion to provoke an intensification and generalization of controls? Would the process of control get out of control? That is my fear and my reason for believing that Cooper's third option may not be available. In which case, of course, governments must decide how much coordination to combine with exchange rate management and the concomitant financing of imbalances, especially those that reflect large capital flows.

In most discussions of these issues, policy coordination is viewed as a precondition for exchange rate stabilization. But the recent report of the Group of Ten (that is, Belgium-Luxembourg, Canada, France, Germany, Italy, Japan, the Netherlands, Switzerland, the United Kingdom, and the United States) concedes that the "convergence" of national policies, whether expressed in terms of targets or instruments, may not be sufficient for stabilization, and my own current work has led me to believe that optimal exchange rate management should be viewed as a partial substitute for the coordination of domestic policies (see Kenen, 1985).

Cooper's chapter here raises many other issues. Let me mention four that call for further reflection.

Cooper notes that the correlation between U.S. and British interest rates has fallen sharply in recent years and that the average difference between them has risen. This was, he says, "a function wholly of differences in the currency of denomination," citing in evidence the persistently close correlation between CD rates in the United States and Eurodollar rates in London. Does this really mean, however, that floating exchange rates have restored some monetary autonomy? The answer, I believe, depends on the way that interest rates affect the real side of the economy. If spending decisions by firms and households depend on the (real) domestic interest rate, Cooper is right. The variability of expectations about future exchange rates allows a central bank to influence expenditure by changing the size of the gap between domestic and foreign interest rates (by conducting itself in a way that affects exchange rate expectations or the size of the risk premium). If, instead, decisions by firms and households depend on the (real) domestic interest rate corrected for exchange rate expectations, more variability in that gap does not necessarily raise the influence of monetary policy on the domestic economy. I am inclined to agree with Cooper, who appears to believe that the *IS* curve should be drawn with reference to the (real) domestic interest rate, but economists must be very clear about this point.

Which brings me to my second point, one concerning the demand for money and thus the *LM* curve. Cooper is right to say that the increased openness of the U.S. economy casts doubt on the validity of the standard demand-for-money function. But he may give too much away when he says that "the only argument in the equation that is not brought into question by greater openness is the interest rate." While I agree with Cooper about the *IS* curve, I am less sure about the *LM* curve. The foreign interest rate and exchange rate expectations may affect the demand for money. I am not impressed by simple currency-substitution models and the statistical evidence that has been adduced to support them. And I have trouble with the notion of "indirect currency substitution" that McKinnon (1984) uses to replace those simple models. Nevertheless, I continue to be intrigued by a remarkable coincidence. The famous mystery of the missing money cropped up just when the world was moving toward exchange rate flexibility. This may, of course, be the impact of a common cause; the acceleration of inflation in the early 1970s could have destabilized the demand for money while also being one reason why governments sought more monetary autonomy by letting their currencies float. But I am not satisfied by this explanation.[1]

My third point pertains to the endnote in Cooper's chapter that deals with the impact of fiscal expansion on the behavior of a floating exchange rate and calls attention to an anomaly. Although fiscal expansion by the United States causes the dollar to appreciate, fiscal expansions by other countries seem to cause their currencies to depreciate.[2] I can think of several complicated explanations, one of them related to my next and final point, that the role of the dollar as an international currency may have macroeconomic implications distinct from those typically assigned to the large size of the U.S. economy. But there may be a simple explanation. The builders of large multi-country models are very careful to impose consistency on the behavior of trade flows; exports from *A* to *B* are always made to equal imports by *B* from *A*. They may not be as careful, however, about imposing consistency on the behavior of capital flows, and their models may behave asymmetrically when the real world does not.

Finally, I call your attention to a single sentence in Cooper's chapter: "The United States is so large a part of the world economy, and the dollar is so widely used, that the United States can influence world monetary conditions to the point of determining them." I have written similar sentences from time to time. Each time, however, I have an uneasy moment, because I would have trouble explaining the point at length. I know that the use of the dollar as an international currency has something to do with the influence of U.S. monetary policy, which cannot be due entirely to the size of the U.S economy, even when size is measured in terms of asset markets as well as goods markets. But I cannot describe precisely the contribution made by the transnational use of the dollar, let alone measure it, and most theoretical models are unhelpful. They virtually preclude a transnational role for a national currency, because they net out all "inside" debts and claims; they focus primarily on changes in supplies of government debt; and the whole Eurocurrency market is made to implode, along with all other forms of intermediation. The same thing is done in most empirical work. Krugman (1984) has shown why foreign exchange markets will want to employ a single vehicle currency. He has dealt with some other aspects of the problem as well, but that sort of analysis has to be carried further before it can shed light on the broad issue. The whole subject calls for much more work.

Notes

1. Note in passing one more problem. Cooper asks whether the demand for money should be treated as a function of output or expenditure—a question that does not arise in a closed economy but can be important in an open economy. Let me ask another question. If the demand for money should depend on output, should it then depend on gross output, including its import content, or on net output (value added)? If the latter, there arises an interesting problem that has not received much attention. Consider an economy that produces and exports a single commodity x, with price p_x, but imports an input y, with price p_y. For simplicity of exposition, suppose that velocity is fixed at v and that the input requirement is fixed at k units of y per unit of x. Then the demand for money is

$$M = v(p_x \cdot x - p_y \cdot y) = v[p_x \cdot x(1 - kp)], \qquad (1.1)$$

where $p = p_y/p_x$. An improvement in the terms of trade (a fall in p) has an odd effect. It raises the demand for money and will thus depress p_x or x unless the central bank raises the supply of money. Putting the point intuitively, a fall in the price of oil should reduce aggregate demand in an oil-importing country by way of its effect on the demand for money, even though it stimulates aggregate demand by way of its income effect.

2. Incidentally, Cooper asserts in that note that fiscal expansion *must* cause the domestic currency to appreciate in portfolio-balance models. That may be true in the particular model he cites, but it is not true in all such models. In Allen and Kenen (1980), the exchange rate can go either way under the influence of an ongoing budget deficit, depending in part on the degree of capital mobility; when the budget deficit is ended and the economy allowed to reach its new stationary state, the value of the domestic currency will be lower, not higher, than in the initial stationary state. (This last result is, of course, consistent with the underlying logic of the portfolio-balance approach; an increase in the supply of dollar bonds causes the dollar to depreciate eventually.)

References

Polly Reynolds Allen and Peter B. Kenen, *Asset Markets, Exchange Rates, and Economic Integration.* Cambridge University Press, Cambridge, England, 1980.

Richard N. Cooper, *The Economics of Interdependence.* McGraw-Hill for the Council on Foreign Relations, New York, 1968.

Deputies of the Group of 10, *Report on the Functioning of the International Monetary System,* 1985; reprinted in *IMF Survey,* International Monetary Fund, Washington, D.C., July 1985.

Peter B. Kenen, "Reforming the International Monetary System: The Need for Consistency in Weighing Options." Paper presented to the New York Academy of Sciences, September 1985 (processed).

Paul Krugman, "The International Role of the Dollar: Theory and Prospect" in J.F.O. Bilson and R.C. Marston, eds., *Exchange Rate Theory and Practice.* University of Chicago Press, Chicago, 1984.

Ronald I. McKinnon, *An International Standard for Monetary Stabilization.* Policy Analyses in International Economics, 5. Institute for International Economics, Washington, D.C., 1984.

Robert A. Mundell, "Capital Mobility and Stabilization Policy under Fixed and Flexible Exchange Rates," *Canadian Journal of Economics & Political Science* 29, November 1963; reprinted in R.A. Mundell, *International Economics,* Macmillan, New York, 1968, chap. 18.

2
International Capital Mobility and Crowding-out in the U.S. Economy: Imperfect Integration of Financial Markets or of Goods Markets?

Jeffrey A. Frankel

C onventional wisdom in the field of international finance holds that the U.S. economy has become so open financially as to be characterized by perfect capital mobility: A highly elastic supply of foreign capital prevents the domestic rate of return from rising significantly above the world rate of return. This view has been challenged recently by the observation that investment rates are highly correlated with national saving rates, and the claim by Feldstein and Horioka that this correlation is evidence of relatively low capital mobility. The experience of the United States in the 1980s seems to confirm this challenge. The decline in U.S. national saving has been partly offset by a capital inflow from abroad, but the effect has not been large enough to prevent U.S. real interest rates from rising and to an extent crowding out domestic investment.

The premise of this chapter is that the Feldstein-Horioka finding regarding crowding-out in an open economy is strong enough to survive the econometric critiques that have been leveled against it, but that it need have nothing to do with the degree of capital mobility in the sense of the openness of financial markets and the equalization of international interest rates expressed in a common currency. It is *real* interest rates that matter for questions of crowding-out, and real interest parity requires not just that nominal interest rates be equalized and expressed in a common currency, but also that purchasing power parity hold. It is well known that purchasing power parity does not in fact hold. Currently, for example, the dollar is expected to depreciate in real terms. Thus real interest rate parity fails and crowding-out takes place *because of imperfect integration of goods markets, not imperfect integration of financial markets.*

I would like to thank Ken Froot, Youkyong Kwon, Tom Walter, and especially Alan MacArthur for their efficient research assistance. I would also like to thank Jim Boughton, Lans Bovenberg, Ken Froot, Frederic Mishkin, Maurice Obstfeld, and Kerry Odell for comments and suggestions. Views expressed here represent the opinions of the author and should not be interpreted as views of the International Monetary Fund.

The first major section of this chapter presents the issues in the context of crowding-out by the U.S. budget deficit in the 1980s. The second section presents regressions of investment against national saving on U.S. historical data. The third discusses three distinct senses in which the term *perfect international capital mobility* has been used: (1) closed interest parity, (2) uncovered interest parity, and (3) real interest parity. It also attempts to see how much of the real interest differential can be explained by expected real depreciation. The final section offers conclusions.

International Capital Mobility and U.S. Crowding-out in the 1980s

It is a commonplace that the U.S. economy has over its history become increasingly integrated into world goods markets and financial markets. As regards goods markets, imports and exports (averaged) as a share of GNP rose gradually at an annual trend rate of .096 percent a year from 1929 to 1984, reaching 9.1 percent of GNP in the 1980s.[1] The percentage of the economy consisting of goods and services that are potentially tradable internationally, as opposed to actually traded, is of course considerably higher. International competition now reaches almost everywhere, beyond U.S. manufacturing into agriculture and services. Long-run trends toward lower transportation costs, lower tariffs, and an increasingly integrated world culture have all played their parts.

U.S. financial markets are considered to be even more closely integrated with the rest of the world than are goods markets. Here the development of the Eurocurrency market, the removal of capital controls when the Bretton Woods system ended, and the continued technological progress in telecommunications and innovation in the banking system worldwide have all been important. Indeed the assumption of perfect capital mobility has for twenty years now been standard in models of floating exchange rates among the United States and most other major industrialized countries, despite some of the surprisingly strong conclusions that typically follow from it.

One strong conclusion that is thought to follow from perfect capital mobility is that a fiscal expansion has no effects—neither a negative effect on investment nor a positive effect on aggregate output. The absence of an effect on investment arises because a potentially infinite capital inflow prevents the domestic interest rate from rising above the world interest rate, so that none of the crowding out of investment that is usual in closed economy models occurs. The absence of an effect on aggregate output arises because the currency appreciates and worsens the trade balance by precisely enough to offset the gain in domestic demand. One can see from a money market equilibrium condition that if the interest rate does not change, because it is tied to the foreign interest rate, and the real money supply does not change, then real income cannot change.[2]

The question of fiscal crowding-out has become especially topical in the 1980s because of the large structural fiscal deficits run by the U.S. federal government. According to some theories an increase in government dissaving should be precisely offset by an increase in private saving, by people putting aside money to help their children pay future taxes, so that there is no effect on total national saving. (National saving is defined as whatever private saving is left over after the government budget deficit has been subtracted out.) Whatever one thinks of the theoretical merits of the argument, the results of the current experiment seem clear. The increase in federal dissaving from the 1970s to the 1980s has not been matched by a rise in private saving. The rate of total national saving has fallen, from 16.1 percent of GNP on average from 1973 to 1980 to 14.5 percent from 1981 to 1984.[3]

As a matter of accounting identity, this fall in national saving must equal the rise in net capital inflow from abroad plus the fall in domestic investment. The question of interest is how the change is divided up between the two. There has in fact been a large net capital inflow, the counterpart of the record current account deficits, but it has not been large enough to prevent the investment rate from falling, from 16.1 percent of GNP from 1973 to 1980 to 15.4 percent from 1981 to 1984.[4]

More visibly, the capital inflow has not been large enough to prevent U.S. real interest rates from rising sharply, even vis-à-vis foreign real interest rates. There are of course different ways of measuring the real interest rate. For questions of saving and investment, the long-term nominal interest rate is to be preferred over the short-term rate. But measuring inflation expectations is more problematic in the long term than in the short term. Table 2–1 reports measures of long-term real interest rates using four measures of expected inflation that are available for both the United States and major trading partners: A three-year lag on past inflation (with weights .5, .3, and .2), forecasts by Data Resources, International (DRI), forecasts by the OECD, and a survey by American Express of opinions among 250 to 300 central bankers, private bankers, corporate treasurers and finance directors, and economists. By any of the four measures there was a clear increase in the U.S. real interest rate after 1980, both absolutely and relative to a weighted average of trading partners. The long-term real interest differential stood at about 3 percent in the first part of 1985, as compared to − 2 percent five years earlier.

For those outside the field of international economics, the novel feature of the 1980s is the magnitude of the U.S. capital inflow and of its counterpart, the notorious record trade deficits. The unfavorable effect of the latter on U.S. export- and import-competing sectors has of course received a great deal of attention; and the favorable effect of the former, keeping interest rates

Table 2–1
Interest Rate Differentials between U.S. and Foreign Assets, and Other Measures of the Expected Rate of Dollar Depreciation, 1976–85
(percent per annum)

		1976–78	1979–80	1981–82	1983–84	1985
Expected nominal rate of depreciation						
1.1	One-year interest differential[a]	−0.48	2.29	3.00	1.73	1.15
1.2	One-year forward discount	0.18	2.57	3.34	1.85	1.32
1.3	Ten-year interest differential	−0.50	0.56	1.91	2.47	2.92
1.4	Economist survey[b]	NA	NA	8.57	8.60	7.12
1.5	American Express survey[c]	0.64	NA	6.67	6.99	NA
Expected inflation rate differential						
2.1	One-year lag	−1.01	3.54	0.88	−0.35	0.06
2.2	Three-year distributed lag	−1.96	2.70	1.89	−0.18	−0.16
2.3	DRI three-year forecast[d]	NA	2.20	0.96	0.23	0.15
2.4	OECD two-year forecast[e]	1.42	2.24	0.62	0.61	−0.20
2.5	American Express survey[f]	−0.75	NA	4.11	2.68	NA
Expected real rate of depreciation						
1.1 – 2.1	One-year real interest differential	0.53	−1.24	2.12	2.09	1.08
1.3–2.2	Ten-year with distributed lag	1.47	−2.15	0.02	2.64	3.08
1.3–2.3	Ten-year with DRI forecast	NA	−1.64	0.95	2.24	2.77
1.3–2.4	Ten-year with OECD forecast	−1.92	−1.68	1.29	1.86	3.12
1.5–2.5	American Express survey	1.39	NA	2.56	4.31	NA
	Dividend/price ratio[g]	NA	1.10	1.79	1.65	1.80
	Earnings/price ratio[g]	NA	1.60	3.99	2.60	3.09

Sources unless otherwise specified: International Monetary Fund *International Financial Statistics* and DRI FACS financial data base, Data Resources, International.

Note: The foreign variables are GNP-weighted averages of the United Kingdom, France, West Germany, and Japan, unless otherwise specified.

[a]Calculated as log (1 + *i*). 1985 contains data through June. Rates for Japan are not available for 1976–77.

[b]Available at 24 survey dates. Source: Economist *Financial Report* (various issues).

[c]Available at 11 survey dates. Source: *American Express Bank Review* (various issues).

[d]Averages of same 24 dates as in footnote [b]. Source: DRI forecasts.

[e]1976–78 data covers only December 1978. 1985 data covers only June 1985. Source: OECD *Economic Outlook*.

[f]Available at same 11 survey dates as in footnote [c] for the United States, United Kingdom, and West Germany. Available at only four survey dates (1976–78) for France.

[g]End-of-quarter averages. 1979–80 includes data only for 1980. 1985 data is for end of first quarter. Foreign ratios represent the aggregate of Europe, Australia, and the Far East. Source: *Capital International Perspective*, Geneva.

from rising as much as they otherwise would, has received some attention as well. But for those inside the field the interesting question is rather: If capital mobility is as perfect as economists have been assuming, why has there been *any* rise in the real interest differential; why has the increase in the net capital inflow not been large enough to prevent *any* crowding out of investment; and why has the increase in the trade deficit not been large enough to counteract the expansionary effects of the fiscal policy so as not to leave *any* net effect on national income?

Correlations of Saving and Investment

The Feldstein-Horioka Methodology

Even before the current episode, Feldstein and Horioka (1980) initiated a controversy on the subject of the implications of perfect capital mobility. They ran cross-sectional regressions of investment against national saving, found coefficients much closer to one than to zero, and interpreted the results as evidence that capital mobility is in fact far less than perfect. The argument was that if a country faced an infinitely elastic foreign supply of capital that prevented the domestic rate of return from rising above the foreign rate, then random variation in propensities to save or in government deficits should be fully offset by international capital flows, and there would be no reason for them to have any effect on investment rates.

The Feldstein-Horioka work has been subjected to a barrage of critiques. Virtually all of them are econometric in nature. Little of the commentary has tried to define better than did Feldstein and Horioka what precisely is the hypothesis that one is seeking to test, or how it relates conceptually to more conventional definitions of capital mobility based on rates of return. Doing so is one of the major aims of this chapter.[5]

But first I will address some of the econometric critiques of the Feldstein-Horioka regressions. Consider the national saving identity with each of its components specified as functions of the rate of return r:

$$I(r) - NS(r, \bar{G}) = KA(r - r^*) \qquad (2.1)$$

where I is investment, NS is national saving, KA is the net capital inflow from abroad, and $\bar{G}$ is government expenditure, or any other determinant of NS thought to be exogenous. Then (assuming also that r^*, the foreign rate of return, is exogenous),

$$\frac{dI}{d\bar{G}} = I_r \frac{dr}{d\bar{G}} = \frac{NS_{\bar{G}}}{1 + (KA_r + NS_r)/(-I_r)} \qquad (2.2)$$

This derivative is in general negative, assuming $NS_{\bar{G}}$ is. But it is zero if $KA_r = \infty$, and is equal to the closed economy crowding-out effect if $KA_r = 0$.

There are three basic econometric difficulties with regressions of investment against national saving. The first, which arises only in time series studies, is the strongly procyclical nature of both saving and investment, even when expressed as shares of GNP (as they always are in these studies). If an exogenous boom causes the saving rate and investment rate both to rise, I do not want to attribute it to low capital mobility. For this reason, Feldstein and Horioka restricted their analysis to cross-sectional data, as did most who followed in their footsteps.[6] The second econometric difficulty is the "large-country problem": The United States and other major countries cannot take the world rate of return r^* as exogenous. Even if perfect capital mobility equates the domestic interest rate to the world interest rate, a fall in domestic saving will reduce domestic investment to the extent that it drives up the world interest rate.[7]

The third econometric difficulty is the general one of endogenicity of the independent variable. The error term in the regression equation consists of all factors determining investment, other than the rate of return (and GNP). If they happen to be uncorrelated with the independent variable, there is no problem. But this is unlikely, especially in light of the identity linking saving and investment.

Probably the most popular criticism of the Feldstein-Horioka regressions is the "policy reaction" argument: Governments react to current account imbalances so as to reduce them. For example, if the government reacts to a trade deficit induced by a random increase in investment, by cutting government expenditure or raising taxes, then national saving and investment will be correlated for reasons having nothing to do with capital mobility.[8] If endogeneity of national saving were the only problem, economists could invert the equation and regress national saving against investment; the hypothesis that capital is in infinitely elastic supply at a given rate of return would still imply a zero coefficient. This test would be equivalent (given the national savings identity) to regressing the current account against investment; the null hypothesis would in that case be a unit coefficient, implying that any exogenous changes in investment are fully financed by borrowing from abroad. This in fact is the equation run by Sachs (1981, 1983). But arguments as to why saving should be endogenous apply also to investment. Clearly the right answer is that national saving, investment, and the current account are all endogenous, and no ordinary least-squares (OLS) regression is appropriate.

If the motivation is to see whether changes in private saving or the government budget would crowd out investment in an open economy, then economists should indeed think of the former as a right-hand side variable and the latter as the left. But the technique that is required is instrumental variables. Total government expenditure is probably not a good enough instrument because under the policy-reaction argument, it is endogenous. Two better candidates are military expenditure and the age composition of the population. The former is most immediately a determinant of the government budget deficit and the latter of private saving. It is possible to think of ways that either could be endogenous; it is conceivable that military expenditure could be cut back in response to trade deficits and that the age composition of the population could respond to the growth rate. It is also possible to think of ways that either could affect investment through routes other than saving and the rate of return. But these two variables seem to meet the criteria for instruments at least as well as most alleged instrumental variables in macroeconomics.[9]

U.S. Saving and Investment Time Series

This section reports Feldstein-Horioka tests on U.S. data. Econometric "fix-ups" for each of the three kinds of problems are attempted. But no claim is made that the results are good tests of the degree of capital mobility. Indeed, it is argued in subsequent sections that they are not. In this chapter in a sense I follow in a tradition of other economists who have criticized Feldstein and Horioka and then found the temptation irresistible to do a few tests of their own on the grounds that the high correlation of savings and investment is an interesting empirical regularity.[10]

If one is concerned with the worldwide degree of capital mobility or crowding out, then cross-sectional studies of the sort performed by Feldstein and Horioka (1980), Penati and Dooley (1984), and others are appropriate. However, if one seeks to isolate such parameters for the United States in particular, and if one wishes to see how they have evolved over time, then time series regression is necessary. I ran instrumental variables regressions of investment against national saving for the United States from 1870 to 1979. I use decade averages of saving and investment rates, hoping to remove the cyclical variation. The data are graphed in figure 2–1.[11] One can see that in the 1890s, U.S. investment fell below national saving, that is, the country began to run current account surpluses, lending abroad in particularly large amounts when Europe was dissaving during World War I. One can also see that both saving and investment fell drastically in the Depression, never fully to return to earlier levels.

Table 2–2 reports the results of the instrumental variables regressions. The coefficient estimate is .96, indicating a very high degree of crowding-out ("low capital mobility"). Despite the very small number of observations (eleven) the standard error is relatively small. Even when corrected for the (marginal) presence of serial correlation, the estimate is high (.91) and one can easily reject the hypothesis of zero crowding-out ("perfect capital mobil-

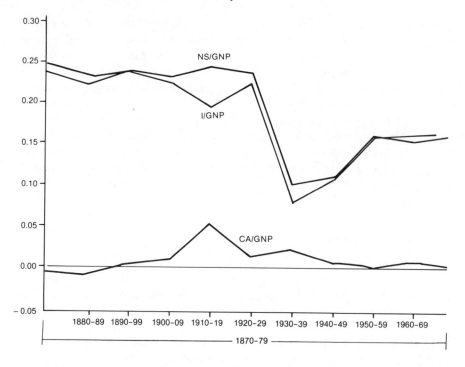

Sources: Roger Ransom and Richard Sutch, "Domestic Saving as an Active Constraint on Capital Formation in the American Economy, 1839–1928: A Provisional Theory." University of California Project on the History of Saving, Working Paper no. 1. University of California-Berkeley, 1983, Tables 4 and E1; and U.S. Department of Commerce, *Historical Statistics of the U.S.*

Figure 2–1. U.S. National Saving (Private Saving plus Government Budget Surplus) (NS), Investment (I), and Current Account (CA) as Shares of GNP, 1870–1979

ity"), though one cannot reject the opposite extreme. To try to see whether the relationship has changed over time, I added a coefficient trend term. Its sign is positive, pointing to an increasing degree of crowding out, but it is not statistically significant, as one would expect from the small number of observations.[12]

A more recent data set would seem more promising for two reasons. First, yearly data are available. Second, it is widely believed that the postwar trend toward increased integration of the economies of the United States and other countries, both with respect to financial markets and goods markets, merely reversed sharp movements in the opposite direction that took place in the interwar period. Thus one looks for a trend beginning in the 1930s at the earliest.

Table 2–2
Instrumental Variables Regression of U.S. Investment against National
Saving, Decades 1870–1979

	Constant	Coefficient	Time Trend in Coefficients	Durbin-Watson Statistic	Autoregressive Parameter	R^2
1.	.000 (.028)	.957 (.144)		1.5		.91
2.	.007 (.914)	.914 (.238)			.20 (.37)	.91
3.	−.025 (.083)	1.035 (.203)	.010 (.030)	1.2		.89

Notes: Standard errors are reported in parentheses.

Dependent variable: productive capital formation/GNP

Independent variable: (gross private saving plus increase in government debt)/GNP

Source: Roger Ransom and Richard Sutch. "Domestic Saving as an Active Constraint on Capital Formation in the American Economy, 1839–1928: A Provisional Theory." University of California Project on the History of Saving, Working paper no. 1. University of California-Berkeley, 1983, tables 4 and E1.

Instrumental variables: (Department of Defense outlays/GNP) and (population 65 years of age and over/population over age 20).

Sources: *Historical Statistics of the U.S.*, Series Y 458–460 and Series A 119 and 133, respectively, Department of Commerce.

Tables 2–3 and 2–4 repeat the regressions for yearly U.S. data in the period 1930–84. In this case, with the greater number of observations, one can reject both extremes of zero and one, even when making the necessary correction for serial correlation. One can also identify a statistically significant time trend of .01 per year in the coefficient. It implies that the degree of crowding out rises over time, from an estimated coefficient of .19 in 1930 (insignificantly different from zero) to an estimated coefficient of .74 in 1984 (insignificantly different from unity). An alternative way to see how the coefficient changes over time is to split the sample. I chose as the breaking point 1958, the year when the European countries restored convertibility of their currencies. The two coefficients are very similar, .75 in the first half of the sample and .78 in the second. In both cases one can easily reject a zero coefficient, but in the 1959–84 period one is unable to reject a coefficient of unity.

One would expect that the foregoing coefficient estimates would be biased upward by the cyclical endogeneity problem, because they are not based on longer-term averages. Table 2–4 reports regressions using yearly saving and investment rates that have been cyclically adjusted. The cyclical adjustment of each is accomplished by first regressing it on the GNP gap, defined as the percentage deviation from the Bureau of Economic Analysis's

Table 2–3
Regressions of Investment against National Saving (Both as Shares of GNP), Yearly Data, 1930–84

	Constant	Coefficient	Time Trend in Coefficient	Autoregressive Parameter	R^2
1930–84	.068 (.017)	.484* (.096)		.80 (.09)	.88
1930–84	.050 (.025)	.176* (.188)	.013* (.003)	.67	.86
1930–58	.021 (.019)	.752* (.104)		.68 (.14)	.93
1959–84	.035 (.029)	.783* (.187)		.55 (.25)	.70

Sources: For gross saving and gross private domestic investment, 1985 *Economic Report of the President,* table B–25. For cyclical adjustment, "Middle Income Expansion Trend," *Survey of Current Business* (U.S. Dept. of Commerce, December 1983). For instrumental variables, *Historical Statistics of the U.S.,* Series Y 458–460 and Series A 119 and 133, Department of Commerce.

Notes: Standard errors are reported in parentheses.

Instrumental variables: Military expenditure/GNP ratio and over-65 population ratio.
*Statistically significant at 95 percent level.

Table 2–4
Regressions of Investment against National Saving (Both as Cyclically Adjusted Shares of GNP), Yearly Data, 1955–84

	Constant	Coefficient	Time Trend in Coefficient	Durbin-Watson Statistic	Autoregressive Parameter	R^2
1955–84		.699* (.190)		.86		.41
1956–84		.803* (.257)			.60 (.22)	.52
1956–84	.003 (.006)	.319 (.429)	.048 (.029)		.77 (.26)	.46
1955–73	−.003 (.002)	.761* (.189)			.27 (.25)	.69
1975–84	.042 (.232)	.181 (.645)			.93	.21

Sources: For gross saving and gross private domestic investment, 1985 *Economic Report of the President,* table B–25. For cyclical adjustment, "Middle Income Expansion Trend," *Survey of Current Business* (U.S. Dept. of Commerce, December 1983). For instrumental variables, *Historical Statistics of the U.S.,* Series Y 458–460 and Series A 119 and 133, Department of Commerce.

Notes: Standard errors are reported in parentheses.

Instrumental variables: Military expenditure/GNP ratio and over-65 population ratio.
*Statistically significant at 95 percent level.

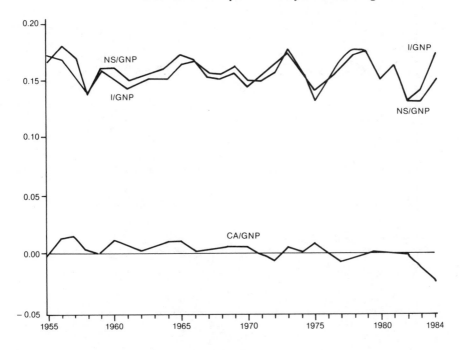

Source: 1985 *Economic Report of the President.*

Figure 2–2. U.S. National Saving (NS), Investment (I), and Current Account (CA) as Shares of GNP, 1955–84

"middle expansion trend" of GNP and taking the residuals. The saving and investment rates are graphed in figures 2–2 and 2–3 for the period 1955–84. They are more stable than earlier in U.S. history.[13] Nevertheless there is enough variation to see that the two series do move together, even after the cyclical variation has been taken out (figure 2–3). The cyclically adjusted investment and saving rates show a regression coefficient of .81. This is similar to the estimate for the much longer 1870–1979 period (.91) in that one can easily reject zero but cannot reject unity. Attempts to find a postwar trend in the coefficient or a break in the data when capital controls were removed in 1974 suggest that the coefficient has been moving closer to one—that is, that the degree of crowding out has increased (or the degree of capital mobility has fallen). But the standard errors are too large, probably because the number of observations and the variation in the data are too small, for the shift to be statistically significant.

The failure to reject complete crowding-out is the same result found by Obstfeld (1985, pp. 39–43) on quarterly U.S. data. The failure to find a drop in the coefficient even in the 1970s is the same result found by Feldstein

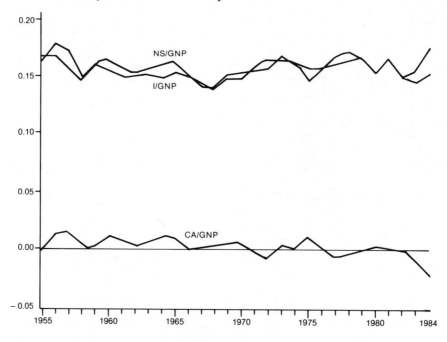

Source: 1985 *Economic Report of the President* and U.S. Department of Commerce, *Survey of Current Business.*

Figure 2–3. U.S. National Saving (NS), Investment (I), and Current Account (CA) as Cyclically Adjusted Shares of GNP, 1955–84

(1983) and Penati and Dooley (1984, pp. 8–10), and interpreted by them as contradicting the popular impression of an increase in the degree of capital mobility among OECD countries.

Obstfeld (1985) attributes the continued high magnitude of the U.S. coefficient in the recent period to the large-country problem. It remains even after the use of instrumental variables and cyclically adjusted numbers. The next step is to relate the *differential* between the U.S. investment rate and the rest of the world's investment rate to the *differential* in national saving rates. Under the null hypothesis, an exogenous fall in the U.S. national saving rate may drive up the world real interest rate and crowd out investment, but there is no reason for the crowding-out to be reflected in U.S. investment *any more* than in the rest-of-the-world investment. Such differential saving rates and investment rates are calculated in table 2–5. The close correspondence between U.S. saving and investment remains: The coefficient in a regression is .740, and is highly significant despite the small number of observations.[14]

Table 2–5
Saving and Investment in the United States versus the Rest of the World, 1970–85

	Investment/GNP			National Saving/GNP[a]			I/GNP Differential (United States versus Rest of World)	NS/Differential (United States versus Rest of World)
	U.S.	Other Industrial Countries	LDCs	U.S.	Other Industrial Countries	LDCs		
1970	.145	.253	.235	.149	.260	.212	−.093	−.070
1971	.154	.253	.237	.155	.265	.215	−.085	−.068
1972	.164	.252	.232	.161	.263	.223	−.071	−.068
1973	.173	.259	.238	.180	.265	.233	−.069	−.058
1974	.159	.255	.261	.165	.246	.290	−.101	−.118
1975	.133	.242	.272	.147	.242	.263	−.134	−.113
1976	.150	.238	.270	.154	.236	.276	−.115	−.115
1977	.169	.236	.275	.163	.239	.275	−.099	−.106
1978	.179	.235	.274	.173	.247	.254	−.089	−.080
1979	.175	.236	.265	.176	.234	.265	−.085	−.084
1980	.153	.237	.265	.155	.227	.273	−.108	−.111
1981	.164	.235	.258	.167	.233	.238	−.091	−.070
1982	.135	.225	.246	.134	.226	.208	−.107	−.076
1983	.143	.218	.238	.132	.227	.212	−.092	−.082
1984	.175	.216	.227	.150	.229	.211	−.051	−.064
1985	.174	—	.220	.142	—	.202	—	—

Source: International Monetary Fund *World Economic Outlook* data base and *International Financial Statistics*.
[a]*National saving* (NS) is calculated as investment (I) + current account (CA).

What Is the Meaning of Capital Mobility?

The apparent finding of a relatively low degree of capital mobility in the saving–investment studies, from Feldstein-Horioka to the results just reported, seems puzzling—even startling—to one accustomed to thinking of capital as perfectly mobile internationally. This is one reason for the succession of econometric critiques of their paper. The instrumental variable results are a partial answer to the critiques (more or less convincing according to whether the military expenditure and age structure variables are considered more or less valid instruments). But even if one believes that problems of econometric endogeneity remain, as is likely, it seems intuitively clear that a degree of domestic crowding out fundamentally exists, and that even if truly exogenous changes in national saving could be isolated, they would not be found to be offset one-for-one by net capital inflow.

Most readers of the Feldstein-Horioka paper and subsequent literature have from the start been vaguely bothered by the connection, or lack of it, between the two authors' use of the phrase *perfect capital mobility* and the use of the phrase that existed previously in the field of international finance. Feldstein and Horioka themselves take pains to say that they are talking about long-term, as distinct from short-term, capital mobility. One problem with this type of argument is that if short-term assets and long-term assets are relatively close substitutes within each country, then international arbitrage of short-term rates of returns would be all that is required. It may be that short-term treasury bills are not in fact close substitutes for long-term bonds, equities, or real capital within a given country; but if so, this is not the fault of international capital mobility.

Penati and Dooley, who generally confirm the findings of Feldstein and Horioka, come closer to describing the connection with traditional notions of capital mobility by emphasizing the distinction between gross flows and net flows:

> It is not necessarily true that a large volume of two-way trade in financial assets is associated with *net* trade in financial assets. But it is the net trade, together with the associated net trade in goods and services, that allows domestic investment to diverge from domestic savings (p. 7).

This is clearly right. But the question that remains to be answered is: If there are no barriers to the gross acquisition of assets across national boundaries, how can there be barriers to the net acquisition of assets? Is not "gross" capital mobility sufficient to equalize interest rates? And if it is, how is it that changes in national saving seem to crowd out investment in their own country?

I turn now to traditional definitions of international capital mobility, where the operational criteria are stated in terms of differential rates of return rather than correlations of saving and investment. Later I will return to the meaning of the correlations.

Three Interest Parity Conditions as Definitions of Capital Mobility

The term *perfect capital mobility* is commonly used in three distinct ways. In each case the operational criterion is a version of international interest rate parity.

Closed Interest Parity

The first definition is the absence of important capital controls, transactions costs, or other barriers separating investors from the assets that they would like to hold.[15] The operative criterion is that arbitrage equalizes nominal interest rates on assets located in different countries, when any exchange rate risk has been removed. This criterion is most often stated as covered interest parity:

$$i = i^* + fd \tag{2.3}$$

where i is the domestic nominal interest rate, i^* the foreign nominal interest rate, and fd the forward discount on domestic currency.

For the criterion to be an interesting one, the interest rates should refer to securities that differ in political jurisdiction, not just in currency of denomination. The best-known study of covered interest parity, Frenkel and Levich (1975), found the relationship to hold well for Europound and Eurodollar interest rates on deposits side-by-side in a London bank. Indeed if one were to find significant deviations from covered interest parity with such a data set, one would be less likely to change one's view of the world than to question the reliability of the data set. The interesting criterion instead uses, for example, London interest rates and New York interest rates. The London interest rate can be either a Eurodollar rate ($i_L^\$$), or a pound rate ($i_L^\pounds$) covered on the forward exchange market. In the former case, one would test the condition

$$i_{NY}^\$ = i_L^\$ \tag{2.4}$$

which one might call "absolute" or "simple" interest parity. In the latter case one would test the condition

$$i_{NY}^\$ = i_L^\pounds + fd \tag{2.5}$$

which is "international" (as opposed to "Euromarket") covered interest parity.

Given that Euromarket covered interest parity holds,

$$i_L^\$ = i_L^\pounds + fd, \tag{2.6}$$

the other two, more interesting, criteria are identical to each other. If one phrase is desired for the two of them interchangeably, it might be "closed interest parity."

Frenkel and Levich (1975, 1977) find that, even for the periods 1962–67 and 1973–75, when Euromarket covered interest parity held well, international covered interest parity, using U.S. and U.K. treasury bills, held significantly less well. They attribute the deviations to what Aliber (1973) called political risk: default, taxation, capital controls, or any other sort of risk attaching to the political jurisdiction of a security as opposed to its currency of denomination. Similarly, Dooley and Isard (1980) find imperfect capital mobility for Germany during the period 1970–74; they use Deutsche mark deposits in Frankfurt versus Euromark deposits in Zurich to test what I have just called absolute or simple interest parity, and find large deviations. Like Aliber and Frenkel and Levich, they attribute the deviations to political risk, specifically allocating primary responsibility to the level of controls in place in Germany at the time (essentially the taxation of interest paid to foreign residents) and secondary responsibility to the uncertainty regarding possible future changes in the level of controls. Fase (1976) finds large deviations from closed interest parity, both simple and covered, for the United States, Canada, Germany, and eight other major countries for the Bretton Woods period of 1961–72.

Germany and the United States removed most of their capital controls in 1974.[16] Using Granger-Sims causality tests on simple interest parity for the dollar (the Eurodollar rate versus the domestic U.S. commercial paper or Treasury bill rate), Hartman (1984) finds a significant strengthening of the link from the 1971–74 period to the 1975–78 period. Boothe et al. (1985, p. 112) find small deviations for the Canadian dollar in the 1975–82 period.

Britain removed its controls in 1979, so that by the 1980s six industrialized countries—the United States, Canada, Germany, the United Kingdom, Switzerland, and the Netherlands—were perceived as having essentially open financial markets. France and Italy, on the other hand, maintain serious controls on capital outflow, as is easily demonstrated by the excess of the Eurocurrency interest rates in London over the domestic rates in France and Italy.

Giavazzi and Pagano (1985, pp. 27–28) find that the deviations from covered interest parity are large enough that domestic arbitrageurs would make guaranteed profits if they could get their money into the Euromarket, on 85 percent of the days in the case of France (September 1982–August 1984, with a mean return of 3.99 percent) and 60 percent of the days in the case of Italy (November 1980–August 1984, with a mean return of 3.51 percent), and that the deviations rise sharply before a devaluation.[17] They also look at Germany and the Netherlands and find deviations that are opposite in sign to those of France and Italy, but that are in any case much smaller in magnitude (the mean returns to covered arbitrage are only 0.34 percent for Germany and 0.14 percent for the Netherlands for the period September 1982–August 1984).

Of the seven summit countries, Japan is the one of controversy. In the late 1970s, Japan maintained strict controls on capital inflow in order to resist the large appreciation of its currency that was taking place. Foreigners were prohibited from acquiring most forms of Japanese securities, such as *gensaki,* a three-month repurchase agreement. In May 1979, in the face of a depreciating yen, the Ministry of Finance removed most of these prohibitions. The controversy arose in 1983, when some American businessmen, alarmed by devastating competition from Japanese exporters, convinced the U.S. Treasury Department that the Japanese government was still using some form of capital market restrictions to keep the value of the yen lower than it would otherwise be. There followed a campaign by the U.S. government to induce the Japanese to adopt a whole list of measures further liberalizing their financial markets. This campaign came to fruition in the May 1984 Yen/ Dollar Agreement between the U.S. Treasury and the Japanese Ministry of Finance.

This episode is a good case study in which to apply the closed interest parity criterion for capital mobility. One can compute the differential between the three-month Euroyen interest rate in London and the *gensaki* rate in Tokyo, and compare its magnitude before and after the purported liberalization. Between the period January 1975–April 1979 and the period May 1979–November 1983, the mean absolute value of the deviation fell from 2.06 percent to 0.31 percent and the variance fell from 3.29 percent to 0.22 percent.[18] The statistics in table 2–6 show that, by the criterion of closed interest parity, Japanese financial markets are now as open internationally as those of the United Kingdom, Germany, and Switzerland.

Table 2–6
Financial Openness for Five Countries: Eurocurrency Three-Month Interest Rate Less Money Market Rate, October 7, 1983–May, 1984

	Japan	United Kingdom	Germany	Switzerland	France
Mean	0.053	0.109	−0.041	0.116	1.813
Mean absolute value	0.101	0.114	0.103	0.161	1.813
Mean square	0.015	0.017	0.020	0.036	5.071
Variance	0.013	0.005	0.018	0.023	1.783

Source: J. Frankel, *The Yen/Dollar Agreement: Liberalizing Japanese Capital Markets* (Cambridge, Mass.: MIT Press, December 1984), p. 24.

Uncovered Interest Parity

The second definition of perfect capital mobility is the absence of imperfect substitutability, attributable in particular to risk, between domestic and foreign assets. The operative condition here is uncovered, or open, interest parity:

$$i^\$ = i^£ + \Delta s^e \tag{2.7}$$

where Δs^e is the expected percentage depreciation of the dollar over the coming period. In other words, investors respond to any differentials in expected returns so as to arbitrage them away. In theory, investors should wish to diversify their portfolios and so should *not* entirely arbitrage away such a differential but rather should leave a risk premium, unless (1) they are risk neutral or (2) exchange risk is completely diversifiable, both extremely strong assumptions. But the magnitude of the risk premium is very much an open matter.

Cumby and Obstfeld (1981, 1984) and others have statistically rejected the hypothesis that the errors made by the interest differential in predicting exchange rate change are random. Given covered interest parity, the tests are equivalent to the (more numerous) tests of the hypothesis that the errors made by the forward discount in predicting exchange rate changes are random. In both cases, the standard finding is statistically significant serial correlation of prediction errors, and even a tendency for predictions to be incorrect as to the *sign* of exchange rate changes. Cumby and Obstfeld, and most others, have concluded from such evidence that uncovered interest parity fails. But as they recognize, the tests are in fact joint tests of uncovered interest parity *and* rational expectations. The evidence cannot distinguish which half of the joint null hypothesis is being rejected.

More information is needed to try to isolate the risk premiums out of the noisy prediction errors (out of the difference between the interest differential and the ex post changes in the exchange rate). The most natural source for such information is the theory of portfolio optimization on the part of investors. The theory says that the risk premium ought to be related to such factors as the degree of risk aversion, the supplies of various currencies that have to be held in investors' portfolios, the variance of the exchange rate in question, and the covariances with returns on other securities and with other investment opportunities. Econometric tests have looked for a systematic relationship between the prediction errors and the variables to which the theory says that the risk premium should be related, and have found no signs of such a relationship.[19] As always, the statistical failure to reject the null hypothesis of a zero risk premium could be due to low power in the test. But there is a surprising, and more far-reaching, point that transcends the particular econometric technique used to estimate variances and covariances of rates of return. It is that conventional estimates of the degree of risk aversion imply that the risk premium must be very small.

It can be shown that if investors optimize with respect to the mean and variance of their wealth, they will allocate their portfolios according to the following equation:

$$x_t = \alpha + [\rho\Omega]^{-1}(rp_t) \tag{2.8}$$

where x_t is the share of the portfolios allocated to foreign assets (or a vector of shares allocated to various foreign currencies); α is the minimum-variance portfolio, which is closely related to the share of consumption allocated to foreign goods (or a vector of such shares); ρ is the coefficient of relative risk aversion; Ω is the variance (or variance-covariance matrix) of the return differential (that is, of the change in the exchange rate if one is looking at short-term financial assets with known nominal returns); and rp_t is the risk premium on foreign assets (or vector), that is, the ex ante return differential or deviation from uncovered interest parity.[20] Intuitively, an increase in the expected return on a particular asset will induce investors to shift a higher share of their portfolios into that asset; but the more important investors consider risk diversification (that is, the larger is ρ or Ω), the less will they shift their portfolios in response to a given change in expected returns.

The unconditional monthly variance of the relative return on dollars has been on the order of .001.[21] The conditional variance, which is what should matter for investor behavior, must be less than or equal to the sample variance. Thus one may take .001 as an upper-bound estimate of Ω. The coefficient of risk aversion, ρ, is thought to be in the neighborhood of two.[22] Taking the product $[\rho\Omega]^{-1}$, it follows from equation 2.8 that asset demands are extraordinarily sensitive to the risk premium. If an increase in the supply of foreign assets x_t equal to 1 percent of the portfolio is to be held willingly, it will have to drive up the risk premium rp_t by .002 percent on a monthly basis, or a mere .024 percent per annum—just 2.4 basis points. It also follows that the magnitude of the risk premiums, not just the variability, is very small.[23]

It must be emphasized that the conclusion that international substitutability is very high, and thus the risk premium very small, depends entirely on the optimal portfolio argument. The hypothesis that investors diversify their portfolios optimally has not itself held up well to statistical tests.[24]

If one were to abandon the optimization hypothesis, one would be hard put to find other sources of information to help isolate the risk premium out of the noisy prediction errors made by the interest differential. About the only apparent alternative is the survey data of exchange rate expectations that made a brief appearance in table 2–1. These data do show a sizable gap between the interest differential and expected rate of depreciation, at least for the 1981–85 period of dollar appreciation. Unfortunately, the implied risk premium goes in precisely the opposite direction from that implied by the Cumby-Obstfeld test and other unbiasness tests on the interest differential or forward discount data. Those tests all imply that when the dollar sold at a discount, as it consistently did during the 1981–85 period, even though it has not depreciated ex post, dollar assets must be carrying a positive risk premium. The risk premium constitutes some positive fraction of the interest differential (100 percent of it, or more, in the case of tests that show predictions in the wrong directions). The natural explanation of why dollar assets might carry a positive risk premium in the mid-1980s is that, as a result of recent enormous federal budget deficits and current account deficits, the supply of dollar assets that the market must hold in its portfolio exceeds the share represented by the minimum-variance portfolio. But the survey data show that for the 1981–85 period, expected depreciation consistently *exceeded* the interest differential, that is, the risk premium on dollars was *negative*. They do not explain any positive fraction of the systematic component of the prediction errors.

I will return to the subject of the survey data subsequently. But for now, especially in light of the fact that the validity of these data as measures of expectations has yet to win widespread acceptance, I take the existing theoretical and empirical evidence as suggesting that international capital mobility is very high, in this second sense of high substitutability in investors' portfolios and a small risk premium.[25]

Real Interest Parity

So far I have concluded that capital is highly mobile between the United States and the other major countries both in the sense of (1) low transactions costs and capital controls, so that closed interest parity holds relatively well between U.S. securities and foreign securities (either denominated in dollars or covered on the forward market) and (2) low-risk premiums, so that uncovered interest parity holds relatively well also (though the evidence here is more widely disputed). How are such conclusions to be reconciled with the results of the Feldstein-Horioka tests already described?

Our third definition of perfect capital mobility is the one that Feldstein had in mind. It is phrased in terms of *real* interest rates, not nominal interest rates. It is, after all, the real interest rate on which saving and investment are thought to depend. The operational criterion is real interest parity:

$$r_{US} = r_{UK} \qquad (2.9)$$

where $r_{US} \equiv i_{US} - \pi^e_{US}$, $r_{UK} \equiv i_{UK} - \pi^e_{UK}$, and π^e_{US} and π^e_{UK} are the countries' expected inflation rates. If infinitely elastic international flows were to tie the domestic real interest rate to the world real interest rate, and if the domestic country were small enough to take the world real interest rate as given, then there should be no crowding out: exogenous decreases in national saving should not drive up the domestic real interest rate and discourage domestic investment. In the Feldstein–Horioka regressions (with valid instrumental variables), the coefficients should be zero.

But, especially given the large-country and other endogeneity problems, a better econometric approach than saving–investment correlations is to test real interest parity directly. Such tests have been performed for the United States and major trading partners in the recent period by Mishkin (1984a, 1984b), Friedman and Schwartz (1982), von Furstenberg (1983), Cumby and Obstfeld (1984), and Cumby and Mishkin (1986). All find significant gaps between domestic and foreign real interest rates. *Since real interest parity is the only definition of perfect capital mobility that could lead one to expect an absence of crowding out, its empirical failure automatically explains the finding of crowding out in the Feldstein-Horioka regressions.* No arguments about econometric endogeneity are required. Furthermore, the general trend in the real interest rate results over time is the same as the general trend in the Feldstein-Horioka regressions. Mishkin (1984, pp. 1352, 1354), for example, found even more significant rejections of real interest parity for the floating rate period after 1973/II than he did for his entire 1967/II–1979/II sample period. This corresponds to the findings of Feldstein (1983) and Penati and Dooley (1984) that the crowding out coefficient did not decline as expected after 1973.

One need not search far for the source of failure of real interest parity. Even if the first two definitions of perfect capital mobility hold completely, so that uncovered interest parity holds,

$$i - i^* = \Delta s^e, \tag{2.10}$$

it is necessary also to assume what is sometimes called ex ante relative purchasing power parity (PPP),

$$\Delta s^e = \pi^e - \pi^{*e}, \tag{2.11}$$

if one is to derive real interest parity

$$i - i^* = \pi^e - \pi^{*e}. \tag{2.12}$$

Whether ex ante relative PPP (also describable as "random walk expectations regarding the real exchange rate") holds is a question regarding the degree of integration of international goods markets (which is thought to be low), not the degree of integration of international financial markets. Here it is important to note that international portfolio investors have reason to arbitrage away gaps in countries' nominal rates of return when expressed in a common numeraire; but they have no reason to arbitrage away a gap between the domestic rate of return expressed in terms of domestic goods and the foreign rate of return expressed in terms of foreign goods. Perhaps the central message of this chapter is that, although Feldstein and Horioka are correct about the existence of crowding out, econometric endogeneity problems notwithstanding, they are wrong to offer this conclusion as evidence of imperfect capital mobility.[26]

It might be protested that my first two definitions of capital mobility refer only to nominal assets—bonds and, especially, shorter-term bills or deposits—and that a perfectly good third definition would refer to real assets—equities and direct investment. But the same argument applies. In the absence of significant barriers to mobility or substitutability (including risk), an international investor should equate the expected rate of return on equities or real investment in one country to that in another *evaluated in a common numeraire,* not each evaluated in terms of local goods prices. If the real return on a country's equities were equal to the real return on its bonds, with each evaluated in terms of local goods prices, and if real interest parity held, then the real returns on equities would be internationally equalized as well. But given the failure of real interest parity, neither foreign direct investment nor any other known force will equalize real returns on capital. Thus equating internationally rates of return on financial assets of any sort will not be sufficient to equate real interest rates; ex ante relative purchasing power parity is needed as well.

Ex Ante Purchasing Power Parity

Not long ago, purchasing power parity was widely accepted. It was argued on a priori grounds that the law of one price should be enforced at least for traded goods: If automobiles were selling at a lower price in Germany than in the United States, international arbitrageurs should buy them in Germany and sell them in the United States, raising the price in one country or lowering it in the other until equality was restored. If PPP were to hold in level form, then it would also hold in expected rate of change form (equation 2.11); goods markets would pose no obstacles to real interest parity.

The empirical evidence against PPP in level form is overwhelming. The enormous real appreciation of the dollar in the 1980s has now convinced the remaining doubters, but abundant statistical evidence was there all along. For example, Krugman (1978, p. 406) computed for the floating rate period July 1973–December 1976 standard deviations of the (logarithmic) real exchange rate equal to 6.0 percent for the pound/dollar rate and 8.4 percent for the mark/dollar rate. He also computed serial correlation coefficients for

Table 2–7
Purchasing Power Parity between the United States and the United Kingdom,
1869–1984

	1973–1984	1945–1972	1945–1984	1869–1984
Mean absolute deviation	.121	.075	.106	.093
Standard deviation	.154	.092	.146	.122
Time trend	− .001*	.006*	− .0004	.009
	(.0003)	(.002)	(.0022)	(.013)
Autoregression				
of deviations from mean	.720*	.706*	.829*	.860*
	(.248)	(.132)	(.090)	(.048)
of deviations from trend	.734*	.710*	.750*	.846*
	(.277)	(.133)	(.106)	(.050)
Regression against nominal exchange rate				
coefficient[a]	1.051*	1.057*	1.005*	.763*
	(.083)	(.073)	(.069)	(.055)
autocorrelation coefficient	.874	.970	.984	.991

Note: Standard errors are reported in parentheses.
*Significant at the 95 percent level.
[a]With constant term and Cochrane-Orcutt correction for autocorrelation.

PPP deviations of .897 and .854, respectively, on a monthly basis, equal to
.271 and .150 on an annual basis. The serial correlation coefficient is of
interest because it is equal to one minus the speed of adjustment to PPP. It
may be best not to rely exclusively on the standard deviation of the real
exchange rate as a summary statistic for the degree of integration of goods
markets because it in part reflects the magnitude of monetary disturbances
during the period.[27]

Table 2–7 shows updated annual statistics on the real exchange rate
between the United States and Great Britain. During the floating rate period
1973–84, though there is no significant time trend, there is a large standard
deviation of 15.4 percent. The serial correlation in the deviations from PPP
is estimated at .720, with a standard error of .248. (The equation estimated
is $[er_{t+1} - \overline{er}_{t+1}] = AR[er_t - \overline{er}_t]$, where er is the real exchange rate and
$\overline{er}$ is the long-run equilibrium level, alternatively estimated as the sample
mean or a time trend, and AR is the autoregressive coefficient.) This means
that the estimated speed of adjustment to PPP is .280 per year and that one
can easily reject the hypothesis of instantaneous adjustment.

From the ashes of absolute PPP, a phoenix has risen. In response to
findings such as those reported here, some authors have swung from one
extreme, the proposition that the tendency of the real exchange rate to return
to a constant is complete and instantaneous, to the opposite extreme that

there is no such tendency at all. The hypothesis that the real exchange rate follows a random walk is just as good as the hypothesis of absolute PPP for implying ex ante relative PPP. But there is even less of an a priori case why PPP should hold in rate-of-change form than in the level form.

Roll (1979) has claimed that the random walk model of the real exchange rate has a basis in efficient markets theory. His argument is apparently that if the expected inflation rate is lower in the United States than in Germany, allowing for expected exchange rate changes, then an arbitrageur can contract to buy automobiles in the United States and ship them to Germany and expect to sell them there at a higher price; such profitable arbitrage would then eliminate the opportunity to begin with, enforcing PPP in expected rate-of-change form. If this arbitrage is intended to be different from the old arbitrage in level form which has been empirically rejected, and Roll clearly intends it to be different, then it is a remarkable strategy to recommend to international traders. Measures of expected real depreciation of the dollar as of 1985 showed a short-term depreciation rate of about 1.0 percent per annum. As of 1985, the level of BMW prices was said to be almost twice as high in the United States as in Germany, as a result of the five-year appreciation of the dollar against the mark. Yet Roll's apparent strategy tells people to buy BMWs in the United States and ship them to Germany because in the three months it takes to complete the shipment their relative prices will have increased 0.25 percent in expected value! The near–50-percent loss would seem to outweigh the 0.25-percent gain.

Even though ex ante relative PPP has little basis in theory, it does appear to have some empirical support. Typically, the estimated speeds of adjustment during the floating rate period, .27 or .28 on an annual basis in table 2–7 (1973–84), while not so low as to be implausible as point estimates, are nevertheless so low that one statistically cannot reject the hypothesis that they are zero. In other words, one cannot reject the hypothesis that the auto-regression coefficient is 1.0.

A 95-percent confidence interval on the autoregressive coefficient covers the range 0.17 to 1.27 (in the no-trend case). If the null hypothesis is an auto-regression coefficient of 1.0, one cannot legitimately use the standard t-test derived from a regression where the right-hand variable is the level of the real exchange rate, because under the null hypothesis its variance is infinite. (This does not invalidate the t-test just reported of the null hypothesis that the tendency to return to PPP was 100 percent, that is, $AR = 0$). There are a number of ways of dealing with this nonstationarity problem. Here one simply applies the corrected Dickey-Fuller cumulative probability distribution for this problem. The t-ratio to test an autoregressive coefficient of 1.0 is 1.13, which falls far short of the Dickey-Fuller 95-percent significance level, 3.00.

This failure to reject a random walk in the real exchange rate is the same result found by Roll (1979), Frenkel (1981, p. 699), Darby (1981), and

Mishkin (1984, pp. 1351–53). Most of these studies used monthly data. On the one hand, the more abundant data reduces the standard error of the estimate but, on the other hand, one is no longer testing whether $AR = .28$ is different from 1.0, but rather whether, say, $AR\ 1/12 = .90$ is different from 1.0, so that it may not be much easier to reject. Another problem is that one cannot be sure that the nature of the true autoregressive process is first-order on a monthly (or continuous-time) basis; the typical finding is that computations on monthly data imply a somewhat more rapid speed of adjustment when annualized than do computations performed directly on annual data, suggesting that the process may not be exactly first order. In any case, the monthly data in the studies cited were generally not powerful enough to reject the random walk.[28]

A more promising alternative is to choose a longer time sample. Table 2–7 also reports statistics for the entire postwar period 1945–84. PPP held slightly better during the Bretton Woods years than it did after 1973, as measured either by the mean absolute deviation and standard deviation of the real exchange rate, or by the ability to reject the hypothesis of zero autocorrelation. But, despite the longer time sample, one is still unable to reject the random walk. The 95-percent confidence interval runs from .65 to 1.01, and the t-ratio of 1.9 falls short of the Dickey-Fuller 95-percent significance level of 2.93.

The last column of table 2–7 presents an entire 116 years of U.S.–U.K. data. With this long a time sample, the standard error is reduced considerably. The rejection of no serial correlation in the real exchange rate is even stronger than in the shorter time samples. More important, one is finally able to detect a significant tendency for the real exchange rate to regress to PPP, at a rate of 14 percent a year. The confidence interval for AR runs from .77 to .95, safely less than unity, and the t-ratio of 2.92 exceeds the Dickey-Fuller significance level of 2.89.

The last row of the table reports regressions of the real exchange rate against the nominal exchange rate. The coefficient is highly significant for the 1869–1984 period. The figures suggest that changes in the nominal exchange rate (for example, due to devaluations under fixed exchange rates or monetary disturbances under floating exchange rates) cause transitory changes in the real exchange rate because goods prices are sticky. Such results specifically rule out the possibility, which is suggested occasionally in the literature, that apparent deviations from PPP might be attributed to random measurement errors in the price data.

In this chapter, my motivation for looking at PPP is to obtain insight into the expected rate of real depreciation, because that is the variable that separates the real interest differential from the risk premium. In rejecting the random walk description of the real exchange rate, one has rejected the claim that the rationally expected rate of real depreciation is zero.

The rationally expected rate of real depreciation estimated from a specific time series process is in any case not necessarily the same as the actual expectation of real depreciation held by investors. People could be either less sophisticated or more sophisticated than the autoregressive model.

Table 2–8 uses the *Economist* and American Express survey data on expectations of exchange rate and price level changes to compute a direct measure of expected real depreciation for the dollar against five individual currencies, and regress it against a measure of current real "overvaluation." Overvaluation is the difference between the current exchange rate and a long-run equilibrium rate calculated by PPP, using as the base the average of the period 1973–80. The equilibrium measure differs from a constant in that it evolves over time at the rate of the inflation differential, and in that when the regression period is confined to the period 1981–84, as is necessarily the case for the *Economist* data set, it shows a large real overvaluation throughout. According to the results in table 2–8, investors show a statistically significant expectation that the real exchange rate will regress back toward PPP.[29] The constant term is also statistically significant.[30]

One can take point estimates from table 2–7 to illustrate what a typical magnitude might be for the rationally expected rate of real depreciation even in the absence of any expected changes in the long-run equilibrium terms of trade. For the 1869–1984 period a 1-percent deviation from PPP, say, an "overvaluation" of the currency, implies a rationally expected rate of subsequent real depreciation equal to 0.14 percent per year. Since the mean absolute deviation from PPP is 9.3 percent, the mean absolute value of the rationally expected rate of real depreciation is 0.14 × 9.3 = 1.3 percent. In the post-1973 period of larger exchange rate fluctuations, the magnitude of expected real depreciation is larger. The most dramatic case is 1984 or 1985, when calculations of real overvaluation of the dollar (relative to PPP) on the order of 30 percent imply that the rationally expected rate of future real depreciation back toward PPP is large enough to explain all of the real interest differential, calculated in the various ways shown in table 2–1.[31]

A more precise decomposition of the real interest differential into a risk premium and expected real depreciation, based on the assumption of rational expectations and the use of ex post data, is difficult. The reason is that the difference between the expected exchange rate change and the ex post exchange rate change, even though random if expectations are rational, is so large as to reduce greatly the precision of any estimates, as Mishkin (1984a) notes. Indeed it was for this reason that Mishkin was unable to reject the hypotheses of a zero risk premium or of zero expected real depreciation considered individually, even though he could easily reject the *joint* null hypothesis in a test of real interest parity, where the exchange rate expectation errors do not interfere.

It should be recalled from the subsection **Uncovered Interest Parity** that,

Table 2-8
Regressive Expectations on the Real Exchange Rate

Measure of Δs^e	Time Sample	Measure of $\pi^e - \pi^{*e}$	Regression Technique	Constant	Coefficient	Dummy 1981–84	Durbin-Watson Statistic	R^2	Degrees of Freedom
Economist survey (3-month)	1981–84 (4/yr.)	DRI forecast	OLS	.018* (.003)	.026* (.010)		1.65	.10	46
Economist survey (6-month)	1981–84 (2/yr. I)	DRI forecast	OLS	.034* (.006)	.061* (.025)		1.30	.19	22
Economist survey (6-month)	1981–84 (2/yr. II)		OLS	.033* (.007)	.038 (.026)		1.54	.06	18
AmEx survey (6-month)	76–8, 81–4 (2/yr.)	AmEx survey	OLS	.014* (.005)	.019 (.037)	.028* (.011)	1.36	.29	22

Source: Expectations measures labeled "Economist" are taken from the *Economist's Financial Report*, various issues. Measures labeled "AmEx" are taken from American Express's *Amex Bank Review*, various issues.

Notes: Dependent variable: Expected rate of real depreciation of dollar, equal to expected nominal depreciation Δs^e minus expected inflation differential $\pi^e - \pi^{*e}$

Independent variable: real overvaluation $(\bar{s} - s)$, measured by PPP for 1973–80

Pooled time series cross-section for dollar against five foreign currencies (mark, pound, yen, French franc, and Swiss franc)

Standard errors are reported in parentheses.

*Significant at the 95 percent level.

on the one hand, the standard tests of unbiasness in the forward discount or interest differential say that the rationally expected rate of depreciation is significantly *less* than that implied by the interest differential, and, on the other hand, that economists' notions of a long-run equilibrium for the dollar, as embodied for example in the *Economist* and American Express survey data, imply that the expected rate of depreciation as of 1985 was considerably *greater*. One cannot prove that expected real depreciation explains 100 percent of the real interest differential, no less and no more. But the calculations of this section are intended to show that plausible magnitudes for the former correspond to plausible magnitudes for the latter, and that deviations from the assumption of perfect capital mobility in the senses of the first two definitions raised earlier in the section **Three Interest Parity Conditions as Definitions of Capital Mobility** are *not* needed to explain deviations from real interest parity.

Conclusion

Regressions of the investment rate against the national saving rate give results for U.S. time series similar to those obtained by Feldstein-Horioka and others for cross-sectional data: a point estimate on the order of .8, significantly different from zero and insignificantly different from 1.0. Econometric problems abound, but cyclically adjusting the saving and investment numbers, using instrumental variables, or working in terms of deviations from world levels does little to reduce the coefficient estimate. The estimate has, if anything, been moving closer to 1.0 in the postwar period. It seems that international capital mobility does not fully prevent exogenous changes in the government budget or in private saving from crowding out domestic investment.

This chapter has argued that neither imperfect capital mobility nor econometric problems are needed to explain the crowding out estimates. "Perfect capital mobility" has multiple definitions: (1) closed interest parity, requiring insignificant barriers such as transactions costs and capital controls; (2) uncovered interest parity, requiring also small exchange risk premiums; and (3) real interest parity, requiring also ex ante relative purchasing power parity. Each criterion can be tested directly. Closed interest parity is observed to hold well among eight of the major industrial countries. Uncovered interest parity is more difficult to test, because investors' exchange rate expectations are not directly observable; nevertheless some theoretical considerations and some evidence from survey data both contradict the view that a large positive component of the interest differential (or forward discount) on the dollar constitutes a risk premium. Thus the first two criteria, the ones that are most properly associated with the degree of integration of financial markets, do seem to hold to within relatively small margins. Real interest parity, the only condition that might lead one to expect an absence of crowding out, is also the condition that clearly fails empirically. This is not surprising, since purchasing power parity is well known to fail empirically, while the argument that ex ante relative PPP could hold nevertheless is extremely weak on both theoretical grounds and empirical grounds. When 116 years of data on the U.S.–U.K. real exchange rate are used, it is possible to reject the random walk characterization and to find a statistically significant speed of adjustment to PPP.

Thus expected real depreciation is an important variable. It seems possible to attribute all of, for example, the 3.0-percent U.S. real interest differential (as of 1985) to expected real depreciation, rather than to a risk premium. This implies that it is possible to attribute the existence of crowding out in an open economy to imperfect integration of goods markets, rather than necessarily to imperfect integration of asset markets as has been suggested in the past.

Notes

1. The share averages .0379 for 1929–44, .0478 for 1945–73 and .0897 for 1974–84. Figures are from the International Monetary Fund's data base. These long-run trends in U.S. trade are examined in Lipsey (1984). See also Cooper (this volume).

2. There are a number of ways that these strong results can be watered down. One way particularly relevant for the United States is the large-country point: to the extent that a fiscal expansion succeeds in driving up the worldwide interest rate, it will have succeeded in raising income and crowding out investment (both effects holding abroad as well as domestically).

3. The decline in saving net of the capital consumption allowance has been even more pronounced. See table 4 in Friedman (1985).

4. The average investment rate in the 1981–84 period encompasses a fall in the first two recession years and a rise in the subsequent two recovery years; investment, like saving, is of course highly procyclical. There has been talk, especially in 1984, of an investment boom. But Bosworth (1985) suggests that the favorable effect that the 1981 corporate tax law changes had on the cost of capital to firms was more than offset by the unfavorable effect of the increase in real interest rates, and that any appearances of an investment boom in 1983–85 were due to the recovery and the existence of new computer technology. See also Friedman (1985). In any case, it must be that the increase in real interest rates has acted to depress investment relative to what it otherwise would be.

5. Two other papers that discuss both the Feldstein-Horioka notion of international capital mobility and the more conventional definitions are Boothe *et al.* (1985) and Obstfeld (1985).

6. Other cross-sectional studies include Fieleke (1982), Feldstein (1983), Penati and Dooley (1984), Murphy (1984), Caprio and Howard (1984), and Summers

(1985). However, Obstfeld (1985) used time series data, as did Sachs (1981) but with the inclusion of a GNP gap variable.

7. Tobin (1983), Murphy (1984), and Obstfeld (1985) criticized Feldstein and Horioka on these grounds.

8. The "policy reaction" argument has been made by Fieleke (1982), Tobin (1983), Westphal (1983), Summers (1985), and Caprio and Howard (1984).

9. Many of the critiques ignore the fact that the original Feldstein and Horioka paper used instrumental variables. (The four instruments were the ratio of retirees over 65 to the working age population, the ratio of younger dependents to the same population, the labor force participation rate of older men, and the benefit/earning "replacement ratio" under social security.)

10. For example, Caprio and Howard (1984), Obstfeld (1985), and Summers (1985).

11. All saving and investment numbers used in this chapter are gross rather than net. Harberger (1980) argued that gross numbers bias upward the Feldstein-Horioka (1980) coefficients estimates, but Feldstein (1983) showed that the same results held with net numbers.

12. We tried splitting the sample of decade data at 1919 to try to see how U.S. capital mobility changed over time, but as one would expect from the very small number of observations, the estimates were so imprecise as to be worthless (-2.69 with a standard error of 2.0, and .75 with a standard error of .38, respectively). Reliable yearly data are not available from before World War I, aside from the problem of cyclical endogeneity.

13. David and Scadding (1974) argue that "Denison's Law," the stability of private saving as a fraction of GNP in the postwar period, applies also to preceding U.S. history, despite shifts from personal saving to durables expenditure and corporate saving. (Their period is 1898–1964.) But as they point out, the stability of private saving in the face of a rising and fluctuating government deficit precludes the stability of aggregate national saving that would be implied by the theories mentioned early in the first section of this chapter.

14. The standard error of the coefficient is .172, the R^2 is .59, and the Durbin-Watson statistic is 1.66. The numbers are not cyclically adjusted, but to the extent that business cycles are internationally synchronized (as they should be under conditions of high capital mobility), cyclical effects should be less important in the differential rates.

15. This is the definition of perfect capital mobility that I argued is the most sensible, to distinguish it from perfect substitutability (the second definition, considered shortly) in Frankel (1983); supporting citations appear there.

16. Dooley and Isard (1980, p. 382–83), Argy (1982, pp. 35, 38, 43, 76–79), and Baumgartner (1977) give the history of German capital controls in the 1970s.

17. Claassen and Wyplosz (1982) and Frankel (1982b) also document the case for France.

18. The sign of the deviation switched, from a mean of -1.84 in the first period to $+0.26$ in the second period. This is evidence that, although the earlier controls acted to prevent capital inflow into Japan (otherwise investors would not have settled for the Euroyen interest rate in London when a higher return was available in Tokyo), those controls that remained after April 1979 acted more to prevent capital *outflow*.

(Otherwise investors would not have settled for the interest rate in Tokyo if a higher Euroyen rate were freely available in London.) It is ironic that the United States in 1983–84 pushed for further Japanese liberalization with the express goal of *strengthening* the yen, when liberalization could be expected to result in greater capital outflow in response to higher interest rates in the United States, and thus to *weaken* the yen. The calculations cited here appear in Frankel (1984, pp. 21–24); the numbers are originally from Morgan Guaranty. See also Otani and Tiwari (1981) and Otani (1983).

19. For example, Frankel (1982a), which also gives further references.

20. Derivations appear in Dornbusch (1983) for the case of two assets and stochastic goods prices, in Krugman (1981) for the case of two assets and nonstochastic goods prices, in Frankel and Engel (1984) for the case of n assets and stochastic goods prices, and in Frankel (1982a) for the case of n assets and nonstochastic goods prices.

21. The period is August 1973–August 1980; Frankel (1985). The calculations assume a constant (conditional) variance.

22. Friend and Blume (1975) estimate ρ to be in the neighborhood of two in the context of investors' portfolio behavior. Stern (1977) provides a survey of estimates in other contexts, most also in the neighborhood of two.

23. Krugman (1981) and Frankel (1985) show that if $\rho\Omega$ is small, then both the level of the risk premium and changes are small. More generally, past tests of biasness in the forward discount or interest differential have not found *unconditional bias;* those who have argued for the existence of a large risk premium have always specified that it be time varying, so as to fluctuate between positive and negative (for example, Hansen and Hodrick (1983)).

24. Frankel and Engel (1984) reject the international optimization hypothesis in a mean-variance framework. Hodrick and Srivistava (1984) do so in a more general intertemporal framework.

25. Frankel and Froot (1985) introduce the survey data, test alternative specifications for the expectations formation process, and test the rational expectations hypothesis. Froot (1985) further investigates whether the standard findings of biasness in the forward discount can be attributed to a risk premium, and allows for measurement error in the survey data.

26. Feldstein and Horioka (1980) and Feldstein (1983) explicitly refer to barriers to integration of financial markets. Among the many subsequent authors who seem automatically to accept the conceptual jump from crowding out to imperfect financial market integration are Tobin (1983), Murphy (1984), Caprio and Howard (1984), and Boothe *et al.* (1985). Obstfeld (1985) and Summers (1985) note the relevance of changes in relative goods prices, though they phrase the distinction differently both from each other and from me here.

27. For example, Krugman found that the standard deviation for the real mark/dollar exchange rate during the German hyperinflation, February 1920–December 1923, was much larger (20.8 percent) than during the 1970s, even though the serial correlation was no higher (.765).

28. Cumby and Obstfeld (1984, p. 146) used a Q-statistic to test for higher order serial correlation in monthly real exchange rate changes and found none. However, they also found that expected inflation differentials are unrelated to expected exchange rate changes, rejecting the random walk characterization of the real exchange rate.

29. Because the data sample is pooled time series cross-section, there is certain to be correlation of the error term across different currencies. The system should be estimated by Seemingly Unrelated Regressions, as is done in Frankel and Froot (1985).

30. The American Express data set covers a longer time period, 1976–84, but fewer observations. The addition of a dummy variable for the strong-dollar period after 1980 eliminates the significance of the regressive coefficient. The results without the dummy variable are significant, but not reported in table 2–8.

31. The 1984 *Economic Report of the President,* chap. 2, found that the expected future real depreciation implicit in the real interest differential roughly coincided with the "real overvaluation" implied by the PPP. But any such calculations are very sensitive to the term of maturity chosen.

References

Aliber, Robert. "The Interest Rate Parity Theorem: A Reinterpretation," *Journal of Political Economy* 81 (1973), pp. 1451–59.

———. "The Integration of National Financial Markets: A Review of Theory and Findings," *Weltwirtschaftliches Archiv* 114, no. 3 (1978), pp. 448–79.

Argy, Victor. *Exchange-Rate Management in Theory and Practice,* Princeton Studies in International Finance 50. Princeton, N.J.: International Finance Section, Princeton University (October 1982).

Baumgartner, Ulrich. "Capital Controls in Three Central European Countries." International Monetary Fund DM/77/12 (February 1977).

Boothe, P., K. Clinton, A. Côté, and D. Longworth. *International Asset Substitutability: Theory and Evidence for Canada.* Ottawa: Bank of Canada (February 1985).

Bosworth, Barry. "Taxes and the Investment Recovery." *Brookings Papers on Economic Activity* (1985), pp. 1–45.

Caprio, Gerard, and David Howard. "Domestic Saving, Current Accounts, and International Capital Mobility," International Finance Discussion Papers no. 244. Washington, D.C.: Federal Reserve Board (June 1984).

Claassen, Emil, and Charles Wyplosz. "Capital Controls: Some Principles and the French Experience." *Annales de l'INSEE* 47–48 (June–December 1982), pp. 237–67.

Cooper, Richard. "The United States as an Open Economy," in this volume.

Cumby, Robert, and Frederick Mishkin. "The International Linkage of Real Interest Rates: The European–U.S. Connection," *Journal of International Money and Finance* 5 (1986), pp. 5–24.

Cumby, Robert, and Maurice Obstfeld, "A Note on Exchange Rate Expectations and Nominal Interest Differentials: A Test of the Fisher Hypothesis," *Journal of Finance* 36 (1981), pp. 697–704.

———. "International Interest Rate and Price Level Linkages under Flexible Exchange Rates: A Review of Recent Evidence" in J. Bilson and R. Marston, eds., *Exchange Rate Theory and Practice.* Chicago: University of Chicago Press (1984).

David, Paul, and John Scadding. "Private Savings: Ultrarationality, Aggregation, and 'Denison's Law," *Journal of Political Economy* (March–April 1974), pp. 225–49.

Dooley, Michael, and Peter Isard. "Capital Controls, Political Risk and Deviations from Interest-Rate Parity," *Journal of Political Economy* 88, no. 2 (April 1980), pp. 370–84.

Dornbusch, Rudiger. "Exchange Rate Risk and the Macroeconomics of Exchange Rate Determination" in R. Hawkins, R. Levich, and C. Wihlborg, eds., *The Internationalization of Financial Market and National Economic Policy.* Greenwich, Conn.: JAI Press (1983), pp. 3–27.

Fase, M.M.G., "The Interdependence of Short-Term Interest Rates in the Major Financial Centers of the World: Some Evidence for 1961–1972," *Kyklos* 29 (1976), pp. 63–96.

Feldstein, Martin. "Domestic Saving and International Capital Movements in the Long Run and the Short Run," *European Economic Review* 21 (1983), pp. 129–151.

Feldstein, Martin, and Charles Horioka. "Domestic Saving and International Capital Flows," *Economic Journal* 90 (1980), pp. 314–29.

Fieleke, Norman. "National Saving and International Investment" in *Saving and Government Policy,* Conference series no. 25. Federal Reserve Bank of Boston (1982).

Frankel, Jeffrey. "In Search of the Exchange Risk Premium: A Six-Currency Test Assuming Mean-Variance Optimization," *Journal of International Money and Finance* 1 (1982), pp. 255–74.

———. "On the Franc," *Annales de l'INSEE* 47–48 (July–December 1982), pp. 185–221.

———. "Monetary and Portfolio-Balance Models of Exchange Rate Determination" in J. Bhandari, ed., *Economic Interdependence and Flexible Exchange Rates.* Cambridge, Mass.: MIT Press (1983).

———. *The Yen/Dollar Agreement: Liberalizing Japanese Capital Markets,* Policy Analyses in International Economics no. 9. Washington, D.C.: Institute for International Economics (1984).

———. "The Implications of Mean-Variance Optimization for Four Questions in International Macroeconomics," *Journal of International Money and Finance,* forthcoming.

Frankel, Jeffrey, and Charles Engel. "Do Asset-Demand Functions Optimize over the Mean and Variance of Real Returns? A Six-Currency Test," *Journal of International Economics* 17 (1984), pp. 309–23.

Frankel, Jeffrey, and Kenneth Froot. "Using Survey Data to Test Some Standard Propositions Regarding Exchange Rate Expectations," National Bureau of Economic Research Working Paper (August 1985).

Frenkel, Jacob. "The Collapse of Purchasing Power Parity during the 1970s," *European Economic Review* 16 (February 1981), pp. 145–65.

———. "Flexible Exchange Rates, Prices, and the Role of 'News': Lessons from the 1970s," *Journal of Political Economy* 89, no. 4 (August 1981), pp. 665–705.

Frenkel, Jacob, and Richard Levich. "Covered Interest Arbitrage: Unexploited Profits?" *Journal of Political Economy* 83, no. 2 (April 1975), pp. 325–38.

———. "Transaction Costs and Interest Arbitrage: Tranquil versus Turbulent Periods," *Journal of Political Economy* 85, no. 6 (December 1977), pp. 1209–26.

Friedman, Benjamin. "Implications of the U.S. Net Capital Inflow" in this volume.

Friedman, Milton, and Anna Schwartz. *Money, Interest Rates, and Prices in the*

United States and United Kingdom: 1867–1975. Chicago: University of Chicago Press (1982).

Friend, Irwin, and Marshall Blume. "The Demand for Risky Assets," *American Economic Review* 65 (December 1975), pp. 900–22.

Froot, Kenneth. "Exchange Rate Survey Data: The Roles of Expectational Errors, the Risk Premium and Measurement Error." Department of Economics, University of California, Berkeley (September 1985).

Giavazzi, Francesco, and Marco Pagano. "Capital Controls and the European Monetary System" in *Capital Controls and Foreign Exchange Legislation,* Occasional Paper. Milano: Euromobiliare (June 1985).

Hansen, Lars, and Robert Hodrick. "Risk-Averse Speculation in the Forward Foreign Exchange Market: An Econometric Analysis of Linear Models" in J. Frenkel, ed., *Exchange Rates and International Macroeconomics.* Chicago: University of Chicago Press (1983).

Harberger, Arnold. "Vignettes on the World Capital Market," *American Economic Review* 70 (1980), pp. 331–37.

Hartman, David. "The International Financial Market and U.S. Interest Rates," *Journal of International Money and Finance* 3 (April 1984), pp. 91–103.

Hodrick, Robert, and Sanjay Srivistava. "An Investigation of Risk and Return in Forward Foreign Exchange," *Journal of International Money and Finance* 3 (1984), pp. 5–24.

Krugman, Paul. "Purchasing Power Parity and Exchange Rates: Another Look at the Evidence," *Journal of International Economics* 8, no. 3 (1978), pp. 397–407.

———. "Consumption Preferences, Asset Demands and Distribution Effects in International Financial Markets," National Bureau of Economic Research, Working Paper no. 651 (March 1981).

Lipsey, Robert. "Recent Trends in U.S. Trade and Investment" in N. Miyawaki, ed., *Problems of Advanced Economics, Proceedings of the Third Conference on New Problems of Advanced Societies,* Tokyo, November 1982. Heidelberg: Springer-Verlag (1984), pp. 58–74.

Mishkin, Frederic. "Are Real Interest Rates Equal across Countries? An Empirical Investigation of International Parity Conditions," *Journal of Finance* 39 (1984a), pp. 1345–58.

———. "The Real Interest Rate: A Multi-Country Empirical Study," *Canadian Journal of Economics* 17, no. 2 (May 1984b), pp. 283–311.

Murphy, Robert. "Capital Mobility and the Relationship between Saving and Investment in OECD Countries," *Journal of International Money and Finance* 3 (1984), pp. 327–42.

Obstfeld, Maurice. "Capital Mobility in the World Economy: Theory and Measurement," paper presented at the Carnegie-Rochester Public Policy Conference (1985).

Otani, Ichiro. "Exchange Rate Instability and Capital Controls: The Japanese Experiense 1978–81" in D. Bigman and T. Taya, eds., *Exchange Rate and Trade Instability: Causes, Consequences and Remedies.* Cambridge, Mass.: Ballinger (1983).

Otani, Ichiro, and Siddarih Tiwari. "Capital Controls and Interest Parity: The Japanese Experience 1978–81, *IMF Staff Papers* (December 1981).

Penati, Alessandro, and Michael Dooley, "Current Account Imbalances and Capital Formation in Industrial Countries, 1949–1981." *IMF Staff Papers* 31 (1984), pp. 1–24.

Ransom, Roger, and Richard Sutch. "Domestic Saving as an Active Constraint on Capital Formation in the American Economy, 1839–1928: A Provisional Theory." University of California Project on the History of Saving, Working Paper no. 1, University of California, Berkeley (1983).

Roll, Richard. "Violations of Purchasing Power Parity and Their Implications for Efficient International Commodity Markets" in M. Sarnat and G. Szego, eds., *International Finance and Trade,* vol. 1. Cambridge, Mass.: Ballinger (1979).

Sachs, Jeffrey. "The Current Account and Macroeconomic Adjustment in the 1970s" in *Brookings Papers on Economic Activity,* vol. 12. Washington, D.C.: Brookings Institution (1981), pp. 201–68.

———. "Aspects of the Current Account Behavior of OECD Economies" in E. Claassen and P. Salin, eds., *Recent Issues in the Theory of Flexible Exchange Rates.* Amsterdam, North-Holland (1983).

Stern, Nicholas. "The Marginal Valuation of Income" in M.J. Artis and A.R. Nobay, eds., *Studies in Modern Economic Analysis.* Oxford, England: Basil Blackwell (1977), pp. 145–76.

Summers, Lawrence. "Tax Policy and International Competitiveness," National Bureau of Economic Research Working Paper (March 1985).

Tobin, James. "Comments on Domestic Saving and International Capital Movements in the Long Run and the Short Run," *European Economic Review* 21 (1983), pp. 153–56.

von Furstenberg, George. "Changes in U.S. Interest Rates and Their Effects on European Interest and Exchange Rates" in D. Bigman and T. Taya, eds., *Exchange Rate and Trade Instability: Causes, Consequences and Remedies.* Cambridge, Mass.: Ballinger (1983).

Westphal, Uwe. "Comments on Domestic Saving and International Capital Movements in the Long Run and the Short Run," *European Economic Review* 21 (1983), pp. 157–59.

Comments

Frederic S. Mishkin

Jeffrey Frankel's chapter is a useful summary and extension of results in the literature on international capital mobility and crowding-out. He looks at the question of whether international capital mobility prevents fiscal policy from having an impact on domestic investment (that is, whether no crowding-out occurs). This question deserves the attention that Frankel devotes to it because it bears on policy issues that are currently very much in the public eye; for example: Do large government deficits crowd out domestic investment so that domestic capital formation is retarded? Can large U.S. budget deficits be the source of the current high real interest rates throughout the world? Can supply-side policies to stimulate domestic saving increase domestic investment and raise the capital stock? How effective are fiscal and monetary policies in influencing the business cycle?

Frankel's analysis leads him to the following conclusions:

1. International capital mobility does not fully prevent fiscal policy from having an impact on domestic investment, so that there is a distinct possibility that large U.S. government budget deficits do crowd out domestic investment.

2. Imperfect goods market integration is the reason why fiscal policy can have an impact on domestic investment.

While in general I agree with Frankel's conclusions, I do not always agree with the methodology used in his empirical analysis. It is important to distinguish between the validity of Frankel's conclusions and his empiricial analysis because a literal reading of his empirical results might lead the reader to a conclusion that I believe is unwarranted. Specifically, a reader might come away from reading Frankel's evidence on saving–investment correlations thinking that there is a causal relationship from domestic saving to domestic investment that is not weakened by the existence of international capital mobility. I found the empirical analysis supporting this view to be unconvincing. Frankel also has some doubts about this evidence because he states, "a better econometric approach than saving–investment correlations is to test real interest rate parity directly." Thus, he and I have less disagreement than my comment suggests because I also find tests of international parity conditions to be the more relevant evidence supporting the two conclusions he reaches.

The Feldstein-Horioka Analysis

Frankel first approaches the effects of international capital mobility by focusing on the Feldstein-Horioka (1980) analysis in which the share of domestic investment in GNP is regressed on the share of national saving. Frankel seems to indicate that the most serious criticism of the Feldstein-Horioka regression analysis is the potential endogeneity of national saving. If this were the most serious criticism, then choosing a "good" set of instruments (ones that are exogenous) and estimating the regression with instrumental variables would solve the problem. I have no objections to the instruments Frankel chooses: Military expenditure and the age composition variables are about as exogenous as economists are ever going to find. However, I think that he has not focused on the most important criticism of the Feldstein-Horioka analysis discussed in the literature.[1]

The most severe problem with the Feldstein-Horioka regressions is not that the national saving variable is endogenous, but is rather that a regression of domestic investment on national saving is not a well-specified model. In my reading of the investment literature I have never seen a structural model that suggests that investment is a function of saving. Finding good exogenous instruments and using them to estimate the relationship between saving and investment with instrumental variables does not solve the basic problem. The regression results on a misspecified model are still uninterpretable, no matter how good the instruments are.

I thus find the results in Frankel's investment–saving regressions to be totally unconvincing. In fact, if they are taken literally, they imply that crowding out in an international context is practically complete and there are almost no effects of international capital mobility on domestic investment. I suspect that Frankel would also not be willing to accept this conclusion, and it is not a position that he advocates in his chapter.

It should be pointed out that my criticism of investment–saving regressions does not imply that government policies that affect domestic saving can have no impact on domestic investment. Such a link may exist, but it must be demonstrated by a more complicated structural model that describes what factors affect saving, which in turn also affects investment.

International Parity Conditions

The second approach for examining international capital mobility is to investigate international parity conditions. Frankel's empirical analysis of the covered interest parity condition is well thought out and it suggests that international capital mobility is very high. I found his discussion of Japan to be especially instructive, because it indicates that despite claims by American businessmen and politicians in 1983 that the Japanese were employing some form of capital market restrictions, the Japanese capital markets had become as open as those in other OECD countries such as Germany and Switzerland.[2]

Frankel's analysis of uncovered interest parity also leads him to conclude that international capital mobility is high. Although I too accept this conclusion, I find the route that he uses to arrive at this conclusion to be unconvincing. Frankel develops a model that indicates that risk premiums in the Eurocurrency market are small. He then takes these small risk premiums as evidence supporting high international capital mobility. My doubts about his reasoning center on two issues: (1) his view that the size of the risk premium provides important information for deciding on the degree of capital mobility and (2) his view that risk premiums are small.

First, a small risk premium is not at all necessary for international capital to be perfect. Large risk premiums in the foreign exchange market are consistent with perfect capital mobility, just as large risk premiums in the bond and stock markets in the United States are consistent with perfect capital mobility within the United States. The presence of large versus small risk premiums in the foreign exchange market thus has little bearing on whether one believes that international capital mobility is high.

Second, the evidence for small risk premiums is by no means clear-cut. An important assumption in Frankel's analysis of the risk premium is that the variance-covariance matrix of return differentials is constant over time—that is, return differentials are covariance-stationary. Models using this assumption have almost uniformly been rejected.[3] Tests of this assumption in a recent paper by Giovannini and Jorion (1985) indicate that it is strongly rejected by the data. Giovannini and Jorion also show that if they allow for variation over time of the variance–covariance matrix of return differentials, they can derive large risk premiums using Frankel's framework. Indeed, in one illustrative example, they find that the risk premium is estimated to be forty times larger when allowance is made for a time-varying variance–covariance matrix.

Giovannini and Jorion's finding that risk premiums can be large is reassuring because Hodrick and Srivistava (1984) and others have shown that risk premiums must be large if expectations in foreign exchange markets are even close to being rational. Since many economists are unwilling to entirely abandon the rational expectations (efficient markets) assumption because they do not see a viable alternative, they are far more comfortable with the view that risk premiums are large rather than small.

The evidence discussed in Frankel's chapter that both he and I find to be the most relevant to the degree of international capital mobility involves the tests of real rate equality. Real interest rate equality across countries is strongly rejected and this leaves open the possibility that domestic fiscal policy can indeed affect domestic investment. Frankel points out that the primary source of the rejection of real rate equality is the failure of ex ante relative purchasing power parity. This parity condition will fail to hold if international goods markets are not well integrated (or equivalently, goods in different countries are far from being perfect substitutes). Since it is plausible that international goods market integration is far weaker than international financial market integration, it is not surprising that ex ante purchasing power parity is rejected by the data. Frankel conducts one test of ex ante purchasing power parity with 116 years of U.S.–U.K. data and rejects this parity condition. His results are consistent with those of Cumby and Obstfeld (1984), who also find rejections of ex ante purchasing power parity when they use powerful statistical techniques on postwar data for several countries.

The evidence on real rate equality and ex ante purchasing power parity thus leads me to Frankel's conclusion that crowding-out can occur because goods markets are not well integrated.[4] However, his chapter does not sufficiently stress several results that are germane to the issue of whether complete crowding-out occurs. First, although Friedman and Schwartz (1982), von Furstenburg (1983), Cumby and Obstfeld (1984), Mishkin (1984), and Cumby and Mishkin (1986) find that real interest rates are not equalized across countries, Cumby and Mishkin (1986) report that there is a strong and statistically significant tendency for real rates to move together in different countries, though the movement is not always one-for-one. This result suggests that international capital mobility *does* affect real interest rate differentials between countries and that complete crowding-out is unlikely. Second, approximately half of the United States's current huge budget deficit is being financed by capital inflows from abroad. This fact also suggests that complete crowding-out does not occur.

Conclusions

My reading of the evidence is as follows: Although zero crowding-out (as a result of perfect international capital mobility) receives little support so that fiscal policy can affect domestic investment, complete crowding-out is also not supported. Since this book is devoted to policy questions, I want to conclude by addressing the question: What does the evidence on international capital mobility and crowding-out imply for government policy.

The conclusion that complete crowding-out is not supported by the data suggests that international capital mobility ameliorates some of the harmful effects of the large budget deficits on the U.S. economy, specifically on real interest rates and on capital formation. The inflows of capital from abroad in the present U.S. situation have surely kept real interest rates lower than they otherwise would have been, which, in turn, has kept domestic investment and capital formation higher. However, the rejection of perfect capital mobility in which fiscal policy is offset by international capital flows suggests that current fiscal policy may be having undesirable effects on the U.S. economy.

It is also important to remember that the United States is a large country. Thus even in the presence of perfect international capital mobility, U.S. fiscal policy can affect the world economy and hence also the U.S. economy. Undesirable effects of U.S. fiscal policy will spill over to the rest of the world. To the extent that international capital mobility helps the United States to suffer less from its fiscal policy excesses, the rest of the world suffers more. Thus, even if the United States were to accept perfect international capital mobility and zero crowding-out, economists should not be complacent about possible harmful effects of U.S. fiscal policy.

Does the evidence on international capital mobility and crowding-out suggest that supply-side policies to stimulate private saving can help increase domestic capital formation? The answer, I believe, is no. First, high international capital mobility will certainly weaken the effects of policy-induced increases in domestic saving on domestic investment. Second, and more important, there is little evidence that saving responds substantially to supply-side incentives. This is particularly evident in recent years when incentives to promote saving have not resulted in a big expansion of private savings. In fact, the private savings rate in the United States has recently been hitting all-time lows. From this perspective, the supply-side revolution has not been a resounding success.

Notes

1. For example, see Tobin (1983) and Obstfeld (1985).
2. This conclusion was also reached in a careful study by Ito (1983).
3. In the exchange rate literature, examples are Hansen and Hodrick (1983) and Hodrick and Srivistava (1984).
4. Although rejection of real rate equality and ex ante relative PPP leaves open the possibility that crowding-out can occur, this rejection does not imply that crowding-out *must* occur. There could be zero crowding-out if deviations from ex ante relative PPP which lead to real rate inequality are never caused by fiscal policy but are rather attributable to some other factor.

References

Cumby, R. and Mishkin, F.S. "The International Linkage of Real Interest Rates: The European–U.S. Connection," *Journal of International Money and Finance* 5 (1986): 5–24.

Cumby, R. and Obstfeld, M. "International Interest Rate and Price Level Linkages under Flexible Exchange Rates: A Review of Recent Evidence" in J. Bilson and R. Marston (eds.), *Exchange Rate Theory and Practice* (Chicago: University of Chicago Press, 1984).

Feldstein, M. and Horioka, C. "Domestic Saving and International Capital Flows," *Economic Journal* 90 (1980): 314–29.

Friedman, M. and Schwartz, A. *Money, Interest Rates and Prices in the United States and the United Kingdom: 1867–1975* (Chicago: University of Chicago Press, 1982).

Giovannini, A. and Jorion, P. "Interest Rates and Risk Premia in the Stock Market and in the Foreign Exchange Market." (New York: Graduate School of Business, Columbia University, mimeo, 1985).

Hansen, L.P. and Hodrick, R.J. "Risk Averse Speculation in the Forward Foreign Exchange Market: An Econometric Analysis of Linear Models" in J.A. Frenkel (ed.), *Exchange Rates and International Macroeconomics* (Chicago: University of Chicago Press, 1983).

Hodrick, R.J. and Srivistava, S. "An Investigation of Risk and Return in Forward Foreign Exchange," *Journal of International Money and Finance* 3 (1984): 5–24.

Ito, T. "Capital Controls and Covered Interest Parity," National Bureau of Economic Research Working Paper no. 1187 (1983).

Mishkin, F.S. "Are Real Interest Rates Equal Across Countries? An Empirical Investigation of International Parity Conditions," *Journal of Finance* 39 (1984): 1345–58.

Obstfeld, M. "Capital Mobility in the World Economy: Theory and Measurement," paper presented at the *Carnegie-Rochester Public Policy Conference* (1985).

Tobin, J. "Comments on Domestic Saving and International Capital Movements in the Long Run and Short Run," *European Economic Review* 21 (1983): 153–56.

von Furstenburg, G. "Changes in U.S. Interest Rates and Their Effects on European Interest and Exchange Rates" in D. Bigman and T. Taya (eds.), *Exchange Rate and Trade Instability: Causes, Consequences and Remedies* (Cambridge, Mass.: Ballinger, 1983).

Part II
Macroeconomic Effects of Increased Openness

3

A VAR Analysis of Economic Interdependence: Canada, the United States, and the Rest of the World

John Kuszczak
John D. Murray

T his chapter uses the techniques of vector autoregression analysis to investigate the international transmission of business cycles among the major industrialized countries which comprise the G-7.[1] Particular attention is given to the dynamic behavior and interactions of the U.S. and Canadian economies during the past twenty years. Though several recent papers have questioned the reliability and usefulness of VAR analysis,[2] the approach would seem to provide a natural and convenient means of (1) measuring the relative importance of domestic and foreign shocks on the evolution of certain key macro variables and (2) comparing the effectiveness of various policy actions under fixed and flexible exchange rate regimes—the two principal objectives of the present chapter.

The chapter begins with an analysis of three closed economy models: Canada, the United States, and Rest of World (ROW). The latter is an aggregate system representing the countries in the G-7 excluding the United States. The regression results, impulse responses, and variance decompositions for these three closed economy models are then compared to three open economy models in which foreign output, prices, interest rates, money, and exchange rates are allowed to affect the domestic economies.

The major conclusions of the chapter can be summarized as follows:

1. Foreign variables exert an important and statistically significant influence on the economies of Canada, the United States, and ROW. Closed econ-

The views expressed in this chapter are those of the authors. No responsibility for them should be attributed to the Bank of Canada. The authors would like to acknowledge the invaluable assistance of Paul Gomme, their research assistant at the Bank of Canada, and Tracey Bartzak, a secretary at the Woodrow Wilson School of Public and International Affairs, Princeton University. They would also like to thank their colleagues for many helpful suggestions, and absolve them of any responsibility for the analysis which follows.

omy models excluding international influences are therefore likely to give a distorted view of the macroeconomic relationships in these economies and could misrepresent the strength and effectiveness of domestic policy actions.

2. While the Canadian economy is evidently more open than the U.S. economy, and therefore more vulnerable to external shocks, at least 20 to 30 percent of the forecast variance of U.S. output and prices can be attributed to innovations in foreign variables.

3. The money equations for both Canada and the United States are very sensitive to movements in foreign interest rates and exchange rates. Due to the astructural nature of VAR models, however, it is impossible to determine whether this sensitivity is caused by currency substitution on the part of private agents (demand-side effects) or the policy actions of monetary authorities (supply-side effects).

4. Over most of the 1962–84 period, Canadian interest rates and money have moved primarily in response to U.S. shocks. This dependence could have been caused by the tight structural relationships binding the U.S. and Canadian economies, or alternatively what Richard Cooper (1985) has termed "goal and policy interdependence."

5. Finally, as an empirical matter the distinction between fixed and flexible exchange rate systems does not seem to have been very important over the 1962–84 period. Tests for structural stability suggest that the time series behavior of Canadian, U.S., and ROW variables remained virtually unchanged following the move to flexible exchange rates in the early 1970s.

The remainder of the chapter is divided into six sections. The first briefly discusses the VAR methodology and the structure of the closed and open economy models. The next describes the data series used in the Canadian and U.S. regressions as well as the trade-weighted indexes that were constructed to estimate for the ROW models. The regression results and variance decompositions of the models are presented in the following section, along with graphs of the impulse responses for selected domestic and foreign shocks. Next comes an examination of the policy implications of our empirical work. The chapter concludes with a brief summary and some suggestions for future research.

Models and Methodology

Two sets of linear, constant coefficient VAR models are estimated in the empirical portion of this chapter. The first set contains three closed economy models representing Canada, the United States, and the rest of the world, respectively. Each closed economy model has four endogenous variables—output, prices, money, and interest rates—which are regressed on a constant term, their own lagged values, and lagged values of the other three endogenous variables in the system.[3] The complete four-equation system for each country can be written in vector notation as

$$y_t^i = \alpha + \sum_{k=1}^{n} \beta(k) y_{t-k}^i + \epsilon_t \tag{3.1}$$

where y_t^i is a 4×1 vector of endogenous variables for country i, α is a 4×1 vector of constant terms, $\beta(k)$ is a 4×4 matrix of estimated coefficients on the lagged values of y_t, and ϵ_t is a white noise error term assumed to be independent and normally distributed with zero mean.

The second set of models has the same basic structure as the first but includes five extra variables: foreign output, prices, money, interest rates, and an exchange rate. These augmented open economy models represent the most important part of our analysis. They are compared to the more familiar closed economy models in the **Results** section and are used to test the statistical significance and economic importance of foreign variables in the three domestic economies.

The structure of the open economy models will vary according to the relationship that the domestic and foreign economies bear to one another. If the international system is truly interdependent, such that shocks to economy A impact on economy B and vice versa (bidirectional causality), the vector y_{t-k} in equation 3.1 will include all nine endogenous variables (four domestic and five foreign). $\beta(k)$, the matrix of parameters on lagged values of y, will also be expanded from dimension 4×4 to 9×9 and will contain few, if any, zero elements. If, on the other hand, the relationship between A and B is best described as one of dependence as opposed to interdependence, lagged values of y from the small (dependent) economy will have no impact on the large economy and at least 5×5 of the coefficients in the $\beta(k)$ matrix of the large economy will have zero values.

All of the models described here have traditional VAR structures in the sense that (1) they impose a common lag length on all explanatory variables, (2) they include the same explanatory variables in each equation, and (3) they use only lagged values of the endogenous variables and a constant term as regressors. This symmetric structure makes it possible to obtain consistent and efficient coefficient estimates by running ordinary least squares on the individual equations, provided the error terms in equation 3.1 are not autocorrelated. One can thereby avoid the necessity of costly systems estimation. The absence of contemporaneous variables on the right side of the equations also eliminates the need to make arbitrary assumptions about the causal relationships of the variables.[4]

There are some notable disadvantages associated with this unrestricted form of econometric analysis, however. First, traditional VAR models are very data intensive. Since the number of coefficients that have to be estimated expands by a factor of $n(2j + 1) + 1$ for every additional variable in the model, we are forced to use very parsimonious specifications.[5] As a consequence, several potentially important variables could be omitted. Second, by admitting only lagged endogenous variables on the right-hand side of each equation (in addition to a constant term), all the contemporaneous shocks which impact on y_t are forced to feed through the residuals, ϵ_t. While this may not pose a problem in the estimation stage of the analysis, the impulse responses and variance decompositions derived from these initial estimates could be seriously affected. If the residuals have high contemporaneous correlations, any adjustment to the order in which the variables are entered in the system could produce dramatic changes in the results. More specifically, certain variables could assume exaggerated importance in the variance decompositions, while other, more significant variables receive little or no weight. This problem arises because the Choleski decomposition which is used to convert the VAR models into their moving average representations attributes all the contemporaneous correlation between two series to the variable that is ordered first in each model.

Some authors have tried to improve the efficiency of their VAR estimates and to save degrees of freedom by assigning different lag lengths to the various regressors. Batten and Thorton (1985), Fackler (1985), and others have proposed a number of heuristic algorithms for this purpose, based on the Akaike Final Prediction Error criterion. Unfortunately these techniques are very cumbersome when more than two or three variables are involved, and typically yield results that are very sample sensitive.

Given the number of models to be estimated here and the large number of variables contained in each, selective adjustment of the lags on individual variables did not seem to be a very practicable approach. Instead, we have tried to keep our models as small as possible by running systemwide significance tests on alternative lag lengths for all the variables in each model. While the lag lengths that are ultimately assigned to the models are probably too long for some series and too short for others, there does not seem to be any obvious alternative to this more aggregative approach.

The second problem mentioned above, concerning the sensitivity of variance decompositions to the ordering of the variables, can be addressed in a somewhat more satisfactory fashion using a strategy recommended by Doan and Litterman (1980). By inspecting the contemporaneous correlations of the residuals in each model it is possible to identify variable combinations that could pose a problem. The variance decompositions and impulse responses can then be recomputed, switching the order of any variables that are highly correlated in order to check the sensitivity of the results. In none of the cases to be reported here did this appear to be a major problem.

Data

In order to implement the VAR modeling techniques and test procedures described under **Models and Methodology**, suitable real world proxies must be found for all the domestic and foreign variables in the models. Though several alternative measures were initially considered, in the end most had to be rejected because they were either not available for all countries or only extended over short time periods. The series which were finally chosen are shown below, along with their mnemonics:[6]

Output = seasonally adjusted index of industrial production (U)

Prices = seasonally adjusted consumer price index (P)[7]

Money = seasonally adjusted demand deposits plus currency (M)

Interest rate = call loan rate on money market instruments (R)

Exchange rate = price of foreign currency in U.S. dollars (S)

All of the series have been defined on a quarterly basis and typically run from 1964.1 to 1984.4. Data for Canada and the United States, however, have been extended back to 1960.1.

Representative aggregate measures of output, prices, money, and the exchange rate were constructed for ROW by combining individual series for Canada, France, Germany, Italy, Japan, and the United Kingdom in four trade-weighted indexes.[8] The specification used to aggregate the series can be written as

$$X_{w,t} = X_{w,t-1} \prod_{i=1}^{6} (X_{i,t}/X_{i,t-1})\tilde{S}_{i,t} \qquad (3.2)$$

where:

X_w = index of aggregate output (prices, money, and the exchange rate) for ROW

X_i = aggregate output (prices, money, and the exchange rate) for the ith country

$\tilde{S}_i$ = ith country's share of world trade

The share weights, $\tilde{S}_{i,t}$, reflect the relative importance of each country in world trade and have been defined such that

$$\sum_{i=1}^{6} \tilde{S}_{i,t} = 1$$

The quarterly values of $\tilde{S}_{i,t}$, which are included in equation 3.2 were obtained by fitting a polynomial time series to annual data extracted from the International Monetary Fund's *World Trade Statistics.* Their average values over the 1964.1–1984.4 sample period are reported below.[9]

Canada	France	Germany	Italy	Japan	U.K.
0.12	0.16	0.26	0.12	0.15	0.19

The index constructed for ROW interest rates uses the same trade-weights as equation 3.2 but has a simpler, linear specification

$$R_{w,t} = \sum_{i=1}^{5} \tilde{S}'_{i,t}(R_{i,t}) \tag{3.3}$$

Only five countries were included in equation 3.3 as reliable interest rate data were not available for Italy prior to 1975.

One final point that should be mentioned regarding the data concerns the procedures used to render the series stationary. VAR analysis assumes that all the stochastic processes in the autoregressive system are variance–covariance stationary. If this condition is not met, little confidence can be placed in the VAR regression results. Since most, if not all, of the data here are highly autocorrelated and tend to drift over time, some form of detrending is obviously required before the models can be estimated.

The two most popular methods of detrending are (1) regressing the data on time (or a function of time), and (2) differencing the data. A priori it is not clear which method is more appropriate, but using the wrong approach could have serious consequences for the empirical work that follows.

After considering various alternatives we eventually decided to transform the data into first-differences of their natural logarithms (which is roughly equivalent to using percentage changes.)[10] Our choice was influenced in part by recent work by Nelson and Plosser (1982). Using a test developed by Dickey and Fuller (1979), the authors have shown that most U.S. time series are well represented as difference stationary processes. In addition, they have found that data that are detrended with time, as opposed to being first differenced, often produce "spurious regression results."[11]

Results

Closed Economy Models

The results for the closed economy models will not be discussed in much detail since there is reason to believe that the models are seriously misspecified. The significance tests reported below show that they exclude several important foreign variables. Nevertheless, these restricted four-equation models do provide useful control solutions which can be used to test the open

Table 3–1
Testing the Lag Structures of Closed Economy Models, 1962.1–1984.4

Canada:		
1962.3–1984.4		
8 vs. 6 lags	$\chi^2(32)^a \; ^5 \; 28.5$	Accept 6
6 vs. 4 lags	$\chi^2(32) = 47.6^*$	Reject 4
United States:		
1962.1–1984.4		
8 vs. 6 lags	$\chi^2(32) = 36.3$	Accept 6
6 vs. 4 lags	$\chi^2(32) = 72.7^*$	Reject 4
Rest of World:		
1965.3–1984.4		
8 vs. 6 lags	$\chi^2(32) = 28.7$	Accept 6
6 vs. 4 lags	$\chi^2(32) = 26.0$	Accept 4
4 vs. 3 lags	$\chi^2(16) = 16.0$	Accept 3
3 vs. 2 lags	$\chi^2(16) = 21.0$	Accept 2
2 vs. 1 lags	$\chi^2(16) = 27.8^*$	Reject 1

[a]Likelihood ratio test statistic distributed as χ^2 with (r) degrees of freedom.
*Significant at the 5.0 percent level.

economy results discussed under **Open Economy Models.** The results are also of some interest in their own right since most of the VAR analyses published to date employ similar closed economy specifications and readers may wish to compare their results with those here.

Parameter Estimates. The first stage of this analysis involves selecting an appropriate lag length for the (endogenous) explanatory variables in each model. As noted earlier, this is done on a systemwide basis (the whole model is tested as opposed to individual equations or variables), using a modified likelihood ratio test first proposed by Sims (1980b).[12] The results are reported in table 3–1.

The lag lengths assigned to the Canadian and U.S. models are much longer than those assigned to the ROW model (six lags versus two). This difference might be explained by the aggregation procedure that was used to create the ROW variables. Averaging the data across six different countries may have removed some of the variation that made longer lags necessary in the other models.

Parameter estimates and summary statistics for the final versions of the closed economy models are presented in tables 3–2 through 3–4.[13] Though it is often difficult to interpret the coefficients in VAR models, plausible stories can be told for most results here.

Table 3-2
Parameter Estimates for the Closed Economy Model of Canada, 1962.3–1984.4

Equation	Constant	$A(L)U_c^a$	$B(L)P_c^a$	$C(L)M_c^a$	$D(L)R_c^a$	R^2	Durbin-Watson Statistic	Standard Error	$Q(27)^b$
U_c	0.017	−0.195	−1.190	0.736	−0.788	0.389	1.99	0.015	13.42
	(2.14)**	(0.55)	(1.91)*	(2.06)*	(1.38)				
P_c	−0.005	0.227	1.10	0.066	0.107	0.843	1.99	0.003	18.51
	(2.68)**	(3.18)**	(29.88)**	(1.76)	(0.57)				
M_c	0.009	−0.062	−0.164	0.723	−1.172	0.394	2.09	0.014	25.54
	(1.19)	(2.13)*	(0.91)	(4.81)**	(4.74)**				
R_c	−0.013	0.397	0.443	0.158	−0.135	0.241	1.98	0.001	11.99
	(2.30)**	(2.32)**	(1.26)	(1.85)*	(1.11)				

[a]Sum of lagged coefficients where lag operators are of order 6. F-statistic testing the joint significance of all lagged coefficients reported in parentheses.

[b]Q(r) = Box-Pierce Q-statistic for autocorrelation, distributed as X^2 with r degrees of freedom.

*Significant at the 10.0 percent level.

**Significant at the 5.0 percent level.

Table 3–3
Parameter Estimates for the Closed Economy Model of the United States, 1962.1–1984.4

Equation	Constant	$A(L)U_{us}$[a]	$B(L)P_{us}$[a]	$C(L)M_{us}$[a]	$D(L)R_{us}$[a]	R^2	Durbin-Watson Statistic	Standard Error	$Q(27)$[b]
U_{us}	0.011 (1.80)**	0.226 (3.70)**	−0.597 (4.13)**	0.315 (1.73)	−1.351 (6.34)**	0.619	2.05	0.014	22.50
P_{us}	−0.002 (0.83)	0.052 (2.23)**	0.842 (10.69)**	0.212 (2.63)**	0.301 (2.66)**	0.724	2.01	0.004	16.34
M_{us}	0.005 (1.97)**	−0.059 (0.88)	0.013 (3.12)**	0.703 (4.01)**	−0.447 (4.01)**	0.461	1.86	0.006	16.76
R_{us}	−0.010 (2.38)**	0.316 (2.37)**	0.108 (4.42)**	0.413 (5.59)**	0.161 (4.70)**	0.551	1.98	0.009	11.69

[a]Sum of lagged coefficients where lag operators are of order 6. F-statistic testing the joint significance of all lagged coefficients reported in parentheses.

[b]$Q(r)$ = Box-Pierce Q-statistic for autocorrelation, distributed as χ^2 with r degrees of freedom.

*Significant at the 10.0 percent level.

**Significant at the 5.0 percent level.

Table 3–4
Parameter Estimates for the Closed Economy Model of Rest of World, 1964.1–1984.4

Equation	Constant	$A(L)U_w$ [a]	$B(L)P_w$ [a]	$C(L)M_w$ [a]	$D(L)R_w$ [a]	R^2	Durbin-Watson Statistic	Standard Error	$Q(27)$ [b]
U_w	0.015 (3.20)**	0.409 (6.47)**	-0.600 (3.79)**	0.012 (0.03)	-0.213 (0.26)	0.310	2.02	0.013	23.62
P_w	0.001 (0.81)	0.033 (2.15)*	0.935 (126.24)**	-0.011 (0.72)	0.167 (2.31)*	0.815	2.10	0.003	37.10
M_w	0.027 (1.52)	0.234 (0.09)	1.116 (0.96)	-0.988 (18.67)**	-2.361 (2.91)**	0.283	2.19	0.049	10.68
R_w	-0.004 (1.80)**	0.245 (3.62)**	0.120 (1.16)	0.008 (0.36)	0.217 (1.56)	0.277	1.99	0.006	25.44

[a]Sum of lagged coefficients where lag operators are of order 2. F-statistic testing the joint significance of all lagged coefficients reported in parentheses.

[b]$Q(r)$ = Box-Pierce Q-statistic for autocorrelation, distributed as X^2 with r degrees of freedom.

*Significant at the 10.0 percent level.

**Significant at the 5.0 percent level.

Real growth (U) is negatively related to increases in interest rates and inflation,[14] and is positively related to money growth and its own lagged values, except in Canada where lagged values of U_c bear a negative but statistically insignificant relationship to current real growth. Inflation on the other hand is positively related to interest rates and lagged inflation, as well as output and money growth—at least in Canada and the United States. The positive sign on lagged interest rates in the Canadian and U.S. price equations is somewhat unexpected, but the same response has been recorded elsewhere by Sims (1980a) and Litterman and Weiss (1983). The result can be interpreted in terms of a Fischer effect (nominal interest rates correctly anticipating future inflation) and/or what Driskill and Sheffrin (1985) have recently labeled a "Patman effect." The latter refers to the direct cost-push effect that higher interest rates might have on prices.

Money growth (M) is depressed by higher interest rates in all three "countries" and generally bears a positive relationship to its own lagged values. M_w in the ROW model is the sole exception. Interest rates (R) tend to rise with higher real growth, inflation, and money, but the relationships are often not statistically significant.

The only troublesome result in tables 3–2, 3–3, and 3–4 is the negative and statistically significant coefficient on U_c in the Canadian money equation.[15] For the most part, however, the qualitative results are very similar across all three models. There are nevertheless two intercountry differences that deserve special attention.

First, the U.S. equations seem to contain more significant variables and generally have greater explanatory power than either the Canadian or ROW equations. This could be taken as evidence that the closed economy specification is more acceptable in the case of the United States, though clearly it is impossible to make any direct comparisons as one is dealing with different dependent variables in each equation. Second, money and interest rates have much less influence in the ROW than in the United States. While this could be a consequence of aggregation, it could also reflect the more heavily regulated nature of Japanese and European financial markets.

Variance Decomposition and Impulse Responses. The variance decompositions of the closed economy models are reported in tables 3–5, 3–6, and 3–7. The statistics measure the proportion of the error variance in each domestic variable that can be attributed to shocks (or "innovations") in output, prices, money, and interest rates over forecast horizons ranging from one to twelve quarters. As one might expect, the most important shocks come from lagged values of the dependent variables themselves. Nevertheless, shocks from other variables typically account for a significant proportion of the error variance in each variable by the twelfth quarter. The one exception is M_w (see table 3–7), which is virtually exogenous.[16]

Table 3–5
Canada: Variance Decomposition of Prediction Errors

Variable	Quarter	Proportion of Error Attributed to Shocks in:				Standard Error
		U_c	P_c	M_c	R_c	
U_c	1	100.0	0.0	0.0	0.0	0.124-01
	4	85.5	4.6	5.1	4.8	0.136-01
	8	78.3	8.8	5.5	7.3	0.170-01
	12	69.2	8.7	9.4	12.7	0.181-01
P_c	1	0.2	93.8	5.6	0.4	0.287-02
	4	6.0	62.3	25.5	6.3	0.476-02
	8	9.0	48.7	31.5	10.8	0.612-02
	12	7.1	36.8	38.3	17.8	0.730-02
M_c	1	0.0	0.0	94.3	5.7	0.116-01
	4	13.5	3.2	59.0	24.2	0.155-01
	8	16.1	4.3	56.4	23.2	0.168-01
	12	15.8	5.3	54.5	24.5	0.173-01
R_c	1	10.5	0.0	0.0	89.5	0.867
	4	18.8	3.3	7.1	70.8	1.060
	8	20.9	4.6	10.3	64.2	1.135
	12	20.7	4.9	10.6	63.7	1.158

Note: Equations were estimated over the sample period 1962.3–1984.4 with six lags on each explanatory variable. The order of the variables in the variance decompositions was *U, R, M,* and *P.*

In order to test the sensitivity of these results to changes in the ordering of the variables, the variance decompositions were rerun reversing the positions of those variables that were most highly correlated. The only variables affected were *R–U* in the case of Canada and the United States, and *R–U* and *R–P* in the ROW (see table 3–8). Since the results did not change significantly after the variables were reordered, they will not be reported here. Evidently, the residual correlations must be much higher than those recorded in table 3–8 before any major changes will appear in the variance decompositions.

The impulse responses for the closed economy models are shown in figures 3–1 through 3–4. Each figure contains three plots, representing the responses of Canadian (-----), U.S. (—·—·—), and ROW (———) variables to innovations in *U, R, M,* and *P.* The adjustment paths are all dynamically

Table 3-6
United States: Variance Decomposition of Prediction Errors

Variable	Quarter	Proportion of Error Attributed to Shocks in:				Standard Error
		U_{us}	P_{us}	M_{us}	R_{us}	
U_{us}	1	100.0	0.0	0.0	0.0	0.117-01
	4	76.2	2.4	6.0	15.4	0.163-01
	8	60.0	7.9	13.3	18.8	0.204-01
	12	54.6	12.4	16.1	16.9	0.219-01
P_{us}	1	0.2	98.8	0.1	0.9	0.381-02
	4	3.2	70.4	17.8	8.6	0.579-02
	8	6.7	60.9	25.0	7.4	0.722-02
	12	6.4	58.0	28.5	7.1	0.770-02
M_{us}	1	1.3	0.0	98.5	0.2	0.493-02
	4	8.4	4.7	77.8	9.1	0.603-02
	8	12.4	11.5	64.8	11.4	0.698-02
	12	12.9	14.3	60.3	12.5	0.728-02
R_{us}	1	19.6	0.0	0.0	80.4	0.796
	4	20.0	9.1	17.6	53.3	1.114
	8	17.0	15.0	17.6	50.4	1.252
	12	18.3	17.9	18.6	45.2	1.340

Note: Equations were estimated over the sample period 1962.3–1984.4 with six lags on each explanatory variable. The order of the variables in the variance decompositions was *U, R, M,* and *P.*

stable and are similar across the three countries, though the cycles are much smoother in the case of ROW and typically display less variability—a consequence of the shorter lags assigned to the ROW model.

In general the impact and short-run effects of the various shocks are consistent with the parameter estimates in tables 3–2 through 3–4. Output in each country increases in response to positive money shocks and decreases in response to higher prices and interest rates. Notice, however, that the contractionary effects of R_{us} and P_{us} on U.S. output are usually delayed by two to three quarters.[17] Money growth is also reduced by interest rates, but increases in response to positive innovations in prices. Interest rates and prices, on the other hand, typically increase in response to innovations in all four domestic variables.

Despite the consistency and apparent plausibility of most of the results,

Table 3–7
Rest of World: Variance Decomposition of Prediction Errors

Variable	Quarter	Proportion of Error Attributed to Shocks in:				Standard Error
		U_w	P_w	M_w	R_w	
U_w	1	100.0	0.0	0.0	0.0	0.120-01
	4	91.9	4.8	0.1	3.2	0.135-01
	8	83.6	10.5	0.2	5.7	0.145-01
	12	81.1	12.4	0.2	6.3	0.149-01
P_w	1	0.6	93.0	0.2	6.2	0.326-02
	4	13.0	68.9	0.9	17.1	0.562-02
	8	20.2	61.0	0.8	18.1	0.715-02
	12	22.1	59.0	0.7	18.1	0.767-02
M_w	1	0.3	0.0	99.2	0.5	0.460-01
	4	0.5	0.5	95.1	3.9	0.567-01
	8	0.8	0.7	94.6	3.9	0.571-01
	12	0.8	0.8	94.4	4.0	0.572-01
R_w	1	9.3	0.0	0.0	90.7	0.565
	4	33.1	0.7	0.4	65.8	0.681
	8	33.1	1.7	0.5	64.8	0.690
	12	33.1	2.3	0.5	64.1	0.694

Note: Equations were estimated over the sample period 1964.1–1984.4 with two lags on each explanatory variable. The order of the variables in the variance decompositions was U, R, M, and P.

several notable intercountry differences can be observed in the plots. Canada, for example, is the only country whose prices fall in response to higher interest rates. As well, the response of money to an interest rate shock in Canada and ROW is much higher than that of the United States. This fact has been noted previously by Abrams and Sellon (1983), and was used by the authors to explain Canada's remarkable ability to consistently meet its monetary targets over the 1975–81 period.[18]

Finally, it is worth noting the negative response of prices in the ROW model to innovations in M_w. We are not aware of any generally accepted theory or institutional peculiarity that would explain why prices might fall in response to a positive money shock. Indeed, since the coefficients on M_w in the ROW price equation are all statistically insignificant, it would be a mistake to attach much importance to this curious result. We mention it only to

Table 3–8
Residual Cross-Correlations for the Closed Economy Models

Canada	U_c	P_c	M_c	R_c
U_c	1.000			
P_c	−0.048	1.000		
M_c	0.013	0.214	1.000	
R_c	0.324*	−0.042	−0.221	1.000

United States	U_{us}	P_{us}	M_{us}	R_{us}
U_{us}	1.000			
P_{us}	−0.048	1.000		
M_{us}	0.113	−0.026	1.000	
R_{us}	0.442*	0.064	0.093	1.000

Rest of World	U_w	P_w	M_w	R_w
U_w	1.000			
P_w	0.078	1.000		
M_w	0.053	−0.052	1.000	
R_w	0.305*	0.261*	−0.050	1.000

*Significant at the 5.0 percent level.

highlight another potential problem associated with VAR analysis. Because the impulse responses and variance decompositions are extracted in a simple, mechanistic fashion, without regard to their statistical significance, it is not unusual to obtain a few unexpected results.

Open Economy Models

Once the five foreign variables are added to the models here, the longest lag length that the equations can reasonably accommodate is four.[19] This restriction is not binding in any of the regressions, which are run over shorter sample periods beginning in either 1970.3 or 1973.1, as the models accept lag lengths as short as one or two (see table 3–9). It does pose a problem in the open economy models for Canada and the United States, which are run over longer sample periods beginning in 1962.1 and 1962.3. These models require at least four lags on each explanatory variable. Though we believe that any biases and distortions that result from these constraints are not serious, we have no formal means of testing their significance.

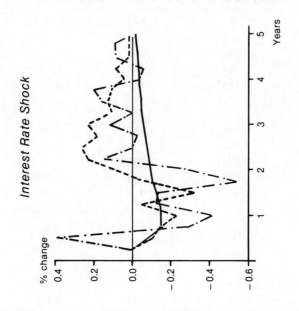

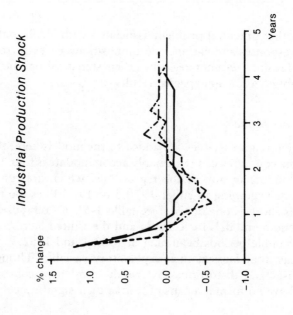

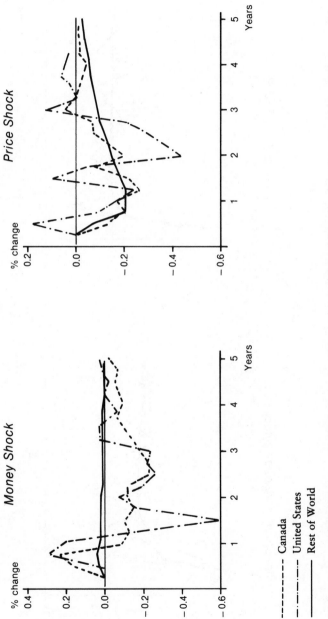

Figure 3–1. Closed Economy Responses in Output to Industrial Production, Interest Rate, Money, and Price Shocks

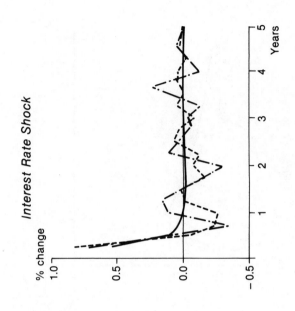

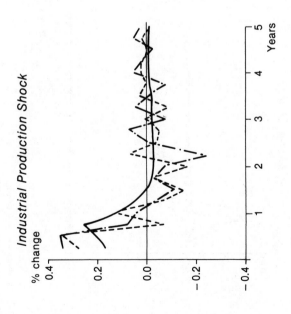

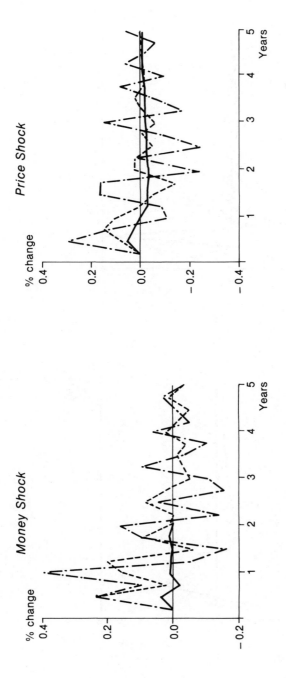

Figure 3–2. Closed Economy Responses in Interest Rates to Industrial Production, Interest Rate, Money, and Price Shocks

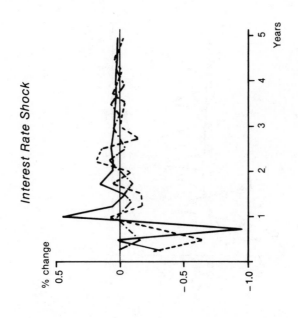

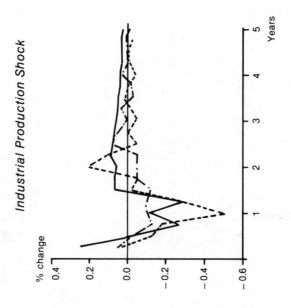

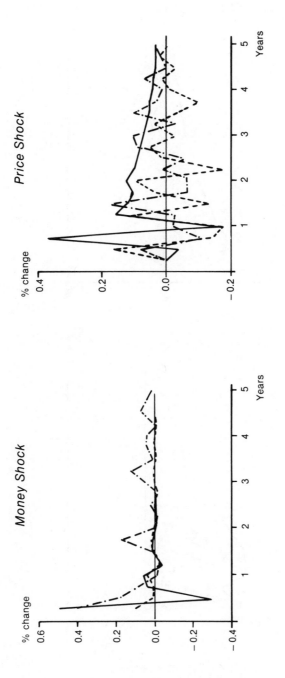

Figure 3–3. Closed Economy Responses in Money to Industrial Production, Interest Rate, Money, and Price Shocks

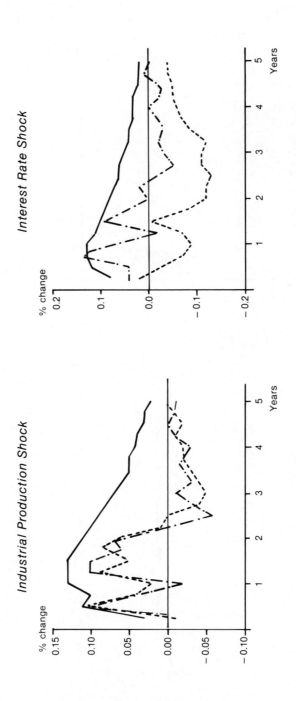

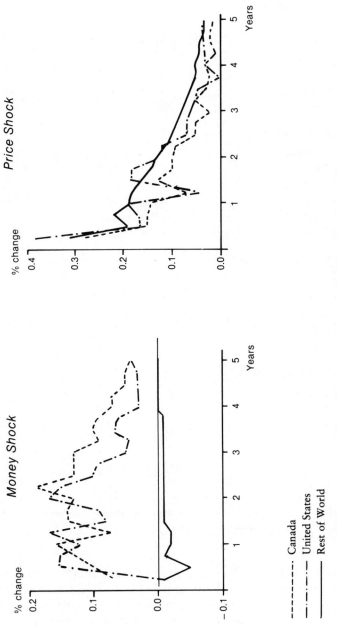

Figure 3–4. Closed Economy Responses in Prices to Industrial Production, Interest Rate, Money, and Price Shocks

Table 3–9
Testing the Lag Structures of Open Economy Models, 1962.1–1984.4

Canada (United States)[a]

1962.3–1984.4

4 vs. 3 lags	$\chi^2(36) = 63.6^*$	Reject 3

1970.3–1984.4

4 vs. 3 lags	$\chi^2(36) = 41.9$	Accept 3
3 vs. 2 lags	$\chi^2(36) = 42.9$	Accept 2
2 vs. 1 lags	$\chi^2(36) = 64.2^*$	Reject 1

United States (Canada)

1962.1–1984.4

4 vs. 3 lags	$\chi^2(36) = 76.9^*$	Reject 3

1970.3–1984.4

4 vs. 3 lags	$\chi^2(36) = 44.2$	Accept 3
3 vs. 2 lags	$\chi^2(36) = 33.4$	Accept 2
2 vs. 1 lags	$\chi^2(36) = 39.6$	Accept 1

United States (Rest of World)

1965.1–1984.4

4 vs. 3 lags	$\chi^2(36) = 88.4^*$	Reject 3

1973.1–1984.4

3 vs. 2 lags	$\chi^2(36) = 33.2$	Accept 2
2 vs. 1 lags	$\chi^2(36) = 30.8$	Accept 1

Rest of World (United States)

1965.1–1984.4

4 vs. 3 lags	$\chi^2(36) = 37.6$	Accept 3
3 vs. 2 lags	$\chi^2(36) = 33.2$	Accept 2
2 vs. 1 lags	$\chi^2(36) = 58.6^*$	Reject 1

1973.1–1984.4

3 vs. 2 lags	$\chi^2(36) = 21.92$	Reject 1
2 vs. 1 lags	$\chi^2(36) = 45.71$	Accept 1

[a]Dependent variables for country x are regressed on lagged variables from x and (y).
*Significant at the 5.0 percent level.

Parameter Estimates. The parameter estimates for the open economy models are reported in tables 3–10 through 3–13. Two sets of results are shown for Canada (tables 3–10 and 3–11): one for a full sample running from 1962.3 to 1984.4, and the other for a shorter sample running from 1970.3 to 1984.4. The latter corresponds to the period of flexible exchange rates in

Canada. Though similar models have been estimated for the United States and ROW, over the period 1973.1–1984.4, only those for Canada are reported below since the same general patterns and relationships are observed in all three models.

The coefficients on many of the domestic variables that were significant in the closed economy models have retained their signs and significance in the open economy models. Several foreign variables also play a significant role, however, and their presence has produced dramatic changes in some important domestic variables. In the case of Canada, lagged domestic interest rates (R_c) now enter the money equation with a positive and statistically insignificant coefficient. Most of their influence appears to have been usurped by R_{us}.[20]

There are other instances, however, in which the addition of foreign variables seems to have enhanced the importance of domestic variables. Notable examples include M_{us} in the U.S. output equation and P_w in the ROW money equation. It is difficult therefore to identify any consistent pattern among the domestic variables in the closed versus open economy models, though the results across countries are once again similar.

While performances of some of the foreign variables in the equations are rather mixed, foreign interest rates and exchange rates have a strong and statistically significant impact in all the open economy models that we have tested. An appreciation of the exchange rate in our Canadian and U.S. models (represented by higher values of S_{c-us} and S_{us-w}) depresses domestic output, prices, and money growth (see tables 3–10 and 3–12). A strong Canadian dollar also lowers short-term interest rates in Canada, but it is not clear how this result should be interpreted. It could reflect expectations of lower inflation following a currency appreciation, or a tendency on the part of Canadian policymakers to lean against the wind and to resist exchange rate pressures with offsetting movements in R_c.[21] A similar response is observed in the U.S. equation for R_{us}, but the coefficient on S_{w-us} is not statistically significant.

Higher foreign interest rates reduce money growth in Canada and the United States, and raise domestic interest rates. They also cause the home currencies in both countries to appreciate. Though this positive reaction is difficult to explain, it is consistent with other published work which has shown that future spot rates are systematically misforecast by movements in international interest rates and the forward premiums on foreign exchange.[22]

Foreign interest rates and exchange rates are less significant in the ROW model (see table 3–13), but the signs on their coefficients are usually the same as those in the Canadian and U.S. models. In any case, likelihood ratio tests indicate that the foreign variables taken as a group are significant in all three models. Therefore, none of the "countries" in this sample is adequately represented by a closed economy specification.

Table 3–10
Parameter Estimates for the Open Economy Model of Canada, 1962.3–1984.4

Equation	Constant	$A(L)U_c{}^a$	$B(L)P_c{}^a$	$C(L)M_c{}^a$	$D(L)R_c{}^a$	$E(L)U_{us}{}^a$
U_c	0.012	−0.618	−2.29	0.540	0.078	0.509
	(1.75)**	(0.81)	(3.07)**	(2.63)**	(0.74)	(0.93)
P_c	−0.002	0.048	0.800	0.053	0.087	0.043
	(1.35)	(1.24)	(6.87)*	(1.43)	(0.75)	(2.00)*
M_c	0.005	0.014	−0.815	0.596	0.567	−0.169
	(0.72)	(1.84)	(1.74)	(3.18)**	(0.99)	(1.84)
R_c	0.004	0.375	−0.155	0.238	−0.249	−0.154
	(1.96)**	(0.96)	(1.61)	(2.89)**	(0.63)	(0.50)
S_{c-us}	0.014	−0.018	0.012	0.328	0.311	−0.717
	(2.90)**	(1.41)	(0.46)	(2.22)*	(0.63)	(3.42)*

[a]Sum of lagged coefficients where lag operators are of order 4. F-statistic testing joint significance of all lagged coefficients reported in parentheses.
[b]Box-Pierce Q-statistic.
  *Significant at the 10.0 percent level.
**Significant at the 5.0 percent level.

Table 3–11
Parameter Estimates for the Open Economy Model of Canada, 1970.3–1984.4

Equation	Constant	$A(L)U_c{}^a$	$B(L)P_c{}^a$	$C(L)M_c{}^a$	$D(L)R_c{}^a$	$E(L)U_{us}{}^a$
U_c	−0.003	−0.298	−1.497	0.767	0.654	0.313
	(0.23)	(0.74)	(3.76)**	(8.45)**	(1.08)	(1.68)
P_c	0.001	0.209	0.860	−0.020	−0.863	−0.136
	(1.31)	(6.57)**	(21.62)**	(2.10)	(0.30)	(4.67)*
M_c	0.015	0.079	−0.636	0.515	0.204	−0.303
	(1.55)	(1.45)	(12.58)**	(5.47)**	(0.29)	(5.33)**
R_c	−0.014	0.317	0.250	0.198	−0.005	−0.119
	(1.93)**	(2.85)*	(0.78)	(1.92)**	(0.42)	(0.48)
S_{c-us}	0.007	−0.146	0.054	0.204	−0.219	−0.067
	(0.65)	(0.18)	(0.04)	(0.96)	(1.41)	(0.07)

[a]Sum of lagged coefficients where lag operators are of order 4. F-statistic testing joint significance of all lagged coefficients reported in parentheses.
[b]Box-Pierce Q-statistic.
  *Significant at the 10.0 percent level.
**Significant at the 5.0 percent level.

$F(L)P_{us}{}^a$	$G(L)M_{us}{}^a$	$H(L)R_{us}{}^a$	$I(L)S_{c-us}{}^a$	$\bar{R}^2$	Durbin-Watson Statistic	Standard Error	$Q(27)^b$
0.768 (1.27)	0.793 (1.63)	−0.798 (0.73)	−0.440 (2.00)*	0.446	1.85	0.014	22.10
0.225 (1.01)	0.039 (0.76)	0.065 (0.98)	−0.071 (2.09)*	0.834	2.13	0.003	17.13
0.474 (1.08)	0.713 (1.19)	−1.587 (2.76)**	−0.165 0.84	0.394	1.95	0.014	24.58
0.557 (2.20)*	−0.343 (3.30)**	0.429 (10.31)**	−0.303 (2.93)**	0.613	1.80	0.007	9.17
−1.150 (2.43)*	−0.036 (0.75)	1.147 (3.87)**	0.320 (1.50)	0.412	1.93	0.010	22.12

$F(L)P_{us}{}^a$	$G(L)M_{us}{}^a$	$H(L)R_{us}{}^a$	$I(L)S_{c-us}{}^a$	$\bar{R}^2$	Durbin-Watson Statistic	Standard Error	$Q(27)^b$
0.149 (0.06)	1.195 (2.52)*	−0.509 (1.03)	−0.076 (0.42)	0.457	1.91	0.016	22.49
0.202 (1.89)	−0.108 (0.28)	0.023 (0.08)	−0.031 (1.86)	0.758	2.04	0.004	1.93
0.109 (0.66)	0.382 (2.67)*	−0.648 (3.36)**	−.082 (1.18)	0.536	2.07	0.013	24.38
0.381 (0.87)	−0.163 (0.99)	0.264 (4.87)**	−0.094 (0.68)	0.503	1.81	0.010	11.65
−0.541 (0.74)	−0.241 (0.49)	0.265 (0.81)	0.459 (5.85)**	0.125	2.11	0.014	9.62

Table 3–12
Parameter Estimates for the Open Economy Model of United States, 1965.1–1984.4

Equation	Constant	$A(L)U_{us}$[a]	$B(L)P_{us}$[a]	$C(L)M_{us}$[a]	$D(L)R_{us}$[a]	$E(L)U_w$[a]
U_{us}	−0.001	0.682	0.927	1.112	−1.601	−0.238
	(0.02)	(1.89)	(1.22)	(2.49)*	(3.36)**	(2.29)*
P_{us}	−0.006	−0.028	0.544	0.286	0.056	0.061
	(2.99)**	(3.60)**	(3.61)**	(5.00)**	(0.19)	(0.49)
M_{us}	0.002	0.121	0.258	0.798	−0.767	0.014
	(0.57)	(0.60)	(1.34)	(5.89)**	(6.87)**	(0.89)
R_{us}	−0.018	0.801	1.379	0.507	−1.424	−0.330
	(2.62)**	(5.01)**	(1.41)	(8.80)**	(5.48)	(1.09)**
S_{w-us}	0.004	0.395	0.687	0.417	−1.354	−0.685
	(0.26)	(0.57)	(1.68)	(1.18)	(2.62)**	(1.20)

[a]Sum of lagged coefficients where lag operators are of order 4. F-statistic testing joint significance of all lagged coefficients reported in parentheses.
[b]Box-Pierce Q-statistic.
*Significant at the 10.0 percent level.
**Significant at the 5.0 percent level.

Table 3–13
Parameter Estimates for the Open Economy Model of Rest of World, 1965.1–1984.4

Equation	Constant	$A(L)U_w$[a]	$B(L)P_w$[a]	$C(L)M_w$[a]	$D(L)R_w$[a]	$E(L)U_{us}$[a]
U_w	0.011	0.116	−0.487	0.005	0.405	0.271
	(1.82)**	(1.62)	(0.89)	(0.03)	(0.81)	(2.48)*
P_w	−0.005	0.473	1.013	−0.018	0.150	−0.028
	(0.30)	(2.54)*	(51.60)**	(0.80)	(1.06)	(0.76)*
M_w	0.043	−0.151	4.408	−1.259	−2.822	−0.271
	(1.78)**	(0.163)	(4.32)**	(22.05)**	(2.32)*	(1.31)
R_w	−0.004	0.216	0.036	0.008	0.023	−0.050
	(1.50)	(3.70)**	(0.19)	(0.32)	(0.23)	(0.77)
S_{w-us}	0.005	0.126	−0.195	0.074	−1.091	−0.216
	(0.39)	(0.40)	(0.04)	(2.34)*	(2.66)*	(1.90)

[a]Sum of lagged coefficients where lag operators are of order 2. F-statistic testing joint significance of all lagged coefficients reported in parentheses.
[b]Box-Pierce Q-statistic.
*Significant at the 10.0 percent level.
**Significant at the 5.0 percent level.

$F(L)P_w{}^a$	$G(L)M_w{}^a$	$H(L)R_w{}^a$	$I(L)S_{us-w}{}^a$	$\bar{R}^2$	Durbin-Watson Statistic	Standard Error	$Q(27)^b$
0.188	−0.008	1.444	−0.438	0.589	2.05	0.015	15.88
(0.94)	(1.06)	(1.15)	(3.60)**				
0.138	0.234	0.669	−0.023	0.846	1.57	0.003	14.81
(0.38)	(10.46)**	(3.32)**	(2.43)*				
0.204	0.011	−0.481	−0.087	0.358	1.99	0.006	19.06
(0.82)	(1.30)	(1.14)	(2.32)*				
−1.125	0.269	2.170	−0.139	0.524	1.82	0.010	16.80
(2.90)**	(1.48)	(3.03)**	(0.96)				
−0.885	−0.060	3.293	0.444	0.254	2.17	0.025	22.79
(0.61)	(1.27)	(2.38)*	(2.87)**				

$F(L)P_{us}{}^a$	$G(L)M_{us}{}^a$	$H(L)R_{us}{}^a$	$I(L)S_{us-w}{}^a$	$\bar{R}^2$	Durbin-Watson Statistic	Standard Error	$Q(27)^b$
−0.192	0.331	−0.215	−0.012	0.356	1.93	0.012	8.72
(0.21)	(1.99)	(0.52)	(0.52)				
−0.128	0.123	0.042	−0.037	0.828	2.16	0.003	34.87
(1.31)	(1.22)	(0.68)	(6.43)**				
−3.86	−0.651	1.020	−0.357	0.290	2.12	0.050	11.10
(2.81)*	(0.71)	(0.53)	(1.03)				
0.074	0.065	0.340	−0.011	0.447	1.91	0.005	17.78
(0.59)	(1.93)	(9.61)**	(0.72)				
0.279	−0.309	0.936	0.432	0.141	1.94	0.003	12.13
(2.35)*	(0.12)	(1.61)	(6.27)**				

The previous discussion was based on regression results that were obtained from models estimated over the full sample period, spanning both fixed and flexible exchange rate regimes. As noted earlier, however, the models have also been estimated over shorter samples corresponding to the most recent period of flexible exchange rates. The Canadian estimates for the shorter sample are reported in table 3–11. As the reader can see, the results are not noticeably different from those reported in table 3–10 for the full sample, suggesting that the major macro relationships linking the U.S. and Canadian economies have remained relatively stable throughout the 1962–84 period. Some differences can be observed in the price and exchange rate equations, but tests for structural stability cannot reject the hypothesis of no significant change between the fixed and flexible exchange rate periods. While this result was not expected, identical results were obtained for the open economy models of the United States and ROW (see table 3–14).[23]

As a further check on the reliability of our regression results, a number of

Table 3–14
Testing the Parameter Stability of Closed and Open Economy Models, 1962.1–1984.4

Closed economy		
Canada: 1962.3–1970.2 vs. 1970.3–1984.4 3 lags[a]	$\chi^2(52) = 70.1^*$	Reject stability
United States: 1962.1–1972.4 vs. 1973.1–1984.4 6 lags	$\chi^2(100) = 74.4$	Accept stability
Rest of World: 1964.1–1972.4 vs. 1973.1–1984.4 2 lags	$\chi^2(36) = 25.5$	Accept stability
Open economy		
Canada/United States: 1962.3–1970.2 vs. 1970.3–1984.4 2 lags	$\chi^2(76) = 70.8$	Accept stability
United States/Rest of World: 1964.1–1972.2 vs. 1973.1–1984.4 1 lag	$\chi^2(40) = 41.8$	Accept stability
Rest of World/United States 1964.1–1972.2 vs. 1973.1–1984.4 1 lag	$\chi^2(40) = 34.2$	Accept stability

[a]Number of lags on each explanatory variable.
*Significant at the 5.0 percent level.

Table 3–15
Granger-Causality Tests, 1962.3–1984.4

United States → Canada[a]		
1962.3–1984.4 (4 lags)[b]	$X^2(80) = 124.7^*$	Reject zero restrictions
1970.3–1984.4 (2 lags)	$X^2(40) = 68.7^*$	Reject zero restrictions
Canada → United States		
1962.3–1984.4 (4 lags)	$X^2(80) = 95.5$	Accept zero restrictions
1970.3–1984.4 (2 lags)	$X^2(40) = 41.0$	Accept zero restrictions
United States → Rest of World		
1965.1–1984.4 (2 lags)	$X^2(40) = 69.3^*$	Reject zero restrictions
1973.1–1984.4 (2 lags)	$X^2(40) = 52.9^{**}$	Reject zero restrictions
Rest of World → United States		
1965.1–1984.4 (4 lags)	$X^2(80) = 122.0^*$	Reject zero restrictions
1973.1–1984.4 (2 lags)	$X^2(40) = 35.7$	Accept zero restrictions

[a]Granger-causality from country x to country y.
[b]"x lags" refers to the number of lags included on each explanatory variable.
  *Significant at the 10.0 percent level.
**Significant at the 5.0 percent level.

Granger-causality tests were run. The first two results, which are reported in table 3–15, can be regarded as a kind of acid test of the VAR methodology, at least as it applies to the present chapter. Canadian variables were added to a closed economy model of the United States, and U.S. variables were added to a closed economy model of Canada, in order to test the exogeneity of the domestic variables in each economy. The test results indicate that U.S. variables are highly significant in the Canadian model (the zero restrictions on the U.S. variables are strongly rejected), but that Canadian variables are not significant in the U.S. model. In terms of our earlier discussion in the section $\Delta\alpha\tau\alpha\ell$ Canada's relationship with the United States might be characterized as one of dependence as opposed to interdependence. (The terms *dependence* and *interdependence* are only used as a convenient means of classifying the causal relationships in table 3–15. They are not meant to imply anything about the political or economic sovereignty of the countries in question.) Though these results are not very surprising, strong evidence of bidirectional causality running between the two countries, or "unidirectional" causality running from Canada to the United States, would have clearly weakened the credibility of the present analysis.[24]

Similar tests on the U.S. and ROW models found evidence of bidirectional causality in the full sample, and unidirectional causality running from the United States to the rest of the world in the shorter sample—results that are also consistent with our priors. Because earlier tests could not reject structural stability over the fixed and flexible exchange rate periods, we will concentrate on the full sample results in the following discussion and assume bidirectional causality between these two countries.

Variance Decomposition and Impulse Responses. The calculation of variance decompositions for open economy models is complicated by the fact that consideration must be given to the order of the variables both within and across countries. In the case of Canada and the United States, the order of the variables across countries does not pose a problem since it is clear that U.S. variables should be given priority. The situation is more ambiguous in the case of the United States and ROW, however. In order to minimize any biases that might be introduced by inadvertently entering the variables in the wrong order, two sets of variance decompositions are calculated, giving the variables in each country an opportunity to go first.

Table 3–16 presents the residual correlations for Canada, the United States, and ROW. Since the highest value that is recorded is 0.51, the variance decompositions are not expected to be very sensitive to changes in the order of the variables.

According the the figures reported in table 3–17, over 50 percent of the forecast variance in Canadian output, prices, interest rates, and money can be attributed to innovations in foreign variables. Indeed, for variables R_c and P_c, the U.S. proportions exceed 60 percent. Greater independence is observed in the flexible exchange rate period (table 3–18), but the differences are not as large as one might have expected, especially for nominal variables such as P_c and M_c.

It is well known that flexible exchange rates will not insulate economies from real external shocks. The primary attraction of flexible exchange rates is the independence that they presumably give policymakers with regard to controlling inflation. This claim would seem to be contradicted by the large proportion of M_c variance that is explained by U.S. output and interest rates. The importance of these U.S. variables in the Canadian money equation could have been caused by (1) currency substitution,[25] (2) exchange rate targeting by Canada's central bank,[26] or (3) an alternative called "goal and policy interdependence," which is more sympathetic to policymakers.[27] While there is some evidence suggesting currency substitution is statistically significant in Canadian money demand equations, it is not generally regarded as economically important. The other explanations focusing on the objectives and reactions of Canadian policymakers represent more plausible alternatives. Discussion of these issues appears in the next section.

Foreign variables also have a significant influence in the variance decompositions of the United States and ROW (see tables 3–19 and 3–20), but the proportion of forecast variance explained by domestic shocks is generally much higher than in Canada.[28]

Table 3–16
Residual Cross-Correlations for Open Economy Models

Canada–United States

	U_c	P_c	M_c	R_c	U_{us}	P_{us}	M_{us}	R_{us}	S_{c-us}
U_c	1.000								
P_c	−0.056	1.000							
M_c	0.172	0.201	1.000						
R_c	0.374*	0.036	−0.092	1.000					
U_{us}	0.342*	0.041	0.065	0.345*	1.000				
P_{us}	−0.091	0.091	−0.021	0.004	−0.029	1.000			
M_{us}	0.260	0.057	0.017	−0.104	0.110	−0.019	1.000		
R_{us}	0.278*	0.166	0.093	0.427*	0.431*	0.076	0.094	1.000	
S_{c-us}	0.088	−0.313*	−0.128	−0.045	−0.024	0.083	−0.074	−0.149	1.000

United States–Rest of World

	U_{us}	P_{us}	M_{us}	R_{us}	U_w	P_w	M_w	R_w	S_{us-w}
U_{us}	1.000								
P_{us}	−0.062	1.000							
M_{us}	0.249	0.084	1.000						
R_{us}	0.490*	0.125	0.249	1.000					
U_w	0.380*	−0.147	0.212	0.188	1.000				
P_w	−0.175	0.258	0.112	−0.082	0.133	1.000			
M_w	−0.319*	−0.142	0.039	−0.027	0.011	−0.065	1.000		
R_w	0.131	0.247	0.028	0.306*	0.223*	0.373*	−0.121	1.000	
S_{us-w}	0.250	0.192	0.115	0.040	0.144	0.511*	−0.354*	0.346*	1.000

*Significant at the 5.0 percent level.

Table 3–17
Canada–United States: Variance Decomposition of Prediction Errors, 1962.3–1984.4

Variable	Quarter	Proportion of Error Attributed to Shocks in:											Standard Error
		U_c	P_c	M_c	R_c	Total Canada	U_{us}	P_{us}	M_{us}	R_{us}	Total U.S.	S_{c-us} [a]	
U_c	1	80.7	0.0	0.0	0.0	80.7	11.7	0.8	4.7	2.1	19.3	0.0	0.107-01
	4	49.6	8.5	7.8	0.7	66.6	11.6	5.4	8.8	5.0	30.8	2.6	0.137-01
	8	30.9	8.3	7.8	0.8	47.8	20.3	6.2	7.0	13.1	46.6	5.6	0.179-01
	12	27.5	7.3	10.5	0.8	46.1	21.5	6.6	9.0	11.6	50.8	5.1	0.193-01
P_c	1	1.2	90.5	4.6	0.0	96.3	0.2	0.6	0.2	2.7	3.7	0.0	0.266-02
	4	1.5	52.0	19.1	0.4	73.0	3.4	9.4	10.3	2.4	25.5	1.5	0.442-02
	8	4.0	28.9	14.9	1.1	48.9	2.4	27.0	18.1	1.9	49.4	1.7	0.601-02
	12	3.1	21.2	12.8	0.8	37.9	3.3	32.4	22.7	2.0	60.4	1.7	0.724-02
M_c	1	2.3	0.0	92.1	4.6	99.1	0.4	0.0	0.0	0.5	0.9	0.0	0.105-01
	4	3.5	4.2	47.8	2.6	58.1	26.2	1.5	3.6	9.0	40.3	1.6	0.177-01
	8	3.7	6.4	38.6	2.4	51.1	26.2	1.8	5.1	12.3	45.4	3.5	0.200-01
	12	3.9	7.1	35.5	2.1	48.6	23.9	7.8	4.8	10.5	47.1	4.3	0.219-01
R_c	1	7.4	0.0	0.0	68.6	76.0	11.9	0.0	2.5	9.5	24.0	0.0	0.559
	4	5.9	2.9	2.1	27.2	38.1	9.2	7.2	8.6	31.9	58.1	3.8	0.912
	8	4.3	5.1	4.9	18.3	32.6	7.8	20.7	11.4	24.0	63.8	3.6	1.124
	12	3.9	4.8	6.3	16.1	31.1	9.0	21.1	11.4	23.7	65.3	3.6	1.283
S_{c-us}	1	0.2	6.4	2.3	0.2	9.1	0.0	0.9	0.4	2.4	3.7	84.8	0.743-02
	4	1.5	5.9	9.6	1.5	18.5	4.8	9.3	3.7	14.4	32.3	46.0	0.107-01
	8	1.2	5.1	13.9	1.2	21.4	16.8	9.1	4.5	11.4	41.8	34.0	0.125-01
	12	1.2	6.3	13.3	1.2	22.0	17.2	9.5	6.0	11.0	43.7	31.7	0.131-01

Note: Equations were estimated with four lags on each explanatory variable. The order of the variables in the variance decompositions was U_{us}, R_{us}, M_{us}, P_{us}, U_c, R_c, M_c, P_c, and S_{c-us}.

[a] The numbers across each row may not sum to 100.0 due to rounding errors.

Table 3–18
Canada–United States: Variance Decomposition of Prediction Errors, 1970.3–1984.4

Variable	Quarter	Proportion of Error Attributed to Shocks in:											Standard Error
		U_c	P_c	M_c	R_c	Total Canada	U_{us}	P_{us}	M_{us}	R_{us}	Total U.S.	S_{c-us} [a]	
U_c	1	81.1	0.0	0.0	0.0	81.1	10.4	2.4	6.1	0.1	19.0	0.0	0.127-01
	4	54.9	2.8	12.7	1.0	71.4	10.8	2.6	10.4	3.1	26.9	1.6	0.159-01
	8	37.9	8.3	10.5	0.7	57.4	15.0	8.5	13.6	4.0	41.1	1.4	0.192-01
	12	33.4	8.5	10.9	0.6	53.4	14.0	12.2	14.4	4.3	44.9	1.3	0.208-01
P_c	1	9.0	86.2	3.9	0.2	99.3	0.1	0.0	0.6	0.0	0.7	0.0	0.314-02
	4	8.5	64.2	6.8	0.7	80.2	2.7	5.4	6.5	0.3	14.9	5.0	0.514-02
	8	9.9	46.4	14.3	0.5	71.1	3.0	8.5	11.4	2.2	25.1	3.8	0.615-02
	12	3.7	12.4	29.4	2.2	47.7	19.4	9.5	8.5	12.2	49.6	2.8	0.718-02
M_c	1	1.6	0.0	87.8	7.1	96.5	0.4	1.9	0.5	0.7	3.5	0.0	0.110-01
	4	3.4	8.4	41.1	2.9	55.8	19.3	2.8	6.7	11.7	40.5	3.9	0.187-01
	8	3.3	13.0	33.0	2.6	51.9	18.2	5.5	9.2	12.0	44.9	3.2	0.211-01
	12	3.7	12.4	29.4	2.2	47.7	19.4	9.5	8.5	12.2	49.6	2.8	0.231-01
R_c	1	3.1	0.0	0.0	81.7	84.4	4.8	0.8	2.1	7.6	15.3	0.0	0.799
	4	11.2	1.4	7.1	43.8	63.7	5.3	4.6	7.8	17.1	34.8	1.8	1.111
	8	9.7	3.5	9.3	36.7	59.2	6.7	4.7	10.9	16.9	39.2	1.5	1.215
	12	8.7	5.3	8.4	31.2	53.6	8.2	7.0	12.4	17.4	45.0	1.3	1.320
S_{c-us}	1	4.7	7.0	0.8	9.3	21.8	0.2	1.7	5.0	0.4	7.3	70.9	0.118-01
	4	4.2	7.9	4.7	7.8	24.6	1.4	5.9	5.3	3.1	15.7	59.7	0.148-01
	8	4.1	7.4	6.3	7.2	25.0	2.6	6.4	6.7	5.8	21.5	53.5	0.157-01
	12	4.0	8.0	6.2	6.9	25.1	3.3	6.9	7.2	6.2	23.6	51.3	0.161-01

Note: Equations were estimated with two lags on each explanatory variable. The order of the variables in the variance decompositions was U_{us}, R_{us}, M_{us}, P_{us}, U_c, R_c, M_c, P_c, and S_{c-us}.
[a] The numbers across each row may not sum to 100.0 due to rounding errors.

Table 3–19
United States–Rest of World: Variance Decomposition of Prediction Errors, 1965.1–1984.4

Variable	Quarter	Proportion of Error Attributed to Shocks in:											
		U_{us}	P_{us}	M_{us}	R_{us}	Total U.S.	U_w	P_w	M_w	R_w	Total ROW	S_{us-w} [a]	Standard Error
U_{us}	1	100.0	0.0	0.0	0.0	100.0	0.0	0.0	0.0	0.0	0.0	0.0	0.110-01
	4	58.6	1.5	2.6	18.5	81.2	7.4	4.1	3.2	1.2	15.9	2.8	0.169-01
	8	44.3	2.7	7.4	13.7	68.1	5.7	8.2	3.8	6.3	24.0	8.0	0.218-01
	12	40.2	3.0	10.3	13.1	66.6	5.6	7.6	4.1	6.2	23.5	9.9	0.225-01
P_{us}	1	0.4	95.7	0.8	3.2	100.0	0.0	0.0	0.0	0.0	0.0	0.0	0.234-02
	4	6.5	24.4	29.5	9.4	69.8	5.2	0.8	15.1	6.4	27.5	2.8	0.466-02
	8	6.1	13.6	30.8	5.0	55.5	10.8	0.9	15.4	4.2	31.3	13.1	0.658-02
	12	6.4	12.5	26.1	4.0	49.0	10.7	1.2	11.9	6.2	30.0	21.6	0.777-02
M_{us}	1	6.2	0.0	93.1	0.7	100.0	0.0	0.0	0.0	0.0	0.0	0.0	0.463-02
	4	7.6	0.8	62.3	16.5	87.2	1.4	1.2	1.4	3.5	7.5	5.1	0.707-02
	8	8.1	3.1	57.4	15.1	83.7	2.6	1.5	2.0	3.8	9.9	6.5	0.707-02
	12	7.7	3.8	48.6	15.7	75.8	3.7	2.7	4.6	4.6	15.6	8.0	0.756-02
R_{us}	1	24.0	0.0	0.0	76.0	100.0	0.0	0.0	0.0	0.0	0.0	0.0	0.755
	4	15.4	0.3	15.7	47.9	79.3	3.9	3.5	8.0	2.1	17.5	3.1	1.155
	8	16.0	3.1	15.8	39.0	73.9	3.2	4.3	5.9	3.4	16.8	9.2	1.361
	12	14.7	3.7	15.5	37.7	71.6	4.2	4.2	6.2	4.8	19.4	8.9	1.449
U_w	1	14.5	1.9	1.5	0.0	17.9	82.2	0.0	0.0	0.0	82.2	0.0	0.932-02
	4	13.7	5.0	6.7	3.6	29.0	58.0	8.1	0.2	2.8	69.1	1.7	0.114-01
	8	11.1	4.4	9.9	4.4	29.8	48.9	7.5	0.9	8.4	65.7	4.5	0.137-01
	12	10.9	4.1	11.5	4.2	30.7	43.5	7.4	1.2	8.6	60.7	8.5	0.460-01
P_w	1	3.0	5.7	2.6	0.0	11.3	5.5	71.3	0.8	11.1	88.7	0.0	0.242-02
	4	3.1	3.5	15.5	1.4	23.5	13.6	39.8	2.1	16.9	72.4	4.0	0.415-02
	8	4.2	3.3	19.3	1.4	24.2	16.4	23.1	2.0	10.9	52.4	19.5	0.584-02
	12	5.6	4.8	17.3	1.1	28.8	14.5	16.5	1.5	9.2	41.7	29.5	0.736-02

M_w	1	10.2	4.1	1.2	2.2	17.7	1.0	0.0	80.2	1.1	82.3	0.0	0.356-01
	4	9.2	2.4	3.6	3.2	18.4	3.7	1.2	69.3	5.5	79.7	1.9	0.540-01
	8	9.0	3.3	4.5	3.5	20.3	6.1	2.8	62.1	5.8	76.8	2.8	0.573-01
	12	8.9	3.5	4.6	3.7	20.7	6.6	3.0	61.0	5.9	76.5	2.9	0.583-01
R_w	1	1.7	4.6	0.3	7.7	14.3	5.3	0.0	0.0	80.4	85.7	0.0	0.378
	4	3.7	3.7	12.5	28.2	48.1	8.7	1.5	1.1	38.4	49.7	2.2	0.567
	8	5.3	3.1	12.2	21.9	42.5	8.4	5.9	1.5	31.8	47.6	9.9	0.660
	12	5.4	3.6	12.6	20.5	42.1	7.9	5.8	2.1	32.2	48.0	9.9	0.697
S_{us-w}	1	6.3	5.0	0.4	0.9	12.6	0.6	17.3	4.8	9.5	31.7	55.1	0.181-01
	4	10.1	5.9	2.1	3.3	21.4	6.6	12.7	6.6	11.2	37.1	41.5	0.232-01
	8	8.9	6.7	2.5	9.9	28.0	6.9	10.7	7.5	12.9	38.0	34.0	0.268-01
	12	9.5	6.7	5.4	9.9	31.5	6.8	10.6	7.2	12.6	37.2	31.5	0.279-01

Note: Equations were estimated with four lags on each explanatory variable. The order of the variables in the variance decompositions was $U_{us}, R_{us}, M_{us}, P_{us}, U_w, R_w, M_w, P_w,$ and S_{us-w}.

[a]The numbers across each row may not sum to 100.0 due to rounding errors.

Table 3-20
Rest of World–United States: Variance Decomposition of Prediction Errors, 1965.1–1984.4

Variable	Quarter	U_w	P_w	M_w	R_w	Total ROW	U_{us}	P_{us}	M_{us}	R_{us}	Total U.S.	S_{us-w}[a]	Standard Error
						Proportion of Error Attributed to Shocks in:							
U_w	1	100.0	0.0	0.0	0.0	100.0	0.0	0.0	0.0	0.0	0.0	0.0	0.932-02
	4	74.8	8.7	0.6	2.8	86.9	0.9	1.4	5.9	3.0	11.2	1.7	0.114-01
	8	63.6	8.5	1.9	8.3	82.3	0.9	1.4	7.7	3.1	13.1	4.5	0.137-01
	12	56.6	7.9	2.9	8.4	75.8	1.4	1.4	9.7	3.1	15.6	8.5	0.146-01
P_w	1	1.8	85.7	0.1	12.4	100.0	0.0	0.0	0.0	0.0	0.0	0.0	0.242-02
	4	10.0	55.0	3.6	16.0	84.6	1.4	1.4	8.2	0.4	11.4	4.0	0.415-02
	8	12.7	35.1	5.1	9.5	62.4	3.9	2.4	11.0	0.7	18.0	19.5	0.584-02
	12	10.9	26.4	5.3	10.1	52.7	4.9	2.7	9.4	0.9	17.7	29.5	0.736-02
M_w	1	0.0	0.0	88.4	1.6	100.0	0.0	0.0	0.0	0.0	0.0	0.0	0.536-01
	4	5.2	0.5	77.2	5.8	88.7	0.7	3.0	4.0	1.7	9.4	1.9	0.540-01
	8	7.3	2.1	69.9	6.0	85.3	0.9	3.6	5.1	2.2	11.8	2.8	0.581-01
	12	8.1	2.2	68.3	6.2	84.8	1.2	3.5	5.1	2.5	12.3	2.9	0.581-01
R_w	1	5.0	0.0	0.0	95.0	100.0	0.0	0.0	0.0	0.0	0.0	0.0	0.378
	4	11.6	1.1	3.0	46.1	61.8	1.4	1.0	12.0	21.7	36.1	2.2	0.567
	8	11.5	4.8	2.9	38.3	57.5	1.9	0.9	13.0	16.7	32.5	9.9	0.660
	12	10.6	4.9	3.8	39.1	58.4	1.9	0.9	13.5	15.5	31.8	9.9	0.697
P_c	1	14.5	7.2	10.3	0.2	32.2	67.8	0.0	0.0	0.0	67.8	0.0	0.111-01
	4	18.5	8.3	8.9	5.8	41.5	35.4	1.0	4.4	14.8	55.6	2.8	0.169-01
	8	16.4	10.7	6.4	9.2	42.7	26.7	1.7	9.9	11.1	49.4	8.0	0.213-01
	12	15.3	9.8	7.6	8.8	41.5	24.0	1.6	12.1	10.8	48.5	9.9	0.225-01
P_{us}	1	2.2	3.6	1.1	8.2	15.1	0.0	81.8	1.1	2.1	85.0	0.0	0.234-02
	4	7.5	3.6	23.4	10.2	44.7	5.0	21.0	23.7	3.1	52.8	2.6	0.466-02
	8	13.8	3.9	20.8	5.6	44.1	4.3	11.6	24.4	2.4	42.7	13.1	0.658-02
	12	12.6	4.3	16.2	9.3	42.5	5.0	9.4	19.7	2.0	36.1	21.6	0.777-02

M_{us}	1	4.5	1.2	0.1	0.2	6.0	6.5	0.0	86.5	1.0	94.0	0.0	0.463-02
	4	3.7	1.3	0.4	4.9	10.3	7.2	1.1	60.7	15.6	84.6	5.1	0.463-02
	8	5.8	2.2	1.5	4.8	14.1	6.7	3.2	55.3	13.9	79.1	6.5	0.707-02
	12	6.0	2.3	4.3	5.1	17.7	6.4	3.2	49.2	15.4	74.2	8.2	0.756-02
R_{us}	1	3.5	4.8	0.0	7.4	15.7	17.9	0.0	0.0	66.4	84.3	0.0	0.755
	4	9.7	3.6	4.3	4.9	22.5	10.8	0.3	16.7	46.4	74.2	3.1	1.155
	8	9.5	4.6	4.2	6.4	24.7	10.5	2.1	16.5	36.9	66.0	9.2	1.361
	12	9.8	4.6	5.8	7.1	27.3	9.7	2.2	16.2	35.7	63.8	8.9	1.450
S_{us}	1	2.1	16.1	10.1	10.4	38.7	5.1	0.1	0.0	1.0	6.2	55.1	0.181-01
	4	9.7	11.8	11.5	10.9	43.9	5.4	1.4	2.1	5.8	14.7	41.5	0.232-01
	8	8.9	9.6	13.5	14.0	46.0	5.3	1.6	2.6	10.6	20.1	34.0	0.268-01
	12	8.8	9.2	12.1	13.5	43.6	5.5	1.8	6.3	10.5	24.1	31.5	0.279-01

Note: Equations were estimated with four lags on each explanatory variable. The order of the variables in the variance decompositions was U_w, R_w, M_w, P_w, U_{us}, R_{us}, M_{us}, P_{us}, and S_{us-w}.
[a] The numbers across each row may not sum to 100.0 due to rounding errors.

The impulse response functions for the open economy models provide a convenient and often more effective means of presenting many of the results described above. Since it is impossible to examine all of the variable combinations that are contained in tables 3–17 through 3–20, we will concentrate on the impulse responses of the Canadian and U.S. money equations. The differences observed in their responses will give some idea of the extent to which monetary policy might have been affected by international influences in the two countries.

Figure 3–5 compares the responses of Canadian (------) and U.S. (—·—·—) money to five foreign shocks. With the exception of the exchange rate shocks the response of Canadian money is always much larger than that of U.S. money. Because these responses are based on the full sample estimates of the Canadian and U.S. models, one might suspect that the results have been biased by Canada's experience during the fixed exchange rate period. However, the same response patterns are observed in figure 3–6 when the shocks are rerun on data drawn exclusively from the flexible exchange period, 1970.3–1984.4.

The sensitivity of Canadian money to foreign shocks seems to be significantly greater than that of U.S. money. Figures 3–7 and 3–8 present the impulse responses of Canadian and U.S. money to domestic shocks, in both closed and open economy models. While the introduction of foreign variables has greatly reduced the influence of R_c, U_c, and P_c on Canadian money, the response of U.S. money to R_{us}, U_{us}, and P_{us} has remained virtually unchanged. Evidently, foreign shocks have not affected U.S. financial markets to the same extent as those in Canada, although several foreign variables enter the U.S. money and interest rate equations with significant coefficients.

Policy Implications

Vector autoregressions are by their nature ill-suited to detailed policy analysis. They are useful descriptive devices that capture the major trends and relationships in economic time series, and that serve as useful checks on other, more structured, modeling procedures. It is therefore difficult to draw any strong conclusions about the causes and consequences of the international relationships identified in the open economy models here. Nevertheless, by combining some institutional knowledge with the results of this empirical analysis, it may be possible to draw some tentative conclusions regarding the importance of economic interdependence from a Canadian perspective.

Narrowly interpreted, the results of subsection **Open Economy Models** would suggest that the behavior of the Canadian economy is largely determined by U.S. variables and that independent macro policies have not played a significant role in either fixed or flexible exchange rate periods. Though one would not want to minimize the importance of open economy considerations in a country such as Canada, researchers may be faced with an "observational equivalence problem" when they try to interpret these results. More specifically, the coincident movement of Canadian and U.S. macro variables may owe as much to the shared policy objectives of U.S. and Canadian monetary authorities as it does to the strong structural relationships binding the two economies. Canadian and U.S. policymakers have typically interpreted economic events in a similar fashion and have often held similar views with regard to what policy actions were appropriate in a given situation. These policy considerations have no doubt contributed to the significance of U.S. variables in the Canadian equations here. Their signficance has also been reinforced by the reaction of Canadian policymakers to short-run movements in U.S. interest rates and attendant fluctuations in the Canadian–U.S. exchange rates.

Research at the Bank of Canada and elsewhere has tended to confirm the impressions of many central bankers that exchange rate markets are subject to "bandwagon" effects and often appear to be driven by extrapolative expectations.[29] In a technical sense, the markets are "irrational" and/or inefficient. This has given rise over the years to a policy reaction on the part of the Bank of Canada in which short-term exchange rate pressures caused by changes in U.S. interest rates are partially resisted by similar movements in Canadian rates. This policy is not intended to peg the exchange rate or to maintain it at an artificial level, but merely to limit the amount of overshooting, though obviously it may be difficult for observers to distinguish between these two types of policies.

This response to exchange rate fluctuations is believed to be desirable for two reasons. First, the exchange rate is an important price in an open economy like Canada and unnecessary volatility could have serious consequences on efficiency. Second, in the inflationary environment of the 1970s and early 1980s, there was concern that "unwarranted" exchange rate movements (depreciations) could fuel inflation expectations.

It is worth noting that this strategy of "short-circuiting" movements in exchange rates and domestic prices with offsetting changes in interest rates was not inconsistent with the Bank's policy of monetary targeting. Rather, it was viewed as a complementary response, helping to keep M-1 on target through much of the 1975–81 period.[30]

Over the long run many of the problems that Canada has experienced in the conduct of monetary policy have been domestic in origin rather than international. These include misperceptions concerning the natural rate of unemployment and the unsettling effects of financial innovations on Canadian money demand. One important recent exception occurred during the 1984 period of high world interest rates when attempts to moderate the

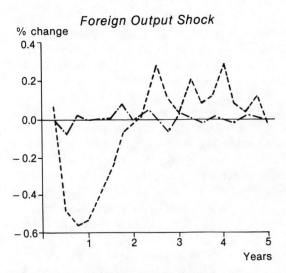

Foreign Output Shock

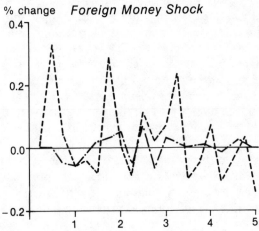

Foreign Money Shock

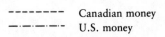

------- Canadian money
—·—·—·- U.S. money

Figure 3–5. Response in Canadian and U.S. Money to Foreign Shocks

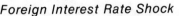

Foreign Interest Rate Shock

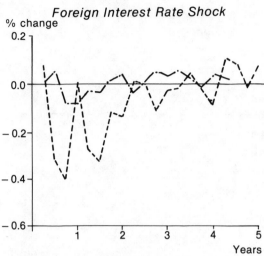

% change

Foreign Price Shock

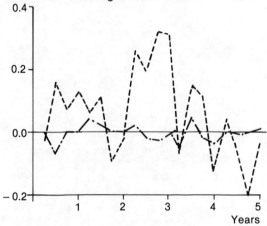

% change

Exchange Rate Shock

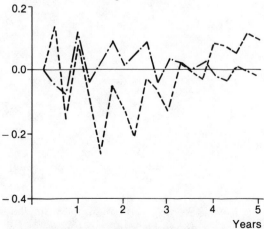

% change

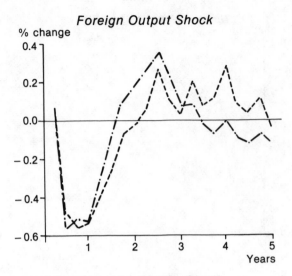

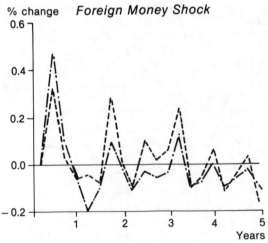

**Figure 3–6. Response in Canadian Money to
Foreign Shocks**

Foreign Interest Rate Shock

Foreign Price Shock

Exchange Rate Shock

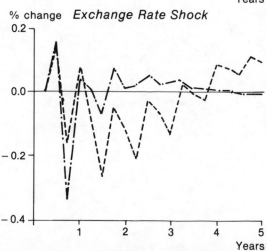

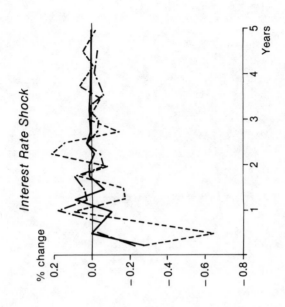

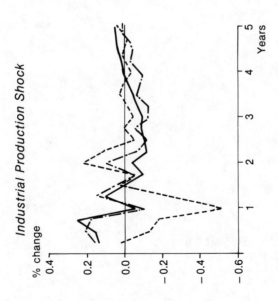

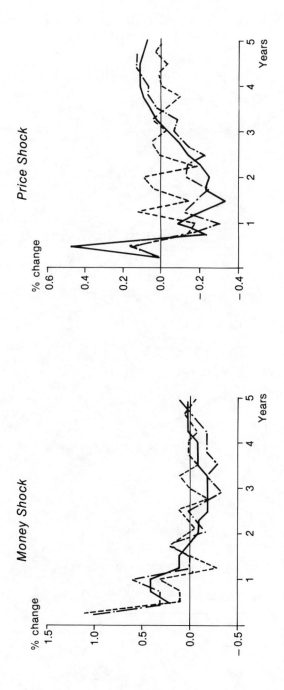

Figure 3–7. Response in Canadian Money to Domestic Shocks

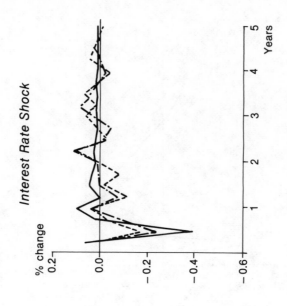

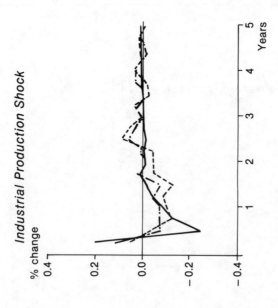

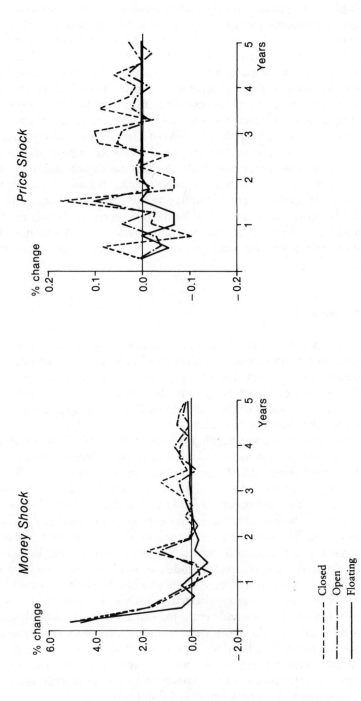

Figure 3–8. Response in U.S. Money to Domestic Shocks

upward movement in Canadian interest rates were frustrated by the reactions of agents in international money markets. This episode can also be linked to domestic policy problems, however. The Bank of Canada had been forced to abandon its *M-1* targets in November 1982, as financial innovations had made *M-1* an unreliable indicator of the ease of restrictiveness of monetary policy. Without a nominal anchor to condition their expectations, market views of future values of the exchange rate were not held with confidence, causing domestic interest rates to rise and the exchange rate to fall.[31]

To summarize, the policy options of a small open economy may not be as circumscribed as the earlier empirical evidence would indicate. Though greater economic integration and international capital mobility occasionally lead to policy complications, monetary policy remains a potent tool whose effectiveness under normal conditions has probably been enhanced (à la Mundell) rather than diminished by the near perfect substitutability of Canadian and U.S. financial instruments. International economic interdependence need not preclude independent policy action by small open economies such as Canada.

Conclusion

Few readers will find the **Results** section surprising or controversial. With the possible exception of the structural stability tests, the evidence is consistent with most of our priors. The primary contribution of this chapter has been to apply VAR modeling techniques to the study of economic interdependence and to quantify some of the concepts and relationships that have heretofore only been discussed in general qualitative terms.

The **Results** section highlighted the differences between small (dependent) economies such as Canada and large (interdependent) economies such as the United States. The **Policy Implications** section tried to show how goal and policy interdependence might have contributed to the strong causal relationships that are observed between Canada and the United States.

Many of these results have been anticipated by earlier papers, but these studies typically offered a partial analysis directed at only one or two variables such as inflation and money.[32] The present chapter has taken a more comprehensive view of interdependence, but has obviously sacrificed some important details and structure in the process. We hope to extend our results in the future by substituting alternative proxies for some of the foreign variables in our regressions and rerunning our models on monthly data. Higher frequency data would allow us to examine the short-run dynamics of our models in greater detail and would provide more degrees of freedom if shorter lag lengths were accepted in the monthly specifications. This in turn would improve the efficiency of our estimates and allow us to experiment with additional variables, including improved fiscal proxies.

Notes

1. The G-7 includes: Canada, France, Germany, Italy, Japan, the United Kingdom, and the United States.

2. See for example Gordon and King (1982) or Offenbacher and Porter (1983).

3. A fifth variable, the nominal value of government debt, was included in some of our preliminary work in an effort to identify the separate effects of monetary and fiscal policies. Unfortunately the addition of this fiscal proxy led to problems of collinearity and significantly reduced the available degrees of freedom, making it difficult to obtain reasonable parameter estimates on other more important variables. Since likelihood ratio tests indicated that government debt was statistically insignificant in all three models, we decided to exclude it in subsequent runs.

4. As shall be seen later, this is only true in the estimation stage of the analysis. It is necessary to make some implicit assumptions about the causal relationships of the variables when the impulse responses and variance decompositions of the models are examined.

5. j is the number of endogenous variables originally in the model and n is the lag length on each variable on the right-hand side.

6. Most of the data were taken from the OECD publication, *Main Economic Indicators* and the Bank for International Settlement (BIS) databank.

7. The consumer price index for the United States is defined exclusive of housing costs.

8. Notice that the indexes for the rest of the world (ROW) have been defined from a U.S. perspective (one including all countries in the G-7 except the United States), since these indexes' primary purpose is to serve as foreign variables in the open economy model of the United States.

9. Masson and Blundell-Wignall (1984) have constructed similar proxies for ROW using a more comprehensive weighting scheme which ranks the countries in terms of their contribution to world trade *and* international financial flows. The weights that they obtain from this more involved procedure are very close to the averages reported in the table.

10. The one exception was interest rates which were simply first differenced.

11. See also Nelson and Kang (1984).

12. The test statistic is distributed as $X^2(r)$ and is computed as

$$V = (T - c)[\log|\Omega^R| - \log|\Omega^U|]$$

where T is the number of observations, c is the number of parameters in the unrestricted model, $|\Omega^R|$ and $|\Omega^U|$ are the determinants of the covariance matrices of the restricted and unrestricted models, and r is the number of restrictions.

13. The Canadian regressions, unlike those for the United States, begin in 1962.3 rather than 1962.1. This was done in order to avoid the instability associated with Canada's 1961–62 exchange rate crisis and the uneasy transition from flexible to fixed exchange rates that followed.

14. The negative signs on lagged inflation are not surprising given the supply shocks of the 1970s. The same effects are observed, however, when the equations are run on pre-1973 data.

15. Financial innovations that have recently lowered the demand for transactions

balances in Canada could be responsible for the negative sign on U_c. See Freedman (1983). This result disappears, however, once foreign variables are added to the model in the section **Open Economy Models.**

16. Contrary to the results reported by Sims (1980a), interest rates and money have almost identical weights in the variance decompositions of U.S. output. Sims' use of monthly numbers and the substitution of 30-day treasury bill rates for the call loan rate could account for this difference.

17. The same "perverse" initial responses to innovations in R_{us} and P_{us} have been reported by Litterman and Weiss (1983).

18. The Canadian authorities, they claim, were able to maintain tight control over aggregate *M-1* through relatively minor adjustments in Canadian short-term interest rates because of the high interest elasticity of Canadian money demand. See also Thiessen (1982).

19. The foreign variables for *U, P, M,* and *R* in the Canadian and ROW models are proxied by U.S. output, prices, money, and interest rates. In the U.S. model, these foreign variables are proxied by the aggregate indexes which were constructed for ROW. S_{c-us}, the exchange rate in the Canadian model, is the U.S. dollar price of one Canadian dollar. S_{us-w}, the exchange rate in the U.S. and ROW models, is the ROW price of one U.S. dollar.

20. Suspecting that this result might have been caused by our choice of interest rates, we reran the Canadian money equation with treasury bill rates and ninety-day commercial paper rates substituted for the call loan rate. The same results were obtained in every case.

21. Canadian policymakers have never considered sterilized intervention to be a viable policy option, except in the very short run, as Canadian and U.S. securities are believed to be almost perfect substitutes. See Boothe *et al.* (1985) and Freedman (1982).

22. Longworth *et al.* (1983), Boothe (1983), and Longworth (1985).

23. There is a possibility that the test statistics are biased toward false "nonrejection" of the stability hypothesis because of the limited number of observations included in each subperiod. However, Litterman and Weiss (1983, p. 7) claim that the bias produced by a low "observation-to-parameter ratio" actually runs in the opposite direction and favors false rejection.

24. Certain Canadian variables did have significant explanatory power in the U.S. equations. Lagged values of M_c, for example, seemed to be a reliable leading indicator of U.S. output. Taken as a group, however, the Canadian variables were insignificant.

25. See Alexander (1981), McKinnon (1982), Miles (1978), and Poloz (1982).

26. See Courchene (1976, 1981) and Bordo and Choudhri (1982).

27. See Cooper (1985).

28. The proportions that are assigned to each country are sensitive to the order in which the countries appear, but the qualitative results in tables 3–19 and 3–20 are generally consistent.

29. See Boothe (1983) and Longworth (1985).

30. A more detailed discussion of the short-circuiting concept is contained in Freedman (1982).

31. Bank of Canada: *Annual Report,* 1984.

32. See for example Batten and Ott (1985), Bordo and Choudhri (1982), Choudhri (1983), and Burbidge and Harrison (1983).

References

Abrams, R.K., and G.H. Sellon. "Monetary Control: A Comparison of the U.S. and Canadian Experiences, 1975–1979." Mimeo, International Monetary Fund, December 1983.

Alexander, W.E. "Foreign Influences on the Demand for Money in an Open Economy: The Canadian Case." *Monetaria* 4, no. 1, January/March 1981, pp. 17–38.

Bank of Canada. *Annual Report, 1984.*

Batten, D.S., and R.W. Hafer. "Currency Substitution and the Link between Money and GNP in the U.S.: 1972–83." Mimeo, Federal Reserve Bank of St. Louis, 1984.

Batten, D.S., and R.W. Hafer. "The Impact of International Factors on U.S. Inflation: An Empirical Test of the Currency Substitution Hypothesis." *Southern Economic Journal,* forthcoming 1986.

Batten, D.S., and M. Ott. "The Interrelationship of Monetary Policies under Floating Exchange Rates." *Journal of Money, Credit, and Banking* 17, no. 1, February 1985, pp. 103–10.

Batten, D.S., and D.L. Thorton. "Lag-Length Selection and Tests of Granger Causality between Money and Income." *Journal of Money, Credit, and Banking* 37, no. 2, May 1985, pp. 164–78.

Boothe, P.M. "Speculative Profit Opportunities in the Canadian Foreign Exchange Market, 1974–78." *Canadian Journal of Economics* 16, no. 4, November 1983, pp. 603–11.

Boothe, P.M., K. Clinton, Agathe Côté, and D. Longworth. *International Asset Substitutability: Theory and Evidence for Canada.* Bank of Canada, February, 1985.

Bordo, M.D., and E.U. Choudhri. "The Link between Money and Prices in an Open Economy: The Canadian Evidence from 1971 to 1980." *Review,* Federal Reserve Bank of St. Louis 64, no. 7, August–September 1982, pp. 13–23.

Burbidge, J., and A. Harrison. "(Innovation) Accounting for U.S.–Canada Business Cycles." Mimeo, McMaster University, April 1983.

Choudri, E.U. "The Transmission of Inflation in a Small Economy: An Empirical Analysis of the Influence of U.S. Monetary Disturbances on Canadian Inflation, 1962–80." *Journal of International Money and Finance* 2, 1983, pp. 167–78.

Cooper, R.N. "Economic Interdependence and Coordination of Economic Policies." In *Handbook of International Economics,* vol. 2, R.W. Jones and P.B. Kenen (eds.), 1985, pp. 1195–234.

Courchene, T.J. *Money, Inflation, and the Bank of Canada: An Analysis of Canadian Monetary Policy from 1970 to Early 1975.* Montreal: C.D. Howe Research Institute, 1976.

———. *Money Inflation and the Bank of Canada, Vol. 2: An Analysis of Monetary Gradualism, 1975–80.* Montreal: C.D. Howe Research Institute, 1981.

Daniel, B.C., and H.O. Fried. "Currency Substitution, Postal Strikes and Canadian Money Demand." *Canadian Journal of Economics* 16, no. 4, November 1983, pp. 112–24.

Dickey, D.A., and W.A. Fuller. "Distribution for the Estimators for Autoregression Time Series with a Unit Root." *Journal of the American Statistical Association* 74, pp. 427–31.

Doan, T., and R. Litterman. *User's Manual RATS Version 4.v.*, VAR Econometrics, 1980.

Driskill, R.A., and S.M. Sheffrin. "'The Patman Effect' and Stabilization Policy." *The Quarterly Journal of Econometrics,* February 1985, pp. 145–63.

Fackler, J.S. "An Empirical Analysis of the Markets for Goods, Money, and Credit." *Journal of Money, Banking, and Credit* 37, no. 1, February 1985, pp. 28–42.

Freedman, C. "The Effect of U.S. Policies on Foreign Countries: The Case of Canada." In *Monetary Policy Issues in the 1980's.* Kansas City: Federal Reserve Bank of Kansas City, 1982, pp. 97–118.

———. "Financial Innovation in Canada: Causes and Consequences." *American Economic Review* 73, no. 2, May 1983, pp. 101–6.

Freeman, G. "International Inflation: Four Commentaries." *Economic Perspectives.* Federal Reserve Bank of Chicago, July 1984.

Gordon, R.J., and S.R. King. "The Output Cost of Disinflation in Traditional and Vector Autoregressive Models." *Brookings Papers on Economic Activity* 1, 1982, pp. 205–42.

Litterman, R.B., and L. Weiss. "Money, Real Interest Rates, and Output: A Reinterpretation of Postwar U.S. Data." National Bureau of Economic Research Working Paper no. 1077, February 1983.

Longworth, D. "Exchange Market Efficiency." *Economic Letters* 8, nos. 2 and 3, 1985, pp. 247–49.

Longworth, D., P.M. Boothe, and K. Clinton. *A Study of the Efficiency of Foreign Exchange Markets.* Bank of Canada, October 1983.

Masson, P., and A. Blundell-Wignall. "Fiscal Policy and the Exchange Rate in the Big Seven: Transmission of U.S. Fiscal Shocks." Mimeo, OECD, May 1984.

McKinnon, R.I. "Currency Substitution and Instability in the World Dollar Standard." *American Economic Review* 72, no. 3, June 1982, pp. 320–33.

Miles, M. "Currency Substitution, Flexible Exchange Rates, and Monetary Independence." *American Economic Review,* 68, no. 3, June 1978, pp. 428–36.

Nelson, C.R., and H. Kang. "Pitfalls in the Use of Time as an Explanatory Variable in Regressions." *Journal of Business and Economic Statistics* 2, no. 1, January 1984, pp. 73–82.

Nelson, C.R., and C.I. Plosser. "Trends and Random Walks in Macroeconomic Time Series: Some Evidence and Implications." *Journal of Monetary Economics* 10, pp. 139–62.

Offenbacher, E.K., and R.D. Porter. "Empirical Comparisons of Credit and Monetary Aggregates Using Vector Autoregression Methods." Special Studies Paper no. 181, Federal Reserve Board, Washington, D.C., October 1983.

Poloz, S. "Unstable Velocity, Volatile Exchange Rates, and Currency Substitution: The Demand for Money in a Multicurrency World." Unpublished doctoral thesis, University of Western Ontario, 1982.

Sims, C.A. "Comparison of Interwar and Postwar Cycles: Monetarism Reconsidered." *American Economic Review* 70, 1980a, pp. 250–57.

Sims, C.A. "Macroeconomics and Reality." *Econometrica* 48, 1980b, pp. 1–48.

Thiessen, G.G. "The Canadian Experience with Monetary Targeting." In *Central Bank Views on Monetary Targeting*. New York: Federal Reserve Bank of New York, May 1982, pp. 100–5.

Comments

Georg Rich

The aim of Kuszczak and Murray's chapter is to explore the economic interdependence among major industrialized countries. To this end, they apply vector autoregressive analysis to key macroeconomic variables for the United States, Canada, and a country called Rest of World (ROW), comprising Canada, France, the Federal Republic of Germany, Italy, Japan, and the United Kingdom. For each of these three countries Kuszczak and Murray consider four endogenous variables: output, the price level, the money stock, and interest rates. Furthermore, they take account of the exchange rates between the U.S. and the Canadian dollar, on the one hand, and between the U.S. dollar and the ROW currency on the other. Following the VAR approach, they regress each endogenous variable on a constant term, its own lagged values, the lagged values of the other domestic endogenous variables, as well as the lagged values of the foreign endogenous variables. These regression equations are in turn used to estimate the relative importance of domestic and foreign shocks as sources of variation in the endogenous variables.

The most important conclusion of Kuszczak and Murray's chapter is that in all three economies domestic variables are highly sensitive to foreign shocks. Not surprisingly, the Canadian economy seems to be much more open than its U.S. and ROW counterparts. Moreover, the shift from a fixed exchange rates system to a floating system does not appear to have loosened the links among the three economies. Thus, Kuszczak and Murray cast doubt on the widely held view that floating exchange rates have enhanced a country's ability to insulate its economy from foreign shocks.

Although these conclusions, for the most part, seem plausible, I find it difficult to comment on Kuszczak and Murray's chapter for two reasons. First, I do not feel qualified to review its theoretical aspects because of my limited knowledge of VAR analysis. Second, estimates obtained from VAR models do not lend themselves to easy interpretation. VAR models impose a minimum of a priori restrictions on the specification and coefficients of the regression equations. The absence of priors would clearly be an advantage if standard structural macroeconomic models did not adequately capture economic interdependence and, therefore, failed to uncover important links between domestic and foreign variables. In this event, VAR analysis might provide some guidance as to how the explanatory power of standard structural models might be improved. However, if based solely on VAR models, an analysis of economic interdependence may well generate misleading results. Unlike structural models, the VAR approach does not offer means of discriminating between spurious and economically significant results. Moreover, if not spurious, the results are frequently consistent with a multitude of structural models. Thus, while VAR models may show *that* two variables are related, they often fail to explain *why* they are related. Let me illustrate these difficulties with two examples drawn from Kuszczak and Murray's chapter.

Canadian Perspective vs. Swiss Perspective

As regards the difference between fixed and floating exchange rates, Kuszczak and Murray's conclusions are colored by Canadian experience. Their results suggest that the Canadian economy was dominated by U.S. variables under both fixed and floating exchange rates. They attribute the close correlation between Canadian and U.S. macrovariables to the similarities of Canadian and U.S. monetary policies, as well as the strong structural relationships between the two countries. Although I admit that the evidence does not point to floating exchange rates acting as a wedge between the Canadian and U.S. economies, I do not believe that Canadian experience may readily be generalized. Kuszczak and Murray's analysis of ROW—which appears to confirm the Canadian results—is not entirely convincing. In my opinion, it is dangerous to draw conclusions from a study of the economic links between the United States and a composite of industrialized countries. The experiences of Japan and Western European countries have been sufficiently diverse to warrant case-by-case consideration. In this context, it is interesting to compare the Kuszczak and Murray chapter with similar research conducted by Genberg and Swoboda for Switzerland.[1] Switzerland, of course, is not part of ROW, as defined by Kuszczak and Murray, but I suspect that most of Genberg and Swoboda's conclusions would also be valid for the Federal Republic of Germany.

Applying VAR analysis to the relationship between Swiss and foreign macroeconomic variables, Genberg and Swoboda find that the sensitivity of Swiss variables to foreign output increased, rather than decreased, after the shift to a floating exchange rate. However, floating exchange rates lessened substantially the dependence of the domestic price level and domestic interest rates on foreign shocks. Thus, they strengthened considerably the ability of the Swiss National Bank—Switzerland's central bank—to influence domestic prices and interest rates. This is comforting knowledge for a central bank that regards price stability as the ultimate objective of monetary policy and does not place much confidence in its ability to manage domestic output either under closed- or open-economy conditions. In light of the Swiss experience, I would maintain that floating exchange rates—despite their shortcomings—have extended the freedom of action of monetary authorities.

Sensitivity to Foreign Shocks

An interesting result reported in the Kuszczak and Murray chapter is the strong sensitivity of the Canadian money stock to changes in U.S. interest rates. They point out that this relationship may reflect currency substitution on the demand side of the money market or such supply-side effects as a strong response of Canadian monetary authorities to movements in U.S. interest rates. As Kuszczak and Murray themselves admit, due to the astructural nature of VAR analysis, they are unable to identify the causes of the observed relationship between the Canadian money stock and U.S. interest rates. Similar problems arise in interpreting the statistically significant link between the U.S. money stock and the exchange rate, as well as the inverse relationship between the ROW money stock and U.S. prices.

From the standpoint of central banks, it is not particularly useful to know that the domestic money stock is sensitive to foreign shocks. What really interests central bankers is the question of whether economic interdependence impairs their ability to achieve such domestic objectives of monetary policy as stable prices and steady economic growth. This question can only be answered by a structural model that allows one to determine the causes of the observed links between the domestic money stock and foreign variables.

Although it is difficult to draw policy conclusions from their chapter, Kuszczak and Murray explore the implications of their results for Canadian monetary policy. In interpreting the strong sensitivity of the Canadian economy to U.S. variables, they play down possible external constraints on Canadian monetary policy, but stress instead shared policy objectives of U.S. and Canadian monetary authorities. Needless to say, since Kuszczak and Murray do not explain the high sensitivity of the Canadian economy to foreign shocks, their emphasis on shared policy objectives may or may not conform to the empirical evidence. Swiss experience certainly suggests that external constraints on monetary policy complicate the central bank's task of achieving its ultimate policy objectives.

Although I had some difficulty in interpreting Kuszczak and Murray's results, I enjoyed reading their chapter. I hope that their competent and interesting work will stimulate further research on economic interdependence, an issue that greatly concerns central banks.

Note

1. Hans Genberg and Alexander K. Swoboda. *External Influences on the Swiss Economy under Fixed and Flexible Exchange Rates.* Diessenhofen: Verlag Rüegger (forthcoming).

4
Implications of the U.S.
Net Capital Inflow

Benjamin M. Friedman

An escalating international imbalance, necessarily including both real
and financial aspects, has become the outstanding failing of U.S.
macroeconomic performance in the 1980s. The half-again real
appreciation of the dollar exchange rate since the beginning of the decade has
severely impaired the ability of U.S. producers to compete for export sales
abroad, or even to protect their traditional domestic markets against foreign
imports. The resulting devastation of the economy's internationally exposed
sectors, especially agriculture and manufacturing, has in turn led to lost profits, lost jobs, and a continuing rash of actual and/or threatened bankrupt-
cies.

At the same time, the financing of a record trade gap by exporting assets
instead of goods and services has sharply altered traditional U.S. financial
relationships. The United States has now dissipated its net international
investment position and, on the current trajectory, will soon become the
world's leading debtor nation. Correspondingly, foreign investors and
foreign financial institutions now play a far larger role in the U.S. financial
markets than they did just a short time ago.

These problematic developments, at least in rough outline, have been the
predictable (and much predicted) consequences of the macroeconomic policy
course followed by the United States since 1981. The extraordinary combination of personal tax cuts, accelerated build-up of military spending, and
resistance to reductions in major nonmilitary government spending programs
such as Social Security and Medicare has led to federal budget deficits far
beyond the nation's prior peacetime experience. Meanwhile, the basic priority of monetary policy has been first to lower, and then to contain, the
economy's rate of price inflation. This fundamental fiscal–monetary imbalance has led to unprecedentedly high real interest rates, and has thereby

I am grateful to Ken Weiller for research assistance; to him as well as Andrew Abel, John Huizinga, Peter Kenen, Jeffrey Sachs, and Lawrence Summers for helpful discussions; and to the
National Science Foundation and the Alfred P. Sloan Foundation for research support.

helped to drive up the real dollar exchange rate. Its predictably negative impact has fallen both on the economy's investment sector and on the internationally competitive sector. The only real surprise has come in the split between these two, with more of the impact falling on the international sector (and correspondingly less on the investment sector) than all but a few observers had predicted at the outset.

The object of this chapter is to explore the implications for the U.S. economy of the financial side of this growing international imbalance. The first section uses basic concepts of national income accounting and balance of payments accounting to review the role of the net foreign capital inflow in financing the economy's stagnant net investment and swollen government deficit. The second section then examines the likely implications of a continuation of this inflow, at magnitudes like those of the recent past, for some time into the future. The discussion here primarily examines the implications, for the pricing of U.S. financial assets, of the growing share of these assets owned by foreign investors. By contrast, the third section considers what would happen if the United States suddenly had to make do without this capital inflow, and includes the results of an attempt to quantify the most important of these effects. The final section briefly summarizes the principal conclusions advanced in the chapter.

Capital Inflows, Investment, and Government Deficits

The deterioration of the U.S. balance of international payments in the 1980s has been spectacular in both speed and extent. As table 4–1 shows, on average during the 1970s a positive balance on services, together with other net receipts, was just sufficient to deliver an essentially balanced current account despite a significant deficit on merchandise trade in the years following the first price increase imposed by the international oil cartel. Indeed, by the end of the decade even the merchandise trade deficit was narrowing despite the further oil price increase imposed in 1979.

The U.S. performance thus far in the 1980s has been dramatically different. By 1983, the trade deficit had jumped to approximately double the level at which it had appeared to plateau during the prior five years, and the further deterioration in 1984 alone represented almost another doubling. Data for 1985 to date indicate yet a further deterioration, albeit not nearly at so dramatic a pace. At the same time, the current account first showed a massive deficit in 1983, and it too has continued to deteriorate ever since.

The fact that producers abroad sell more goods and services to Americans than U.S. producers sell to foreigners automatically and necessarily has a financial counterpart. Precisely because foreign producers are *selling* their goods to Americans, rather than donating them in some eleemosynary fash-

Table 4–1
U.S. Trade and Current Account Balances, 1951–85
(billions of dollars)

	Trade Account		Current Account	
	Amount	*% of GNP*	*Amount*	*% of GNP*
Average, 1951–60	$ 2.9	0.7%	$ 0.6	0.1%
Average, 1961–70	4.1	0.7	3.3	0.5
Average, 1971–80	– 10.5	– 0.5	– 0.4	0.0
1971	2.6	0.3	2.3	0.2
1972	– 2.3	– 0.2	– 1.4	– 0.1
1973	– 6.4	– 0.5	– 5.8	– 0.5
1974	0.8	0.1	7.1	0.5
1975	– 5.1	– 0.4	2.0	0.1
1976	8.7	0.6	18.1	1.2
1977	– 9.1	– 0.5	4.2	0.2
1978	– 30.5	– 1.6	– 14.5	– 0.8
1979	– 33.6	– 1.6	– 15.4	– 0.7
1980	– 30.3	– 1.3	– 1.0	0.0
1981	– 24.2	– 0.9	1.9	0.1
1982	– 28.4	– 1.0	6.3	0.2
1983	– 60.4	– 1.8	– 41.6	– 1.3
1984	– 106.2	– 2.9	– 101.5	– 2.8
1985	– 119.4	– 3.1	– 116.3	– 3.0

Source: U.S. Department of Commerce, *Survey of Current Business* (various issues).
Note: Data for 1985 are through 1985:Q2 for the trade account, and through 1985:Q1 for the current account, at seasonally adjusted annual rates.

ion, they receive payment. That payment may occur directly in the form of a dollar deposit on some U.S. bank remitted to the foreign seller. Alternatively, the American buyer may pay the foreign seller in the seller's own currency by first purchasing the needed amount of that currency in the foreign exchange market. In either case, some foreigner—either the seller of goods or the seller of currency—then holds an additional dollar deposit in the amount corresponding to the U.S. import.

When U.S. imports exceed U.S. exports, the amount of dollar deposits acquired in this way by foreign holders exceeds the amount of foreign currency deposits acquired by U.S. holders. On a net basis, therefore—that is, even after U.S. holders use the foreign exchange market to swap the foreign currency they have received back into dollars—foreign holders still have a remaining amount of dollar deposits conceptually equal to the U.S. current account deficit. They need not continue to hold these assets in deposit form, of course, and no individual foreigner need hold any additional dollar assets at all. All foreign investors together, however, must increase their net hold-

Table 4–2
U.S. Net Exports and Net Foreign Investment, 1984
(billions of dollars)

Balance of payments accounts	
Balance of goods and services	– $90.1
Merchandise exports	220.3
Other exports	142.1
Merchandise imports (–)	– 328.6
Other imports (–)	– 123.9
Government grants abroad (–)	– 8.5
Other flows abroad (–)	– 2.9
Balance on current account	– 101.5
Statistical discrepancy	24.7
Net capital flow	– 76.8
U.S. assets abroad	20.4
Foreign assets in the U.S. (–)	– 97.3
Relationship to national income accounts	
Balance on goods and services (balance of payments accounts)	– $90.1
Net gold exports (–)	1.2
Net capital gains in services income (–)	9.1
Government interest in services imports	19.8
Other accounting differences	– 4.2
Balance on goods and services (national income accounts)	– 64.2
National income accounts	
Balance on goods and services	– $64.2
Merchandise exports	219.2
Services exports	145.0
Merchandise imports (–)	– 325.5
Services imports (–)	– 103.0
Net transfers abroad (–)	– 9.6
Government interest payments abroad (–)	– 19.6
Net foreign investment	– 93.4

Source: U.S. Department of Commerce, *Survey of Current Business* (various issues).
Note: Figures may not add up perfectly because of rounding.

ings of dollar assets by just the amount by which U.S. imports exceed U.S. exports.

By presenting the relevant data for 1984, table 4–2 illustrates this essential connection between the U.S. export–import balance and foreign holders' net acquisition of dollar assets. After adjustment for statistical discrepancy, 1984's $102 billion current account deficit in the conventional balance of payments accounts corresponded to a "net capital flow" of – $77 billion—

that is, an excess of $77 billion in foreign holders' accumulation of dollar assets over U.S. holders' accumulation of assets abroad. Because of both conceptual and statistical differences (primarily involving treatment of the statistical discrepancy, but including other items as well), the corresponding "net foreign investment" flow in the conventional national income accounts was – $93 billion—that is, an excess of $93 billion in foreign saving applied to U.S. uses over U.S. saving applied to foreign uses.

Even in an economy the size of the United States, the presence of net capital inflows from abroad in this magnitude makes a substantial difference for the overall balance of saving and investment. Table 4–3, using national income accounting concepts, shows the U.S. balance of net saving and net investment for 1984. The economy's $272 billion of net private saving, including personal saving plus corporate retained earnings, represented the amount that the economy's private sector as a whole made available in 1984 to finance new investment beyond what was necessary just to maintain the nation's depreciating stocks of business and residential capital. Nevertheless, because of the need to finance a $176 billion federal government deficit, a deficit only partly offset by an aggregate $53 billion surplus for all state and local governments, the economy's total net saving was only $149 billion.

The economy's total net investment, which equals total net saving except for a small statistical discrepancy, was therefore only $141 billion in 1984.[1] By contrast, net private domestic investment, including business and residential fixed capital formation as well as business inventory accumulation,

Table 4–3
U.S. Net Saving and Investment, 1984
(billions of dollars)

Total net saving	$148.6
Net private saving	271.6
Personal saving	156.1
Corporate saving	115.4
State-local government surplus	52.9
Federal government surplus	– 175.8
Total net investment	$141.2
Net private domestic investment	234.6
Fixed investment	176.4
Inventory accumulation	58.2
Net foreign investment	– 93.4
Statistical discrepancy	$7.4

Source: U.S. Department of Commerce, *Survey of Current Business* (various issues).
Note: Figures may not add up perfectly because of rounding.

amounted to $235 billion. The two totals were consistent because, instead of devoting part of net saving to net investment abroad, the United States *dis*-invested abroad by $93 billion. That is, it accumulated $93 billion less in assets abroad than foreign holders accumulated in the United States. In other words, by importing more goods and services than it exported, the United States was able to take advantage of the corresponding net capital inflow to supplement the saving available from domestic sources.

Placed in this context, the $93 billion net capital inflow in 1984 was of substantial importance. It has lately become fashionable in the business press to describe this inflow from abroad as having financed more than half of the federal government's deficit. Given the inherent fungibility of financial flows at this level of aggregation, it would be equally correct to say that the capital inflow had financed more than half of the nation's net fixed capital formation—or, similarly, more than all of the U.S. business sector's net investment in new plant and equipment.[2] A less misleading description would be merely to say that the $93 billion net capital inflow had supplemented a net domestic saving total of only $149 billion.

This massive U.S. reliance on foreign capital is unprecedented in the twentieth century. Table 4–4 reviews the main 1951–85 movements of the U.S. balance of net saving and investment, in a form comparable to table 4–3, but stated in percentages of gross national product so as to abstract from the economy's growth. Despite substantial variation since World War II in such factors as tax rates, price inflation, real rates of return, and income growth trends—all of which could in principle affect saving behavior—the U.S. economy's net private saving rate has remained steady throughout this period. Its postwar mean has been 7.2 percent, with a standard deviation around the mean of only 1 percent, and it has displayed no significant time trend during this period (once the data are corrected for cyclical variation). The saving rate has varied in a modestly procyclical pattern, however, and this variation accounts for the slightly higher than average level during the 1960s and (in part) for the distinctly lower than average level during the early 1980s.

Table 4–4 makes clear the extraordinary stance of U.S. fiscal policy during the 1980s. In contrast to a nearly balanced federal budget on average throughout the 1950s and 1960s, and a deficit equal to less than 2 percent of gross national product on average during the 1970s, the federal budget deficit has now been approximately 5 percent of gross national product—above the prior record for any peacetime year—in each of the past four consecutive years. By contrast, state and local governments have increasingly run budget surpluses during this period, as current pension surpluses have grown faster than operating deficits. With net private saving slightly lower than the historical average, and the federal deficit ballooning far beyond the aggregate state-local government surplus, both total net saving and total net investment dur-

Table 4–4
U.S. Net Saving and Investment as Percentages of GNP, 1951–85

	1951–60	1961–70	1971–80	1981	1982	1983	1984	1985
Total net saving	6.9%	7.5%	6.1%	5.2%	1.6%	1.8%	4.1%	3.0%
Net private saving	7.2	8.0	7.1	6.1	5.4	5.9	7.4	6.5
Personal saving	4.7	4.7	4.9	4.6	4.4	3.6	4.3	3.3
Corporate saving	2.5	3.3	2.2	1.4	1.0	2.3	3.1	3.2
State-local government surplus	-0.2	0.1	0.9	1.3	1.1	1.3	1.4	1.4
Federal government surplus	-0.2	-0.5	-1.9	-2.2	-4.8	-5.4	-4.8	-4.9
Total net investment	7.0	7.5	6.3	5.4	1.6	1.8	3.8	2.8
Net private domestic investment	6.7	7.0	6.2	5.2	1.8	2.9	6.4	5.7
Plant and equipment	2.7	3.5	3.0	3.1	2.0	1.5	4.8	4.9
Residential construction	3.2	2.5	2.5	1.3	0.6	1.8		
Inventory accumulation	0.8	1.1	0.7	0.9	-0.9	-0.4	1.6	0.8
Net foreign investment	0.3	0.5	0.1	0.2	-0.2	-1.0	-2.6	-2.9
Memoranda: Capital consumption	8.9	8.5	9.9	11.2	11.7	11.4	11.0	11.0
Gross private saving	16.1	16.4	17.0	17.2	17.1	17.3	18.4	17.6

Source: U.S. Department of Commerce, *Survey of Current Business* (various issues), and author's estimate.

Notes: Data are averages (except for 1981–85) of annual flows. Data for 1985 are through 1985: Q2 at seasonally adjusted annual rates. Total net saving and total net investment differ by statistical discrepancy. Detail may not add to totals because of rounding.

ing the 1980s have fallen far short of prior U.S. norms. Instead of the typical 7-percent rate that characterized the prior three decades, total net investment averaged only 3.1 percent of gross national product during 1981–85, and only 2.5 percent for 1982–85.

Increasingly since 1982, however, a negative net foreign investment position has cushioned the impact of this change on the U.S. economy's domestic capital formation. U.S. net foreign investment was last positive—that is, the United States last devoted more saving to foreign uses than it imported saving from abroad for domestic uses—in 1981. Since then the nation's net foreign investment has been negative, and increasingly so each year as the current account balance has deteriorated.

To be sure, the 1980s have hardly been a banner period for capital formation in the United States, even with the aid of so much foreign saving. Net private domestic investment has averaged only 4.4 percent of gross national product during this period, well below the 6–7-percent range typical of the prior three decades. Nor has business investment in plant and equipment fared particularly well (presumably at the expense of homebuilding), despite the tax incentives legislated in 1981.[3] The absence of greater strength in business fixed capital formation, in turn, has probably played at least some role in disappointing hopes that the U.S. economy's productivity growth might show renewed strength in the 1980s.[4] Nevertheless, even this meager investment performance would presumably have been still more disappointing in the absence of the swelling foreign capital inflow.

The continuing and increasing reliance on foreign capital to finance its massive government deficit and modest net capital formation raises two sets of issues for the United States. First, what consequences follow if the capital inflow continues? Second, what if it doesn't? The next two sections address these questions.

What if the Capital Inflow Continues?

Financial flows represent changes in stocks of assets owned and liabilities owed. As table 4–2 shows, during 1984 foreign holders collectively accumulated $97 billion of assets in the United States, including debt liabilities issued by U.S borrowers as well as equity claims and real estate, while U.S. holders accumulated only $20 billion of analogous assets abroad. These totals, though certainly substantial enough, are still but one year's contribution to the building over time of assets internationally owned and liabilities internationally owed. If U.S. exports of goods and services continue to fall short of U.S. imports by anything like the deficit experienced in 1984, these internationally relevant asset and liability stocks will continue to grow, not just absolutely but also in comparison to the size of the U.S. economy.

Table 4–5 shows the 1970–84 evolution of the stock of assets abroad owned by U.S. holders, the stock of assets in the United States owned by foreign holders, and the U.S. "net international investment position" consisting of the difference between the two. These asset stocks (measured in dollars) grow from year to year not only with the capital flows that finance the U.S. balance of payments but also as a result of valuation changes due to either asset prices or exchange rates. In 1984, for example, U.S. holdings of assets abroad increased by $21 billion as a result of a $20 billion capital flow, enhanced by $6 billion due to increases in foreign asset prices (and other statistical adjustments), and reduced by $5 billion due to the falling value of most foreign currencies in dollar terms. Similarly, in 1984, foreign asset holdings in the United States increased by $99 billion as a result of a $97 billion capital flow, enhanced by $2 billion due to increases in U.S. asset prices.

The most dramatic development of the 1980s documented in table 4–5 is the dramatic reduction, in just two years, of the positive U.S. net international investment position. During the nineteenth century the United States, in a pattern that has since become typical of many developing countries, financed its initial industrialization with large inflows of foreign capital. Once its industrial development was under way, however, the United States began to export capital rather than import it. By 1914, this new capital outflow had sufficiently accumulated to render U.S. holdings of assets abroad greater than foreign holdings of assets in the United States—that is, to give the United States a positive net international investment position. A continuing excess of U.S. accumulation abroad over foreign accumulation in the United States, on average over nearly seven decades, brought the U.S. net international investment position to $147 billion (nearly 5 percent of U.S.

Table 4–5
U.S. Net Investment Position, 1970–84
(billions of dollars)

	U.S. Assets Abroad[a]	Foreign Assets in the U.S.[a]	Net U.S. Position[a]
1970	$165.4	$106.9	$ 58.5
1975	295.1	220.9	74.2
1980	606.9	500.8	106.1
1981	719.9	579.0	140.9
1982	839.0	692.0	147.0
1983	893.8	787.6	106.2
1984	914.7	886.4	28.3

Source: U.S. Department of Commerce, *Survey of Current Business* (various issues).
[a]At year-end.

gross national product) by year-end 1982. The capital flows required to finance just the last two years of U.S. imports in excess of U.S. exports reduced this net position to only $28 billion by year-end 1984. By the end of 1985, the net position will be negative, and at current rates it will grow to − $400–500 billion (in today's prices) by the end of the decade.

The dissipation of the U.S. net international investment position — and, still worse, the continuing movement of the United States into net debtor status — bears potentially worrisome implications for the freedom of U.S. economic policy and for the nation's ability to achieve a rising standard of living. At the most obvious level, net debtor status implies the need not just to service debt obligations owed abroad but to nurture foreign leaders' confidence in the nation's ability to meet its obligations, and hence their willingness to hold them. To be sure, the situation of the United States would be unlike that of many of today's troubled debtor nations, in that the great majority of U.S. liabilities are denominated in the United States's own currency. Even so, a net external debt of $400–500 billion (in constant prices) would represent 11–14 percent of 1990 gross national product if the U.S. economy achieved an average 3-percent real growth for the remainder of the decade, or roughly 100 percent of 1990 total exports if the export share of total output remains as it is today.

Moreover, even apart from the strains that would be implied by the sheer magnitude of the debt service obligation due to such a large net external debt position, it is worrisome that, in contrast to the experience of prior years, the recent accumulation of U.S. assets held abroad has been almost entirely due to private rather than official (that is, government) holders. During 1971–78, for example, foreign official holders accumulated a total of $147 billion of U.S. assets, while foreign private holders accumulated a total of $118 billion of U.S. assets. During 1979–84, the foreign official and foreign private accumulations have totalled $26 billion and $489 billion, respectively. As a result, private holders accounted for 78 percent of the $886 billion of U.S. assets held abroad as of year-end 1984. On the other side of the account, it is also worrisome that almost half of all U.S. holdings of assets abroad ($443 billion out of $915 billion at year-end 1984) now consist of bank loans to foreign borrowers, many of whom are unable to meet their own obligations except in the highly artificial sense implied by the recent widening circle of reschedulings.[5]

Even if foreign holders continue not to question the creditworthiness of U.S. obligors, so that neither actual defaults nor crises of confidence disrupt financial flows and, consequently, economic activity, the net debtor status of the United States poses a significant challenge to the nation's ability to achieve increases over time in its standard of living. As the direct connection between net capital inflows and the balance of payments on goods and services suggests, a nation's net debtor or creditor status determines its ability to consume (or invest) in relation to what it produces. If asset returns are approximately equalized in international markets, a creditor nation earns a positive net flow of income by virtue of owning more than it owes internationally. It may then apply that income to finance consumption in excess of domestic production. As table 4–1 shows, on average during the 1970s, the United States maintained an approximately balanced current account, despite a significant trade deficit, because of service income including earnings on its relatively large positive net international investment position. As recently as 1982, the United States ran a $6 billion current account surplus, despite a $28 billion trade deficit, almost entirely because of earning $85 billion on assets abroad while having to pay only $55 billion on foreign holdings of U.S. assets.

As the U.S. net international investment position has eroded since 1982, so too has the positive net flow of income earned on international asset holdings. In 1984, the United States earned $87 billion on assets abroad (including "payments" of interest on rescheduled debts held by U.S. banks), while paying $68 billion. Hence in 1984 again, the United States could still use investment income to finance at least part of its shortfall of goods exports behind goods imports.

Now, however, as the United States becomes a net debtor, it will have to produce more than it consumes (and invests) if it is not to spiral explosively into ever greater indebtedness relative to the economy's productive capacity. What makes this prospect all the more problematic is that the United States has not been using the bulge in financial capital inflows to facilitate a bulge in the formation of either physical or human capital resources, as rapidly developing countries typically do. As table 4–4 shows, U.S. investment in productive physical capital has been below average during these years. Nor has spending for research and development or for education shown any unusual strength. Instead of mortgaging part of the future income from its investments — a familiar activity that may or may not be sensible, depending upon the relative returns and the associated risks involved — the United States has been mortgaging its future income in order to finance a combination of government and private consumption.

Finally, the increasing accumulation of foreign asset holdings in the United States can significantly affect U.S. financial markets, and hence the resulting outcomes for U.S. economic activity more broadly, in still another way. Because the capital inflow required to finance today's U.S. export-import imbalance is so large, foreign holdings of U.S. assets are rising not just in relation to U.S. holdings of assets abroad but also in relation to the overall size of the U.S. financial markets. Throughout the 1960s, total foreign asset holdings in the United States (including foreign direct investment) represented only some 3 percent of the total of financial assets held and traded in U.S. markets.[6] As table 4–6 shows, the share of U.S. financial assets held by

Table 4–6
Foreign Holdings of U.S. Financial Assets, 1960–84
(billions of dollars)

	Amount[a]	% of U.S. Market[a]
1960	$ 40.6	3.1%
1965	57.7	3.0
1970	98.3	3.8
1975	187.7	5.2
1980	390.7	6.1
1981	420.1	6.1
1982	440.0	5.8
1983	512.8	6.1
1984	618.8	6.7

Source: Board of Governors of the Federal Reserve System, *Flow of Funds* (various issues.)
Notes: Foreign holdings exclude gold and Special Drawing Rights (SDR), and include interbank claims net of foreign interbank liabilities. U.S. market size includes foreign plus all domestic nonfinancial sectors.
[a]At year-end.

foreign investors has risen rapidly since then, and it is continuing to do so. As of year-end 1984, foreign holdings accounted for nearly 7 percent of all U.S. financial assets.[7]

This increasing foreign ownership of U.S. financial assets will affect the equilibrium of asset prices and asset returns determined in U.S. markets, and hence also affect U.S. nonfinancial economic activity, unless foreign investors turn out to exhibit portfolio preferences identical to those of American investors. When the investors who collectively hold the assets in any market are heterogeneous, in general the resulting equilibrium set of asset prices and returns is some weighted combination of the equilibrium prices and returns that would result if each group, in turn, uniquely constituted the entire market. For example, as Lintner (1969) showed, when investors have differing degrees of risk aversion, the resulting equilibrium price of risk is a weighted (harmonic) mean of each investor's own degree of risk aversion, with the weights corresponding to each investor's relative share of total asset holdings. Changes in different investors' relative market importance in this sense therefore lead to changes in the overall market price of risk.

More generally, if the market consists of investors, indexed by i, each of whose single-period asset preferences are of the form

$$A_{it}^D = W_{it} \cdot (B_{it} r_t^e + \pi_{it}) \qquad (4.1)$$

where A^D is a vector of asset demands (satisfying $A^{D'} 1 = W$), W is the investor's total wealth, $\mathbf{r}^e$ is a vector of expected asset returns, and $\mathbf{B}$ and $\boldsymbol{\pi}$ are, respectively, a matrix and a vector of coefficients determined by the investor's risk preferences and assessments of the risks associated with the various available assets,[8] then the asset market partial equilibrium condition

$$\sum_i \mathbf{A}_{it}^D = \mathbf{A}_t^S \tag{4.2}$$

for vector $\mathbf{A}^S$ of asset supplies outstanding, determines the market-clearing structure of expected asset returns as

$$\mathbf{r}_t^e = \left(\sum_i \mathbf{W}_{it} \mathbf{B}_{it} \right)^{-1} \left(\mathbf{A}_t^S - \sum_i \mathbf{W}_{it} \boldsymbol{\pi}_{it} \right). \tag{4.3}$$

If investors' risk preferences and/or risk assessments differ, then the nonproportionate growth of different investors' wealth positions over time changes the resulting asset return structure.[9]

Foreign investors in U.S. asset markets may exhibit portfolio preferences different from those of American investors for a variety of easily understandable reasons. First, in a world still of limited (though increasing) capital mobility, the relevant set of available assets for foreign investors differs from the corresponding set for Americans. Because of the consequent differences in the set of relevant asset return covariances, even the same assets may have different risk properties as seen by the two respective groups of investors. Second, investors with incomes largely originating in different countries face different sets of macroeconomic risks, due to the countries' differing policy regimes, industrial structures, dependence on imported oil and other raw materials, and other analogous characteristics. Again, even identical assets may therefore have different risk characteristics from the perspective of investors in different countries.[10] Third, there is no reason to expect such aspects of underlying preferences as risk aversion to be uniform across countries with widely differing societal structures and traditions.

For any or all of these reasons, foreign investors participating in the U.S. financial markets may prefer either more or less risky assets overall, may prefer either more debt securities or more equity securities, may prefer either more long-term or short-term debt, or may prefer either more volatile or less volatile equities, in comparison to American investors. If so, then the rapidly increasing share of U.S. financial assets held by foreign investors implies that their portfolio preferences will assume greater importance—in the sense of equation 4.3, foreign investors' W_i will rise, relative to that for U.S. investors—in determining the yield and price relationships that prevail in U.S. markets.

Table 4–7 compares the composition of foreign holdings of U.S. finan-

Table 4–7
Foreign versus Domestic Holdings of Financial Assets, 1984
(billions of dollars)

	Foreign Holders		Domestic Holders	
	Amount[a]	% of Total[a]	Amount[a]	% of Total[a]
Checkable deposits and currency	$ 19.7	4.4%	$ 582.2	7.1%
Large time deposits	39.4	8.8	392.3	4.8
Short-term U.S. government securities	72.0	16.0 ⎤		
Long-term U.S. government securities	120.8	26.9 ⎦	1,709.5	20.8
Other short-term paper	40.9	9.1	266.4	3.2
Corporate bonds	61.8	13.8	588.1	7.2
State-local government securities	0.0	0.0	543.6	6.6
Mortgages	0.0	0.0	2,028.9	24.7
Corporate equities	94.5	21.0	2,090.3	25.5
Total	449.1	100.0	8,201.3	100.0

Source: Board of Governors of the Federal Reserve System, *Flow of Funds* (various issues).

Notes: Short-term U.S. government securities include marketable securities only. Other short-term paper includes commercial paper and bankers acceptances. Foreign holdings of corporate equities exclude foreign direct investment. Totals exclude small time and saving deposits, money market mutual funds, interbank claims, and other miscellaneous assets.

[a]At year-end.

cial assets to the corresponding composition of financial asset holdings by all domestic U.S. investors, for year-end 1984.[11] Although the absence of foreign ownership of some specific assets stands out, the rough outlines of the two aggregate portfolios are quite similar. The respective fractions invested in equities, for example, are within four percentage points.[12] Similarly, the respective fractions invested in bank-issued claims (plus currency) are essentially identical.

The most significant difference between foreign and U.S. financial asset holdings shown in table 4–7 is in the maturity composition of debt instruments. As of year-end 1984, foreign investors held $152 billion of short-term debt instruments issued in U.S. markets (including negotiable time deposits, but excluding checkable deposits and currency) versus $183 billion of long-term instruments, for a roughly 5-to-6 short-to-long maturity structure. Determining the analogous ratio for domestic investors is more problematic because of the unavailability of current data on the maturity composition of the relevant holdings of U.S. government securities,[13] but a plausible inference based on what data are available suggests that the corresponding totals for domestic investors are $1.4 trillion of short-term debt instruments versus $4.1 trillion of long-term instruments, for a 1-to-3 short-to-long maturity structure.

If foreign investors continue to represent an increasing share of U.S. financial asset holdings, and if their portfolio preferences remain unchanged, over time the market-clearing relationship among asset returns is therefore likely to require a greater premium of expected returns on long-term debts over expected returns on short-term debts than has been the case on average in the past. Such a change in the prevailing structure of interest rates (and asset returns more generally) will not only bear a variety of implications within the U.S. financial markets—for example, for the relative attractiveness of different forms of saving, and hence of different kinds of saving institutions—but also, and more importantly, exert effects on U.S. nonfinancial economic activity. In particular, evidence on both business and household financing patterns suggests that such a widening of average maturity premiums, if not offset by other factors, is likely in turn to shift the composition of aggregate demand away from fixed capital formation toward other applications.[14] Hence it will further compound the economy's recent problem of poor investment performance shown in table 4–4.

What if the Capital Inflow Does Not Continue?

The entire question of implications of continuing massive inflow of foreign capital into the United States will, of course, become moot if the capital inflow soon shrinks—that is, if the United States manages to regain a much greater degree of balance between its exports and its imports. A decline in the real exchange value of the dollar, due either to a shift in the mix of U.S. fiscal and monetary policies or to a change in international portfolio preferences, is probably the most obvious development that would bring about such an outcome. There are other possibilities too, however. For example, U.S. producers could become more competitive abroad, even at the current dollar exchange rate, if they developed new products eagerly sought by foreign buyers, or if trade negotiations succeeded in lessening restrictions impeding U.S. exports. Alternatively, U.S. producers could regain domestic sales if additional protectionist measures enacted by the United States further excluded foreign imports.[15]

In light of the increasingly important role played by the net capital inflow in the U.S. balance of saving and investment, discussed at length under **Capital Inflows, Investment, and Government Deficits,** any imminent shrinkage of this inflow would have serious repercussions for major aspects of U.S. economic activity. Even so, unraveling those repercussions is far from straightforward. For example, as that section notes, the business press has recently emphasized the role of the capital inflow in financing the federal government's budget deficit. The standard implication drawn in such evaluations is that, in the absence of the capital inflow, the government deficit would absorb a larger share of domestic net private saving, leaving less available to finance domestic capital formation. Whether such an outcome would in fact follow from a shrinking of the capital flow, however, depends crucially on what caused the capital flow to shrink in the first place. If the exogenous event at the beginning of the causal chain were a return to the typical pre-1980s fiscal policy, for example, then the smaller budget deficit would itself offset all or part of the lost foreign capital.

In evaluating such questions, therefore, it is essential not only to separate what is exogenous from what is endogenous but also to specify clearly the exact experiment under consideration. The most useful way to begin is with the balance of saving and investment in the form implicit from table 4–4 (excluding the statistical discrepancy)

$$PS = DI + GD + FI \tag{4.4}$$

where PS is net private saving, DI is net private domestic investment, GD is the combined deficit of federal and all state and local governments, and FI is net foreign investment (that is, the negative of the foreign capital inflow). Because this identity must hold at all times, no one of the four variables indicated can vary without a precisely offsetting variation in one or more of the other three. More specifically, in the context of thought experiments in which all four of these variables are endogenous, no exogenous shock—neither a change in U.S. fiscal and monetary policies, nor a change in foreign investors' willingness to hold dollar assets—can affect any one of the four without affecting one or more of the others in a precisely offsetting way.

Table 4–8 indicates the nature of these offsetting movements in the respective elements of the balance of saving and investment in response to U.S. fiscal and monetary policies, based on seasonally adjusted quarterly data spanning 1970–84. The first column of the table reports results from ordinary-least-squares regressions of the form

$$Y_{it} = \alpha_i + \sum_{j=0}^{3} \beta_{ij} FP_{t-j} + u_{it} \tag{4.5}$$

where y_i is in turn each of the four saving or investment variables shown in equation 4.4, measured as a percentage of gross national product; FP is the federal government budget deficit calculated on a 6-percent unemployment basis, and also measured as a percentage of gross national product;[16] α_i and

Table 4–8
Estimated Effects on the Balance of Saving and Investment

Dependent Variable	Independent Variable			
	FP		MP	
PS: $\hat{\beta}_0$	− .09	(− 0.4)	− 10.42	(− 2.7)
$\Sigma \hat{\beta}_j$	− .68	(− 2.9)	3.72	(8.0)
SE ($\bar{R}^2$)	1.10	(.08)	.79	(.53)
DI: $\hat{\beta}_0$	− 1.24	(− 3.6)	− 1.78	(2.6)
$\Sigma \hat{\beta}_j$	− .80	(− 2.1)	6.38	(7.5)
SE ($\bar{R}^2$)	1.74	(.28)	1.45	(.50)
GD: $\hat{\beta}_0$	1.48	(5.9)	9.48	(1.4)
$\Sigma \hat{\beta}_j$	.86	(3.2)	− 4.68	(− 5.7)
SE ($\bar{R}^2$)	1.26	(.49)	1.39	(.38)
FI: $\hat{\beta}_0$	− .31	(− 2.0)	1.17	(0.3)
$\Sigma \hat{\beta}_j$	− .86	(− 5.4)	2.07	(5.0)
SE ($\bar{R}^2$)	.74	(.33)	.70	(.39)

Notes: Ordinary-least-squares regression results for equation (4.5) (column 1) and equation (4.6) (column 2).

Quarterly data, 1970:Q1–1984:Q4, seasonally adjusted.

Numbers in parentheses by coefficient estimates are t-statistics.

All variables except MP are stated as percentages of GNP.

Definitions of variables symbols:

PS = net private saving
DI = net private domestic investment
GD = federal plus state-local government deficit
FI = net foreign investment
FP = high-employment federal deficit
MP = logarithm of trend-adjusted ratio of money stock to GNP

the β_{ij} are fixed coefficients to be estimated; and u_i is a disturbance term corresponding to y_i. For each of the four regressions, the table presents only partial results consisting of the estimated $\hat{\beta}_0$ and $\Sigma_{t=0}^3 \hat{\beta}_j$, the associated t-statistics, and the standard error of estimate (SE) and associated $\bar{R}^2$. The second column reports analogous results for regressions of the form

$$y_{it} = \alpha_i + \sum_{j=0}^3 \beta_{ij} MP_{t-j} + u_{it} \qquad (4.6)$$

where MP is a monetary policy index indicating the logarithm of the (quadratic) trend-adjusted value of the M-1 money stock relative to gross national product.[17]

Because of the restriction imposed by the identity in equation 4.4, ordinary-least-squares estimates of any system of equations of the form

$$\mathbf{y}_t = \boldsymbol{\alpha} + \mathbf{B}\mathbf{z}_t + \mathbf{u}_t \tag{4.7}$$

where

$$\mathbf{y} = \begin{bmatrix} PS \\ -DI \\ -GD \\ -FI \end{bmatrix} \tag{4.8}$$

and z is any vector of driving variables, necessarily satisfy the "adding-up" conditions

$$\hat{\boldsymbol{\alpha}}'1 = \hat{\boldsymbol{\beta}}_j'1 = \mathbf{u}_t 1 = 0 \tag{4.9}$$

where $\hat{\boldsymbol{\beta}}_j$ is the jth column of matrix $\mathbf{B}$.[18] As comparison down the two columns of table 4–8 shows, after appropriate sign changes the two sets of $\hat{\beta}_0$ values and $\Sigma_j \hat{\beta}_j$ values satisfy these conditions to within the accuracy implied by the omission of the statistical discrepancy.

The two sets of regression results reported in table 4–8 therefore indicate answers to the question of how the elements of the U.S. balance of saving and investment vary together, based on two separate thought experiments. First, what if the driving variable is a change in U.S. fiscal policy, as represented by an increase in the high-employment federal deficit relative to gross national product? As the $\hat{\beta}_0$ values in the first column show, the overall actual government deficit responds immediately and sharply to the high-employment deficit; with essentially no response in private saving, the immediate result is both to crowd out domestic investment ($\hat{\beta}_{DI,0} = -1.24$) and, to a much lesser extent, to draw in foreign capital ($\hat{\beta}_{FI} = -.31$).[19]

The corresponding one-year cumulative effects of a change in fiscal policy tell a roughly similar story, albeit with some interesting differences. Over a year private saving declines ($\Sigma\hat{\beta}_{PS,j} = -.68$). The crowding out of domestic investment becomes smaller ($\Sigma\hat{\beta}_{DI,j} = -.80$), while the impact on the foreign capital inflow becomes larger ($\Sigma\hat{\beta}_{FI,j} = -.86$), so that after a year the two effects are approximately equal magnitude. Overall, the entire set of estimates broadly corresponds to the U.S. experience thus far during the 1980s. Read in the opposite direction, they provide a plausible enough first answer to the question of what would happen as the result of a tightening of U.S. fiscal policy.

The second column of table 4–8 tells a roughly analogous story about the effects of an easing of U.S. monetary policy.[20] The estimated immediate impact of greater money growth is to depress both private saving and domestic investment; the accompanying effects on the government deficit and on net foreign investment are insignificantly different from zero.[21] Over a year an easier monetary policy stimulates private saving ($\Sigma \hat{\beta}_{PS,j} = 3.72$) and stimulates domestic investment by much more ($\Sigma \hat{\beta}_{DI,j} = 6.38$). Because the government deficit narrows ($\Sigma \hat{\beta}_{GD,j} = -4.68$), net foreign investment increases—in other words, the capital inflow becomes smaller ($\Sigma \hat{\beta}_{FI,j} = 2.07$).

Univariate regressions such as those reported in table 4–8 do not clearly separate the effects of fiscal and monetary policies because they do not hold one policy constant while analyzing the other. Table 4–9 presents corresponding partial results (for convenience, omitting the initial impact estimates) from ordinary-least-squares regressions of the form

$$y_{it} = \alpha_i + \sum_{j=0}^{3} \hat{\beta}_{ij} EX_{t-j} + \sum_{j=0}^{3} \gamma_{ij} RE_{t-j} + \sum_{j=0}^{3} \delta_{ij} MP_{t-j} + u_{it} \quad (4.10)$$

where EX and RE are federal government expenditures and revenues, respectively, with both calculated on a 6-percent unemployment basis and measured as percentages of gross national product, and all other variables are as in equations 4.5 and 4.6.[22] The underlying sample again consists of seasonally adjusted quarterly data spanning 1970–84.

On balance, the one-year cumulative effects of fiscal and monetary policies reported in table 4–9 are consistent with the separate effects reported in table 4–8, although fewer of these effects are statistically significant in the multivariate context. Over a year the partial effect of greater high-employment federal government expenditures is to enlarge the overall actual government deficit with essentially no offsetting increase in private saving. The result is to crowd out domestic investment ($\Sigma \hat{\beta}_{DI,j} = -1.07$) and, to a much lesser extent (and not significantly), to draw in foreign capital ($\Sigma \hat{\beta}_{FI,j} = -.23$). The partial effect of greater high-employment federal government revenues is to enlarge the overall actual government deficit by much less than one-for-one, although again with no increase in private saving.[23] The result is primarily to increase net foreign investment ($\Sigma \hat{\gamma}_{FI,j} = .85$) and, to a lesser extent (and not significantly), to crowd out investment ($\Sigma \hat{\gamma}_{DI,j} = -.35$). Finally, the partial effect of more rapid money growth is primarily to stimulate both private saving ($\Sigma \hat{\delta}_{PS,j} = 5.00$) and domestic investment ($\Sigma \hat{\delta}_{DI,j} = 4.08$). To a rough approximation, these results again correspond to the now familiar analysis of the deterioration of the U.S. trade balance and of U.S. capital

Table 4–9
Estimated Joint Effects on the Balance of Saving and Investment

Dependent Variable	$\Sigma \hat{\beta}_j$		$\Sigma \hat{\gamma}_j$		$\Sigma \hat{\delta}_j$		SE	$\bar{R}^2$
PS	.10	(0.3)	.02	(0.1)	5.00	(8.1)	.67	.66
DI	-1.07	(-1.7)	-.35	(-0.9)	4.08	(3.1)	1.43	.51
GD	1.28	(2.5)	-.35	(-1.0)	-1.28	(-1.2)	1.15	.57
FI	-.23	(-0.9)	.85	(5.1)	2.02	(3.8)	.58	.58

Notes: Ordinary-least-squares regression results for equation (4.10).
Quarterly data, 1970:Q1–1984:Q4, seasonally adjusted.
Numbers in parentheses are *t*-statistics.
All variables except *MP* are stated as percentages of GNP.

Definitions of variable symbols:

EX = high-employment federal expenditures
RE = high-employment federal revenues
PS = net private saving
DI = net private domestic investment
GD = federal plus state-local government deficit
FI = net foreign investment
FP = high-employment federal deficit
MP = logarithm of trend-adjusted ratio of money stock to GNP

formation in the 1980s, in terms of the radical turn during this period in the U.S. fiscal–monetary policy mix.

Apart from a change in U.S. fiscal or monetary policy, the most obvious possible cause of a decline in the real dollar exchange rate—and hence a narrowing of the U.S. trade deficit and a corresponding shrinkage of the foreign capital inflow—is a change in the willingness of foreign investors to hold dollar-denominated assets.[24] Even so, carrying out an analysis of the effects of shifting foreign portfolio preferences corresponding to the analysis of fiscal and monetary policies in tables 4–8 and 4–9 is highly problematic. Presumably, foreign investors' asset preferences respond to a variety of influences—for example, both interest rates and exchange rates—that in turn either directly depend on the outcomes for the major elements of the saving–investment balance or, at the least, are jointly determined with them. To the extent that such codetermination is present, such variables are not valid right-hand-side variables in any system like equation 4.8, and the resulting estimates would be biased.

What would be necessary, instead—as in the analysis of fiscal and monetary policies—is to identify some genuinely exogenous influence to serve as the initial point of the causal chain constituting the thought experiment at issue. If some exogenous factor increases the aggregate demand for net dollar assets, therefore leads to a rise in the dollar exchange rate, therefore leads to a larger trade deficit, therefore leads to a large net capital inflow, and therefore affects some or all of the other elements in the U.S. balance of saving and investment, it is that exogenous factor—not the capital inflow, nor the trade deficit, nor the exchange rate—which constitutes the valid right-hand–side variable for these purposes. Unfortunately, attempts along these lines based on two separate approaches, both aimed at isolating independent components of movements in either exchange rates or interest rate differentials, proved insufficient.[25] A structural modeling approach, such as that applied by Sachs (1985), is apparently necessary to unravel the effects of shifts in foreign portfolio preferences.

Summary of Conclusions

The rapidly growing net inflow of capital from abroad, mirroring the extraordinary deterioration of the U.S. export–import balance, has played a major role in equilibrating overall saving and investment in the United States in the face of unprecedentedly large and persistent federal government budget deficits during the 1980s. As of the middle of the decade, this capital inflow is more than half as large as the total net saving of the United States. By relying on it in this way, the United States has already dissipated the positive net international investment position it had built up over the previous seven decades. On the current trajectory, the United States will soon be the world's leading debtor nation.

Because of the sheer size of the foreign capital inflow, the share of U.S. financial assets held by foreign investors is also growing rapidly. To the extent that foreign investors' portfolio preferences differ from those of U.S. investors, their increasing relative importance in this sense will change the equilibrium price and yield relationships determined in U.S. markets. The most readily apparent difference between foreign and domestic patterns of asset holdings in this regard is that foreign investors, on average, hold far less of their portfolios in long-term debt instruments and, correspondingly, far more of their portfolios in short-term debt instruments, than do American investors. The increasing share of foreign ownership of U.S. financial assets is therefore likely to raise the expected return premium on long-term debt, and hence to shift the composition of U.S. financial activity away from capital formation.

The foreign capital inflow—and with it the U.S. export–import balance—may change in response to a variety of possible influences, including especially either fiscal and monetary policies in the United States or shifts in foreign investors' portfolio preferences for dollar assets versus assets denominated in other currencies. Empirical estimates indicate that a tightening of U.S. fiscal policy would significantly stimulate U.S. capital formation as well as shrink the U.S. capital inflow (that is, improve the U.S. export–import balance). Similar estimates indicate that an easing of U.S. monetary policy would also significantly stimulate capital formation and shrink the capital inflow. The difficulty of isolating genuinely independent movements of exchange rates and international interest rate differentials precludes deriving similar estimates for the analogous effects of a shift in portfolio preferences.

Notes

1. The statistical discrepancy in the national income accounts is not the same as that in the balance of payments accounts.

2. Data indicating the split between net business investment in plant and equipment and net residential investment, within the $176 billion total shown in table 4–3, are not yet available. Extrapolations based on prior years' allocation of the relevant depreciation flows suggests that each component probably represented about one-half of the total.

3. See again note 2.

4. Growth of output per manhour in the U.S. economy's nonfarm business sector averaged 2.7 percent per annum during 1948–65, but then declined to 1.8 percent per annum during 1966–77. Productivity then remained flat during 1978–82. Despite the usual cyclical increase at the outset of the current business expansion, productivity growth during the expansion to date (1983:Q1–1985:Q2) has averaged 2.3 percent

per annum, actually somewhat below the comparable average for prior postwar expansions.

5. Other problems of asset valuation and reporting suggest that the data in table 4–5 may over- or underestimate the U.S. position. These data value U.S. direct investment abroad and foreign direct investment in the United States at cost, and hence presumably undervalue both, but the former exceeds the latter by a large margin ($233 billion versus $160 billion at year-end 1984). Similarly, the data value U.S. gold holdings ($12 billion at year-end 1984) at only $42.22 per ounce. Yet another potential problem, of course, is the accumulation of unreported flows in both directions. The accumulated statistical discrepancy since 1970 has been a $150 billion inflow, part of which has probably been a capital inflow.

6. Even this low percentage represents a small overstatement in that foreign direct investment ($7 billion out of the $41 billion total for 1960, for example) includes some real estate holdings, while the comparison base consists of financial claims only.

7. The totals shown in table 4–6 are smaller than the foreign holdings shown in table 4–5 for several reasons, especially the netting of interbank claims. Other differences include the treatment of U.S. corporations' borrowing abroad via Netherlands Antilles subsidiaries and (since 1981) the operation of U.S. banks' international banking facilities (IBFs). Isard and Stekler (1985) have shown that adjusting for these factors (especially IBFs) substantially diminishes the apparent accumulation of foreign claims during 1981–82, but does so to a much smaller extent thereafter.

8. The linear homogenous form in equation 4.1 follows, for example, from the assumptions of constant relative risk aversion and joint normally (or lognormally) distributed asset return assessments. If all assets are risky, for example, the specific relationship is

$$\mathbf{B} = - \frac{1}{\rho} [\Omega^{-1} - (1'\Omega^{-1}1)^{-1}\Omega^{-1}1\ 1'\Omega^{-1}]$$

$$\boldsymbol{\pi} = (1'\Omega^{-1}1)^{-1}\Omega^{-1}1$$

where ρ is the coefficient of relative risk aversion and Ω is the variance–covariance matrix associated with $\mathbf{r}^e$. See Friedman and Roley (forthcoming) for further details of the derivation and underlying assumptions.

9. See Friedman (1982) for an analysis along these lines in a general equilibrium model (that is, one including simultaneous determination of financial and nonfinancial market outcomes), but in a closed-economy context.

10. In terms of the familiar generalization of the capital asset pricing model due to Breeden (1979), the point is simply that the consumption stream to be hedged is typically different for residents of different countries.

11. Foreign holdings here exclude $154 billion of foreign direct investment, as well as a variety of miscellaneous claims that are not typically traded in the market (for example, $23 billion of trade credit). Domestic holdings analogously exclude claims not typically traded (for example, $633 billion of trade credit, and $1.7 trillion of small time and savings deposits).

12. Note again, however, the exclusion of $154 of foreign direct investment.

13. In 1982, the U.S. Treasury discontinued the regular Treasury *Survey of Ownership*.

14. See, for example, the results in Friedman (1982). Moreover, this factor acting to enlarge the maturity premium on long-term debts will work in the same direction as the independent changes in risk structures analyzed by Bodie *et al.* (1984).

15. In the case of U.S. protectionism, the ultimate effect on the U.S. trade balance would, of course, depend on the absence of a like response by foreign countries.

16. It is not in general the case that government expenditures and revenues have just offsetting effects, so that on purely a priori grounds it is more appealing to present results for expenditures and revenues separately, rather than for the deficit as in table 4–8. Nevertheless, regressions corresponding to those in table 4–8, but using as independent variable either government expenditures or government revenues (both calculated on a 6 percent unemployment basis) uniformly exhibit larger standard errors than those reported in table 4–8 based on the deficit variable. By contrast, the multiple regressions reported in table 4–9 treat expenditures and revenues separately.

17. The variable is the residual from the ordinary-least-squares regression

$$\ln \frac{M - 1}{\text{GNP}} = \alpha + \beta_1 t + \beta_2 t^2.$$

I am grateful to Ken Weiller for the use of this variable; see Weiller (1985).

18. The analogy to the basic insight of Brainard and Tobin (1968) is readily apparent.

19. The greater than one-for-one response of both the overall deficit and domestic investment is surprising. These current-quarter results probably reflect simultaneity biases, due, for example, to the use of fiscal policy for purposes of countercyclical stabilization. See the discussion of such biases in Goldfeld and Blinder (1972).

20. The absolute magnitudes of the coefficient estimates are larger here, because the *MP* variable is a logarithm rather than a percentage of GNP.

21. Here, too, the estimated current-quarter effects presumably reflect simultaneity biases, including the countercyclical use of monetary policy as well as the endogeneity of the money stock in the usual sense; see again Goldfeld and Blinder (1972).

22. Here, unlike in the results for equation 4.5 reported in table 4–8, treating government expenditures and revenues separately leads to regressions with smaller standard errors, in three of the four cases, than those for analogous regressions combining the two into a single deficit variable.

23. The unresponsiveness of private saving to government expenditures or government revenues in these estimates (and, still worse if it were credible, the finding of a negative response of private saving to the deficit in table 4–8) is a manifestation of the now familiar empirical contradiction of the Barro (1974) hypothesis. For a recent more detailed look at the evidence on this issue, see Blinder and Deaton (1985).

24. Marris (1985a, 1985b) in particular has emphasized this prospect.

25. The first of these approaches attempted to isolate the component of the movement of exchange rates or interest rate differentials that is not attributable either to ordinary U.S. business fluctuations or to variations in U.S. fiscal and monetary policies, and hence that may plausibly represent other exogenous influences like changing portfolio preferences. The method used was to proxy these influences by the *residuals*

from preliminary regressions relating exchange rates or interest rate differentials to the *FP* and *MP* variables used in equations 4.5 and 4.6, together with the U.S. unemployment rate, growth rate of real GNP, and inflation rate. The second approach focused more directly on foreign fiscal and monetary policies by using the *fitted values* from preliminary regressions relating exchange rates or interest rate differentials to indexes of foreign fiscal and monetary policies, analogous to the *FP* and *MP* variables, constructed on a GNP-weighted basis for six countries other than the United States.

References

Barro, Robert J. "Are Government Bonds Net Wealth?" *Journal of Political Economy* 82 (November–December 1974), 1095–117.

Blinder, Alan S., and Angus S. Deaton. "The Time Series Consumption Function Revisited." *Brookings Papers on Economic Activity* (no. 2, 1985), 465–511.

Bodie, Zvi, Alex Kane, and Robert McDonald. "Why Haven't Nominal Rates Declined?" *Financial Analysts Journal* 40 (March–April 1984), 16–27.

Brainard, William C., and James Tobin. "Pitfalls in Financial Model-Building." *American Economic Review* 58 (May 1968), 99–122.

Breeden, Douglas. "An Intertemporal Capital Asset Pricing Model with Stochastic Consumption and Investment Opportunities." *Journal of Financial Economics* 7 (September 1979), 265–96.

Friedman, Benjamin M. "Effects of Shifting Saving Patterns on Interest Rates and Economic Activity." *Journal of Finance* 37 (March 1982), 37–62.

———. and V. Vance Roley. "Aspects of Investor Behavior under Risk" in Feiwel (ed.), *Essays in Honor of Kenneth Arrow,* forthcoming.

Goldfeld, Stephen M., and Alan S. Blinder. "Some Implications of Endogenous Stabilization." *Brookings Papers on Economic Activity* (no. 3, 1972), 585–640.

Isard, Peter, and Lois Stekler. "U.S. International Capital Flows and the Dollar." *Brookings Papers on Economic Activity* (no. 1, 1985), 219–36.

Lintner, John. "The Aggregation of Investors' Diverse Judgments and Preferences in Purely Competitive Security Markets." *Journal of Financial and Quantitative Analysis* 4 (December 1969), 347–400.

Marris, Stephen N. *Dollars and Deficits: The World Economy at Risk.* Washington, D.C.: Institute for International Economics, 1985a.

———. "The Decline and Fall of the Dollar: Some Policy Issues." *Brookings Papers on Economic Activity* (no. 1, 1985b), 237–44.

Sachs, Jeffrey D. "The Dollar and the Policy Mix: 1985." *Brookings Papers on Economic Activity* (no. 1, 1985), 117–85.

Weiller, Kenneth J. "Government Deficits, Debt and the Real Exchange Rate in a Two-Country Model: Theory and Evidence." Mimeo. Department of Economics, Harvard University, 1985.

Comments

John Huizinga

B enjamin Friedman's preceding chapter investigates recent U.S. international capital transactions along three dimensions. In the section **Capital Inflows, Investment, and Government Deficits** it characterizes the current situation, using national income identities to describe how increased U.S. net capital inflows have been balanced by changes in net private savings, government budget deficits, and net private domestic investment. Its next section addresses the question, what important consequences are likely to occur if the current level and direction of capital flows continue? The following section asks, if certain policy actions are implemented to eliminate existing capital flows, how will these policies affect net private savings, net private domestic investment, and the government budget deficit? In what follows I summarize what I think the chapter's major conclusions are, explain where I disagree with the chapter, and also raise some issues that I feel are relevant but are not discussed in it. Before turning to specifics, however, let me say that the chapter is informative and easy to read, while providing interesting food for thought.

According to the data presented under **Capital Inflows, Investment, and Government Deficits,** the dramatic increase in U.S. current account deficits, and therefore the associated increase in capital inflows, began in 1983 and has continued through 1985. During the period 1983–85, net private savings averaged 6.6 percent of gross national product, dropping somewhat from the average of 7.3 percent over the period 1950–82. Net private domestic investment was also low by historical standards, averaging 4.3 percent of gross national product from 1983–85 compared to 5.7 percent from 1950–82. In contrast, government budget deficits as a fraction of gross national product rose more than five-fold, increasing from an average of .7 percent over the period 1950–82 to an average of 3.7 percent from 1983–85.

This characterization of recent U.S. net capital inflows, private savings, private domestic investment, and government deficits appears to accurately reflect the facts of interest. Admittedly, the contention that private domestic investment actually has fallen recently could be challenged on a variety of grounds. It may be unwise to compare investment over a relatively short horizon (such as 1983–85) with investment over a relatively long horizon (such as 1950–82 or even decades such as 1961–70) given that investment is so cyclically sensitive. The fact that the United States has been moving from long-lived to short-lived capital and the fact that there have been changes in the price of consumption goods relative to investment goods can also make it difficult to compare investment to gross national product ratios from different points in time. However, these considerations are unlikely to be so important that they could overturn what should be the main message from the analysis of capital inflow, investments, and deficits. Large capital inflows into the United States are not merely replacing diminished private savings in order to maintain the existing level of private domestic investment and government deficits. Nor are they supplementing an unchanging amount of private savings in order to allow increased private domestic investment. Rather, large capital inflows are occurring at a time when the United States has chosen to run historically large government budget deficits.

What important consequences are likely to occur if the current level and direction of capital flows continue? The chapter outlines three. First, these flows could have worrisome implications for the ability of the United States to achieve a rising standard of living. This point is best understood when it is kept in mind that continual capital inflows will eventually turn any nation into a net debtor. As a net debtor, the profile of future consumption and investment must be reduced for a given profile of future production in order to service the debt. Viewed in this way, it is easy to see why it is important to characterize what has been happening with U.S. private domestic investment. If investment has been rising, increased future U.S. production could be available to finance increased debt service obligations and there might not be any reduction of future consumption.

Should changes in the future standard of living be of major concern to the United States today? Obviously it depends on how long the capital flows continue and on their magnitude. According to the figures in table 4–5, the United States has gone from a net creditor of $147 billion dollars in 1982 to a net creditor of $28 billion in 1984. Has this made a noticeable change in the U.S. standard of living? Probably not. Despite the large change in the stock of assets, data in the 1984 *Economic Report of the President* indicate that U.S. net investment income has gone from about $28 billion in 1982 to $20 billion in 1984, representing a change from 1.0 percent of net national product to 0.6 percent. I think this type of comparison, between the flow variables net investment income and net national product, is more relevant for analyzing welfare than the comparison between the flow variable total exports (or gross national product) and the stock variable net U.S. asset position, which is the one highlighted in the preceding chapter. Thus, I agree wholeheartedly with the proposition that continued capital inflows into the United States will, given the lack of a noticeable increase in net private domestic investment, diminish the future standard of living, but I disagree with the idea that this reduction will be of major importance in the near future. The remarkably large capital flows experienced recently have had a fairly small impact on resources at the nation's disposal.

The second implication of continued capital inflows that Friedman discusses is their impact on U.S. economic policy. The issue of primary concern here is whether, when the United States becomes a net debtor, it will need to carry out policies that will instill confidence in foreign lenders, presumably to ensure that the real return the nation must pay on its net debt is not too high.

The chapter points out several factors that play a role in determining the importance of this concern. For instance, there has been an increasing trend of foreign private citizens replacing foreign governments as the source of financing for U.S. trade imbalances. This trend presumably raises the probability of an increase in returns being necessary to induce the rest of the world to maintain their net creditor position, *if* assets in the United States become less attractive, because private investors' portfolio decisions are probably less dependent on political factors and more dependent on economic factors than the portfolio decisions of foreign official investors. However, the interaction between U.S. economic policy and the future attractiveness of U.S. assets is not investigated in much detail here so that it is unclear exactly which policies the United States might want to but cannot implement due to concerns over how the policies would alter the attractiveness of U.S. assets to foreign investors.

I think two aspects of the recent capital flows deserve more attention than is given in the chapter. The first is that the increased capital inflow has in large part gone through the private banking sector. Over 40 percent of the net capital inflow during 1983 and 1984 was bank reported, according to figures in the May 1985 *Federal Reserve Bulletin*. Most of this was net own claims as opposed to net custody claims (that is, it was reported by the banks as being for their own accounts as opposed to their custody accounts). In contrast, capital inflows associated with foreign net purchases of U.S. treasury obligations, the second largest category, comprised less than 30 percent of the capital inflow during this period. Thus, although the results presented in table 4–7 indicate that foreign lending to the United States through purchases of U.S. government securities has historically been the most important, this trend is changing. To the extent that U.S. policy is guided by an attempt to instill foreign investors' confidence, it is confidence in the U.S. banking system that appears to be of increasing concern.

The second aspect of recent capital inflows that I think deserves more attention is the interaction between the maturity structure of the debt being incurred and the incentives to return to a higher level of inflation. As noted in this **Comment** and in the preceding chapter, most U.S. liabilities are nominal (as opposed to real) and, in addition, are U.S.-dollar–denominated. This raises the possibility that one interaction between the capital flows and U.S. economic policy is to provide an incentive to create unexpected inflation and thereby diminish the real value of U.S. indebtedness. The extent to which this incentive exists depends in large part on the maturity structure of the national debt, with a relatively short maturity debt creating less of an incentive to unexpectedly raise the inflation rate. Based on the data provided in table 4–7, the ratio of short-term debt to long-term debt is 5-to-6, creating the impression that the United States could benefit from its relatively unique position of being able to borrow in a currency whose value it directly controls. The figures of table 4–7 probably overstate the incentive to create unexpected inflation since, according to note 11, they omit $1.7 trillion of small time and savings deposits and a large fraction of this total is presumably short-term time deposits whose market rates of interest quickly react to changes in inflation. Nonetheless, the incentive to inflate away foreign debt might well be one of the more important consequences of continued capital inflows for U.S. economic policy.

The final implication of continued capital flows to be considered in the chapter is also related to the maturity structure of U.S. liabilities. It is claimed that foreign investors have a preference for short-term assets over long-term assets, relative to domestic investors, and that this may necessitate a premium being paid on long-term assets in order to maintain capital market equilibrium. I do not think that historical evidence would support much concern over this possibility. The most relevant evidence in this regard probably comes from Operation Twist in the late 1960s, when a change in excess demand for longer-maturity assets was presumably brought about by the Fed conducting open market purchases of longer-term government securities instead of treasury bills. The policy had little if any effect on the term structure of interest rates or on the premium associated with long- versus short-maturity assets.

The final section of the chapter addresses the question, if capital inflows do not continue, how will net private savings, net private domestic investment, and the government budget deficit be affected? The important point is made that since there are a variety of changes that could lead to the elimination of the capital inflows, the question cannot be answered without first specifying what causes the capital flows to cease. Three possibilities are considered: changes in full-employment government expenditure, changes in full-employment tax receipts, and changes in monetary growth relative to trend. The empirical results presented are based on reduced-form regressions using quarterly data, estimated over the period 1970–84.

It is estimated that capital inflows can be curtailed by increased money growth, decreased government expenditures, or increased tax collections. Increased money growth impacts on the other accounts in a way consistent with the predictions of textbook macro models: lowering government deficits (presumably through increased output and endogenous tax collections), raising private savings (again, presumably through increased output), and raising domestic investment (presumably through either increased output or lower interest rates). The estimated impacts and the predictions of textbook macro models also are in agreement for decreased government expenditures: lower government deficits, higher domestic investment, and lower private savings. Only increased tax collections are estimated to have effects qualitatively different from those predicted by a textbook macro model: lower government deficits but, in contrast to predictions, lower domestic investment and higher savings. Quantitatively, the most surprising results are the lack of any noticeable effects of government expenditure and tax receipts on private savings.

When describing these results, the chapter acknowledges that the endogeneity of the policy variables may limit one's ability to interpret the regressions as telling about the outcomes of exogenous policy changes. I share this concern, and would add another. Even if the policies considered here could be treated as exogenous, can one really think of the reduced forms estimated here as being stable over time? I would expect that the reduced-form equations could show a fair amount of instability given that the time period of 1970–84 saw the end of the Bretton Woods era of fixed exchange rates, the dramatic changes of monetary operating procedure in 1979 and 1982, and the oil embargo of 1973–74. Furthermore, even if the reduced-form equations have been stable up until now, do people have any reason to expect that they will continue to be unchanged? The well-known Lucas critique warns that predictions based on a reduced-form equation estimated while one policy regime is in place can be very misleading about how the economy will operate when another policy regime becomes operative. If the policies used to stop the capital inflows are inherently different from the ones observed to date, predicting how savings, investment, and government deficits will be affected is not possible based solely on reduced-form estimates.

Part III
Policy Responses to
Increased Openness

5

International Interdependence and the Constraints on Macroeconomic Policies

Jacob A. Frenkel

his chapter examines within a theoretical framework some of the constraints that the openness of the economy impose upon policy making.[1] The open economy is linked to the rest of the world primarily through three key linkages: through international trade in goods and services, through international mobility of capital, and through international exchanges of national monies. Macroeconomic policies for open economies differ, in fundamentally important ways, from the corresponding policies for closed economies. The openness of the economy imposes constraints on the effectiveness and proper conduct of macroeconomic policies but it also provides policymakers with information that may be usefully exploited in the design of policy.

In order to set the stage for the analysis and in order to illustrate how the degree of integration in world capital markets impacts on the proper policy mix, my next section analyzes the famous "policy assignment problem." The main message of this analysis—which is carried out within the analytical framework of the Mundell-Fleming model of the 1960s vintage—is that from some points of view an increased degree of capital market integration may simplify rather than complicate the solution to the policy assignment problem.

On the other hand the analysis also demonstrates the severe constraint that a pegged exchange rate system imposes on the conduct of monetary policy. This constraint is illustrated further under **Aspects of the Monetary Approach to the Balance of Payments.** That framework also serves to illustrate the more fundamental restrictions on the conduct of fiscal and monetary policy—restrictions that stem from the interdependence among the various policy instruments.

The research reported here is part of the National Bureau of Economic Research's program in International Studies and Economic Fluctuations. Any opinions expressed are those of the author and not necessarily those of the National Bureau of Economic Research.

The analysis is extended in the subsequent section in order to examine the implications of capital mobility and portfolio balance. The purpose of that analysis is twofold. First, it illustrates the channels through which monetary and fiscal policies operate, as well as the constraints that the international mobility of capital impose on the effectiveness of monetary and fiscal policies. Second, it provides for a useful framework for the comparison between the mechanisms and the speed of adjustment of the economic system under fixed and flexible exchange rate regimes. The section concludes with a more general discussion of the interaction between exchange rate regimes and the constraints on the conduct and effectiveness of macroeconomic policies.

The topic of exchange market intervention is discussed in the next section, where it is argued that the evidence on the relative ineffectiveness of sterilized intervention implies that the open economy constraints on the conduct of monetary policy are unlikely to be alleviated through sterilization policies. The chapter concludes with a discussion of some policy implications.

At the outset it is relevant to note that recent developments in the theory of macroeconomic policy have established conditions for the effectiveness of policies in influencing output and employment which emphasize the distinction between anticipated and unanticipated policy actions, the importance of incomplete information, and the consequences of contracts that fix nominal wages and prices over finite intervals. This chapter, which focuses on the international constraints on macroeconomic policies, does not analyze how these conditions are modified in an open economy. Rather, since the main concern of this chapter is with macroeconomic policy, a principal objective of which is to influence output and employment, it will be assumed that requisite conditions for such influence are satisfied.

The Constraints on Macroeconomic Policies: The Assignment Problem

The basic theory of macroeconomic policy for the open economy has been advanced by the contributions of James E. Meade and Robert A. Mundell. The key characteristic of these contributions is the perception that considerations concerning the openness of the economy and the implications of the openness to the conduct of policies are fundamental and belong to the center stage of the analysis. This notion is in sharp contrast with the conventional view (which was particularly popular in the United States) that the foreign trade sector is an appendix to the economy which could otherwise be analyzed as if it were closed. More recent developments associated with the implications of the monetary approach to the balance of payments—and more generally with the role played by "rational expectations," which tend to nullify the intended effects of policies—have led to doubts about the efficacy (and wisdom) of stabilization policies and have resulted in "policy pessimism."

This section surveys some of the elementary issues relevant for the analysis of policies. Special emphasis is given to the nature of the constraints that the openness of the economy imposes on policymaking. A convenient starting point is Mundell's analysis of the proper assignment of fiscal and monetary policies to the attainment of internal and external balance.

The Assignment Problem: Mundell's Solution (1962)

Mundell's analysis of the assignment problem serves as a convenient starting point since it was developed against a similar background of policy pessimism. The relevant question at the time was: How can a small open economy that gives up the use of its exchange rate as a policy instrument (by deciding to peg the rate) and that gives up the use of tariffs, quota, and other measures of commercial policy (by abiding by the rules of GAAT), attain simultaneously internal balance and external balance with the use of fiscal and monetary policy? In providing the answer to this question Mundell first recognized that an application of Jan Tinbergen's (1952) policy principle, which states that to attain two independent targets there must be at least two policy instruments, implies that with the aid of two policy instruments (fiscal and monetary policies) *there is* a way to attain simultaneously internal and external balance. He then extended Tinbergen's principle by developing the effective market classification principle which guides the policymaker (according to the stability criterion) in pairing the two instruments with the objectives on which they have the most influence. To illustrate Mundell's framework, consider the following fully employed small open economy.

Let government spending be G and let private aggregate demand be $E(y,r)$ where y denotes income and r denotes the rate of interest. Assume that aggregate demand depends negatively on the rate of interest. Both the private sector and the government divide their spending between imported goods and domestically produced goods. For simplicity of exposition suppose that both the private sector and the government spend a fraction m on imports and $(1 - m)$ on domestically produced goods. Internal balance is attained when aggregate demand for domestic goods equals aggregate supply as in equation 5.1:

$$(1 - m)[E(\bar{y}, r) + G] + \bar{x} = \bar{y} \qquad (5.1)$$

where $\bar{y}$ denotes full employment income and where $\bar{x}$ denotes the (exogenously given) level of exports representing foreign demand for domestic output.

External balance is specified as balance of payments equilibrium in which the sum of the surpluses in the current account and the capital account is zero so that there is no need for international reserve flow. Thus, external balance is attained when

$$\bar{x} - IM + z(r) = 0 \tag{5.2}$$

where IM denotes imports and where $z(r)$ denotes the surplus in the capital account which is assumed to depend positively on the rate of interest. Recalling that imports are a fraction m of the sum of private and government spending, one can write the condition for external balance as

$$\bar{x} - m[E(\bar{y}, r) + G] + z(r) = 0 \tag{5.3}$$

If monetary policy is defined in terms of changes in the rate of interest and fiscal policy in terms of the rate of government spending, it is clear that in general equations 5.1 and 5.3 can be solved with the appropriate choice of the policy instruments r and G. This is the implication of Tinbergen's principle.

The effective market classification principle can be demonstrated using Mundell's diagram. In figure 5–1 the locus XX describes combinations of monetary and fiscal policy which maintain internal balance. Using equation 5.1 the slope of that locus is:

$$\left. \frac{dr}{dG} \right|_{XX} = \frac{1}{-E_r} > 0 \tag{5.4}$$

where E_r denotes the partial derivative of private aggregate demand with respect to the rate of interest. In the same figure, the locus FF describes combinations of monetary and fiscal policies that ensure external balance. Using equation 5.3, the slope of that locus is:

$$\left. \frac{dr}{dG} \right|_{FF} = \frac{1}{-E_r + z_r/m} > 0 \tag{5.5}$$

A comparison of the slopes of the XX and FF schedules indicates that as long as $z_r > 0$ (that is, as long as there is some degree of international capital mobility), the XX schedule is steeper than the FF schedule. The explanation is obvious. A rise in government spending creates an excess demand in the market for goods and induces a deterioration in the balance of trade. The rise in aggregate demand and the deterioration in the balance of trade can be offset by a rise in the rate of interest. The latter, however, also induces an improvement in the capital account of the balance of payments. The relative

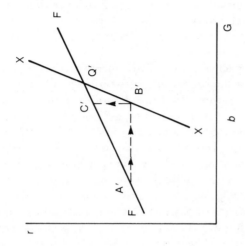

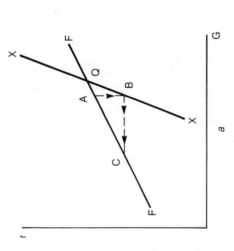

The *XX* and the *FF* schedules denote internal and external balance, respectively. In panel *a* monetary policy is allocated to the attainment of internal balance and fiscal policy to the attainment of external balance. In panel *b* monetary policy is allocated to the attainment of external balance and fiscal policy to the attainment of internal balance.

Figure 5–1. Mundell's Analysis of the Assignment Problem

slopes of the two schedules reflect the fact that changes in the rate of interest have a relatively stronger effect on the external balance than on the internal balance. This differential effect arises because the rate of interest affects the capital account in addition to its effect on the balance of trade through the induced changes in aggregate demand.

The differential impact of the two instruments on the two targets has important implications for the proper allocation of responsibilities between the monetary and the fiscal authorities. Consider for example points A and A' in panels *a* and *b* in figure 5–1. These points correspond to a position of external balance that is combined with an excess supply of domestic output. Internal balance could be restored by an expansionary monetary policy which lowers r as in panel *a*, or alternatively by an expansionary fiscal policy which raises G as in panel *b*. These policies yield equilibrium at points B and B' respectively, which correspond to a position of internal balance combined with a deficit in the balance of payments. The deficit can be eliminated by a fiscal contraction which lowers G as in panel *a* or by a monetary contraction which raises r as in panel *b*. The external balance is restored at points C and C'. As is evident, the path that is followed in panel *a* leads away from the global equilibrium at point Q while the path that is followed in panel *b* leads progressively toward the global equilibrium, Q'. The key difference between the two panels is in the allocation of instruments to targets. In panel *a* the responsibility for external balance was given to the fiscal authority while the responsibility for internal balance was given to the monetary authority. In contrast, panel *b* corresponds to the opposite allocation where fiscal policy deals with internal balance while monetary policy with external balance. The allocation of instruments according to the effective market classification principle ensures that path *b* will be followed and yields Mundell's famous propositions that monetary policy ought to be aimed at external balance and fiscal policy at internal balance. *This principle imposes a severe constraint on the conduct of policy.* A failure to follow this prescription may yield a progressively worsening situation.

Further Developments of the Assignment Problem:
The Role of Capital Mobility

The analysis in the preceding section introduced both the concept of the assignment problem and the notion of Tinbergen's principle about the relationship between the number of targets and the number of independent policy instruments. It also introduced Mundell's principle of the effective market classification. The specific model, however, is subject to a major limitation in that it defines monetary policy in terms of the changes in the rate of interest rather than in terms of open market operations. The difference between the two definitions of monetary policy is fundamental since when capital is highly mobile, the monetary authorities may not be able to alter the rate of interest or even to alter the supply of money. In this section I modify the analysis of the assignment problem.[2] The modification defines monetary policy in terms of open market operations which alter the domestic source component of the monetary base. The analytical framework is that of the standard pegged exchange rates variable output open economy version of the *IS-LM* model as developed by Mundell (1961, 1963) and Fleming (1962), extended by McKinnon and Oates (1966), elaborated further by Swoboda (1972), and surveyed by Mussa (1979).

Equilibrium in the market for domestic output is described by equation 5.6, where G denotes government spending on domestic goods and where, for simplicity, imports depend only on income.

$$E(y, r) + \bar{x} - IM(y) + G = y. \tag{5.6}$$

Money market equilibrium is described by equation 5.7 where $L(y, r)$ denotes the demand for money and $D + R$ the supply of money; D denotes the domestic source component of the monetary base and R denotes international reserves. The exchange rate is normalized to be unity and the money multiplier is assumed to be unity.

$$L(y, r) - (D + R) = 0 \tag{5.7}$$

Finally, external balance is attained when the balance of payments is balanced as in equation 5.8:

$$\bar{x} - IM(y) + z(r) = 0 \tag{5.8}$$

From equations 5.6 and 5.7 the impact effects of fiscal and monetary policies on income and the rate of interest can be expressed as

$$dy = -\frac{L_r}{\Delta} dG - \frac{E_r}{\Delta} dD \tag{5.9}$$

$$dr = \frac{L_y}{\Delta} dG - \frac{s + m}{\Delta} dD \tag{5.10}$$

where $\Delta = -(s + m)L_r - E_r L_y > 0$, s and m denote the marginal propensities to save and import respectively, L_r denotes the negative effect of a change in the rate of interest on the demand for money, and L_y denotes the inverse of the velocity of circulation.

In general these changes in income and the rate of interest will not persist for the long run since as long as the balance of payments is imbalanced, the money supply is being changed, and, as a result, income and the rate of interest are altered. From equation 5.8, the change in reserves (the balance of payments) can be expressed as

$$\frac{dR}{dt} = -mdy + z_r dr \tag{5.11}$$

where dR/dt denotes the change in reserves per unit of time. Using equations 5.9 and 5.10 in 5.11, the equilibrium change in reserves can be written as

$$\frac{dR}{dt} = \frac{mL_r + z_r L_y}{\Delta} dG + \frac{mE_r - z_r(s+m)}{\Delta} dD. \tag{5.12}$$

Equation 5.12 with $(dR/dt) = 0$, expresses the combinations of fiscal and monetary changes that are necessary for the maintenance of external balance.

The internal balance condition is defined in terms of the attainment of a given level of income so that $dy = 0$. From equation 5.9, the slope of the internal balance schedule XX in figure 5–2 is

$$\left.\frac{dD}{dG}\right|_{XX} = \frac{-L_r}{E_r} < 0. \tag{5.13}$$

This slope indicates that in order to maintain a given level of income, an expansionary monetary policy must be accompanied by a contractionary fiscal policy. All points to the right of the XX schedule correspond to an excess demand for output while points to the left correspond to excess supply.

From equation 5.12 (with $dR/dt = 0$) the slope of the external balance schedule FF is

$$\left.\frac{dD}{dG}\right|_{FF} = \frac{mL_r + z_r L_y}{(s+m)z_r - mE_r} \gtrless 0. \tag{5.14}$$

All points above the FF schedule correspond to a deficit in the balance of payments and all points below the schedule correspond to a surplus. As may be seen, the slope of the external balance schedule depends on the degree of capital mobility. If the degree of capital mobility is relatively low, $mL_r + z_r L_y < 0$ and the schedule is negatively sloped. Conversely, when the degree of capital mobility is relatively high, $mL_r + z_r L_y > 0$ and the schedule is positively sloped. The economic interpretation is straightforward. A rise in government spending raises income and the rate of interest. The rise in income induces a deterioration in the balance of trade while the rise in the rate

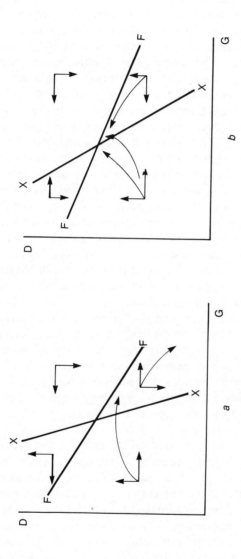

The *XX* and the *FF* schedules denote internal and external balance, respectively. In panel *a* monetary policy is allocated to the attainment of internal balance and fiscal policy to the attainment of external balance. In panel *b* monetary policy is allocated to the attainment of external balance and fiscal policy to the attainment of internal balance.

Figure 5–2. The Assignment Problem with Low Capital Mobility

of interest induces an improvement in the capital account. If capital is highly mobile, the improvement in the capital account will exceed the deterioration in the balance of trade; the balance of payments will be in surplus which could be corrected by an expansionary credit policy. In contrast, if the degree of capital mobility is relatively low, the deficit in the balance of trade will exceed the surplus in the capital account, and the overall balance of payments will be in deficit which could be corrected by a contractionary credit policy.

The following analysis shows that the solution to the assignment problem depends in a fundamental way on the degree of capital mobility. Consider first the case where capital is relatively immobile. In that case the external balance schedule is negatively sloped and, as can be seen by a comparison of equations, 5.13 and 5.14, the external balance schedule is flatter than the internal balance schedule. Figure 5–2 describes the implications of two alternative assignments of fiscal and monetary policies. As may be seen, the implications of Mundell's analysis remain intact. When fiscal policy is assigned to attaining external balance and monetary policy is assigned to attaining internal balance as in panel *a*, the system becomes unstable as the situation gets progressively worse. In contrast, under the opposite assignment, as in panel *b*, the system is stable and the point of global equilibrium is reached.

Consider next the case in which capital is highly mobile. In that case the *FF* schedule is positively sloped and the implications of the two alternative assignments of fiscal and monetary policies are described in figure 5–3. A comparison of panels *a* and *b* of figure 5–3 shows that in contrast with the previous analysis, both solutions to the assignment problem lead to a *stable* system. It is in this context that one may argue that a liberalization of capital flows and a removal of controls may contribute to greater flexibility in the use of fiscal and monetary policies for the small open economy. The reason is that when capital is highly mobile, these policies do not need to be rigidly tight for the attainment of specific targets, as in the case in which the degree of capital mobility is not too high.

The key difference between the two solutions lies in the dynamics. As is seen, in panel *a* of figure 5–3, the direction of the path to global equilibrium is clockwise while the direction of the path in panel *b* is counterclockwise. The difference between the two paths may be significant once one considers the delays and the costs that are associated with changes in the course of macroeconomic policies. For example, it is reasonable to assume that it is relatively easy to agree on the proper policies when the attainment of both targets require expansionary or contractionary actions. The problem arises in the case of a conflict. When the attainment of one target calls for an expansionary policy while the attainment of another target calls for a contractionary policy, the choice between panels *a* and *b* may be significant. As is evident from panel *a* following the phase during which fiscal and monetary policies move in the same direction (an expansion or a contraction), there is

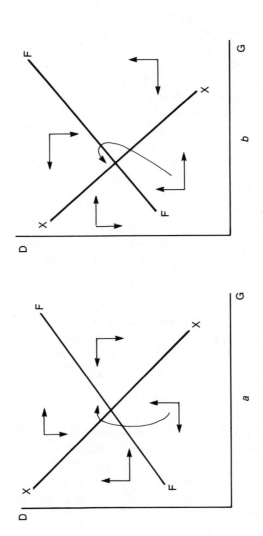

The *XX* and *FF* schedules denote internal and external balance, respectively. In panel *a* monetary policy is allocated to the attainment of internal balance and fiscal policy to the attainment of external balance. In panel *b* monetary policy is allocated to the attainment of external balance and fiscal policy to the attainment of internal balance.

Figure 5–3. The Assignment Problem with High Capital Mobility

always a phase during which fiscal policy continues in its course while monetary policy changes direction. In contrast in panel *b* fiscal policy is always the instrument which changes direction following the phase in which both instruments operated in the same (expansionary or contractionary) direction. To the extent that in circumstances of conflict between policies, it is easier to alter the monetary instrument than it is to alter the fiscal instrument (which might require legislation), the path in panel *a* might be superior to the path in panel *b,* and the proper allocation of instruments to targets would not be the conventional one. In that case fiscal policy would be assigned to the external target while monetary policy would be assigned to the internal target. *Nevertheless, and in contrast with the standard analysis, if capital is highly mobile this alternative assignment would still yield a stable path. Hence, under such circumstances the open economy constraint on the policy mix may not be as severe.*

The analysis in this section examined the implications of the open economy *IS-LM* model for the solution to the assignment problem. Before leaving this model it is worth pointing out some of its key features. First, and most important, the specification of the model recognizes that under a pegged exchange rate system the money supply is endogenous. This simple proposition follows from Tinbergen's principle concerning the necessary relationship between the number of instruments and targets. Once the monetary authority commits the money supply process to the maintenance of a specific target exchange rate, it cannot use this instrument to achieve other targets. Under these circumstances the money· supply instrument has to be set at that level which is consistent with the maintenance of the given exchange rate. Further, the model incorporates explicitly considerations of money market equilibrium. This brings to the forefront the notion that under a pegged exchange rate system, the nominal quantity of money is determined by the private sector's demand and, therefore, open market operations may not succeed in altering the nominal quantity of money. The effects of such policies may only be reflected in changes in the asset *composition* of the central bank. For example, an open market purchase which raises D (the domestic source component of the monetary base) results in a reduction in R (international reserves) without inducing a change in the money supply. *This dependence of the balance of payments (the change in international reserves) on the relationship between the demand for money and the rate of credit expansion is one of the major constraints that a pegged exchange rate system imposes on the conduct of macroeconomic policy.* This constraint is among the key characteristics of the monetary approach to the balance of payments. The· next section uses some elements in order to illustrate additional constraints on the conduct of macroeconomic policies in the open economy.

Aspects of the Monetary Approach to the Balance of Payments: The Constraints and Interdependencies of Policies

The monetary approach to the balance of payments states that the balance of payments is essentially (though not exclusively) a monetary phenomenon. Since in recent years there have been numerous expositions of the monetary approach (see for example the expositions in Johnson, 1958, Dornbusch, 1980, and Frenkel and Mussa, 1985), I will only sketch here some of its policy implications.

Consider the following simple monetary model. Let the demand for money L be proportional to income as in equation 5.15:

$$L = kY \tag{5.15}$$

and, as before, let the supply of money M be

$$M = R + D \tag{5.16}$$

Money market equilibrium requires equality between the demand the supply of money as in eqaution 5.17:

$$kY = R + D \tag{5.17}$$

By differentiating equation 5.17 with respect to time, one can express the rate of change of international reserves (the balance of payments) as

$$\frac{dR}{dt} = k\lambda Y - \frac{dD}{dt} \tag{5.18}$$

where λ denotes the percent rate of growth of income, $k\lambda y$ denotes the flow demand for money, and dD/dt denotes the rate of credit expansion. Equation 5.18 states that in the absence of credit expansion, the flow demand for money is satisfied by an equal accumulation of international reserves which is brought about through a surplus in the balance of payments. Furthermore, for a given flow demand for money, any attempt to increase the supply by credit expansion will be offset by a corresponding decline in international reserves. This reiterates the fundamental fact that *the necessary consequence of pegging the exchange rate is a loss of control over the supply of money.*

This analysis has emphasized the intimate relationship between the demand for money, monetary policy, and the balance of payments. What are the effects of other macroeconomic policies? In order to examine these issues, one extends the analytical framework so as to incorporate government spending, taxes, and the budget. Assume that government spending G is a constant fraction g of national income

$$G = gy \tag{5.19}$$

and assume that the proportional income tax rate is τ. Assume further that international reserves are held in interest earning assets which yield a rate of return of r percent per unit of time. It follows that the government budget constraint is

$$G = \tau Y + rR + dD/dt \tag{5.20}$$

which states that government spending, G, can be financed by taxes, τy, by the return on reserve holdings, rR, and by credit expansion, dD/dt. Substituting equation 5.19 and 5.20 into 5.18 yields

$$\frac{dR}{dt} = [k\lambda - (g - \tau)] Y + rR \tag{5.21}$$

Equation 5.21 indicates that a rise in government spending worsens the balance of payments while a rise in the growth of income, in the tax rate, and in the return on reserve holdings improves the balance of payments. Further, *ceteris paribus* a balanced-budget rise in government spending (so that $dg = d\tau$) will not affect the balance of payments. This analysis demonstrates the intimate relationship between the budget deficit, the rate of credit expansion, and the balance of payments, which are interconnected by the budget constraints of the government and of the private sector. *These constraints imply that in a fundamental sense not all policy instruments are independent* and, therefore, it may not always be appropriate to treat monetary and fiscal policies as two independent instruments of policy.

It should be emphasized that these interrelationships are *not* specific to the monetary approach to the balance of payments. Rather, they are a reflection of the fundamental identities of national income accounting according to which national product must equal the sum of private aggregate demand E (absorption), government spending G, and net foreign demand—the surplus in the balance of trade $(X - IM)$.

$$y = E + G + (X - IM). \tag{5.22}$$

By subtracting total taxes (denoted by T) from both sides of 5.22 and rearranging, we obtain

$$(X - IM) = [(y - T) - E] + (T - G) \qquad (5.23)$$

which expresses the surplus in the current account (which equals the balance of payments in the absence of capital movements) as the sum of private savings (the excess of disposable income over spending) and public savings (the budget surplus). The same idea is expressed in equation 5.21, in which private savings is the flow demand for money $k\lambda Y$, while the budget surplus is $rR + (\tau - g)Y$.

From the policy perspective, equation 5.23 emphasizes that what matters for determining the current account of the balance of payments is the total level spending rather than the composition of spending between domestic and foreign goods. It follows that for a given level of income, the only effective balance of payments policies are those which are either expenditure-reducing or expenditure-increasing policies. Under these circumstances expenditure-switching policies which alter the composition of spending between imports and domestically produced goods will not be effective. Since this policy implication is derived directly from the identities of national income accounting, they are not specific to the monetary approach and should characterize any model with similar features.

The emphasis on the relationship between total income and total expenditures is the key insight of Alexander's (1952) absorption approach to the balance of payments. As a policy matter, however, there may be room for expenditure switching policies once the existing structure of relative prices in the economy does not correspond to the equilibrium price structure. To illustrate the point and to introduce the notion of relative prices, it is necessary to disaggregate total output as in Dornbusch (1974). Consider an economy that produces traded and nontraded goods, and denote the relative price of nontraded goods by p_N. The value of output (using traded goods as a numeraire) is

$$y = y_T + p_N y_N \qquad (5.24)$$

where y_T and y_N denote the rates of production of traded and nontraded goods respectively. The value of private spending is

$$E = E_T + p_N E_N \qquad (5.25)$$

where E_T and E_N denote private spending on traded and nontraded goods, respectively. Government spending G is also allocated between the two goods so that

$$G = G_T + p_N G_N \qquad (5.26)$$

where G_T and G_N denote government spending on traded and nontraded goods, respectively. Subtracting equation 5.25 from 5.24 yields

$$y - E = (y_T - E_T) + p_N(y_N - E_N) \qquad (5.27)$$

To introduce the effects of government spending, subtract total taxes T from both sides of 5.27 and add and subtract government spending to the right-hand side using equation 5.26. After rearranging this yields

$$(X - IM) = [(y - T) - E] + (T - G) + p_N[(E_N + G_N) - y_N] \qquad (5.28)$$

where the balance of trade $(X - IM)$ was substituted for the excess supply of traded goods $y_T - (E_T + G_T)$.

It is clear from equation 5.28 that the balance of trade (or the balance of payments in the absence of capital movements) can be described and analyzed in terms of three basic magnitudes: (1) the excess of private disposable income over expenditures, (2) the excess of public income over expenditures (the budget surplus), and (3) the excess demand for nontraded goods. The first two components have been discussed and introduced in equation 5.23. The third component reflects a "disequilibrium" relative price structure that prevents market clearing for nontraded goods. The first two components reflect the traditonal factors emphasized by the absorption approach. They relate to *aggregate* private and government spending which could only be influenced by expenditure-increasing or by expenditure-reducing policies. On the other hand the third component could be influenced by expenditure-switching policies that alter the relative price structure. This formulation highlights the fundamental constraint on open economy macroeconomic policy. *These constraints are "model free." They stem from the fundamental identities of national income accounting* that link the trade balance to the government budget, to the discrepancies between aggregate spending and disposable income and between demand and supply of home goods.

The foregoing analysis of the constraints on the conduct of macroeconomic policy in the open economy focused on the general implications of the "assignment problem" and of the national income accounting identities as reflected by the propositions of the "absorption" and "monetary" approaches to the balance of payments. The next section examines in greater detail some of the constraints that are imposed by the integration of international capital markets.

Capital Mobility and the Constraints on Macroeconomic Policies under Fixed Exchange Rate Regimes

As indicated in my opening paragraphs, one of the central linkages between national economies operates through the international mobility of capital which links interest rates on financial assets. In addition, by permitting countries to finance current account imbalances, this mobility provides for a channel through which macroeconomic disturbances are transmitted internationally. What are the constraints that such mobility of capital imposes on the conduct of policy?

International Capital Mobility and Domestic Stabilization

International capital mobility imposes a severe constraint on the use of monetary policy for domestic stabilization purposes. Under a fixed exchange rate, an increase in the domestic credit component of the money supply in a small open economy may temporarily reduce interest rates on domestic securities, but it will induce a capital outflow and a corresponding loss of foreign exchange reserves that will rapidly reduce the money supply back to its previous equilibrium level. Monetary expansion by a large country, which affects conditions in world financial markets, can be somewhat more effective in influencing domestic prices, output, and employment. However, even a large country will suffer a loss of foreign exchange reserves that is inversely related to its size in the world economy. Sterilization operations of a central bank may temporarily insulate the domestic money supply from changes in foreign exchange reserves, but, in the long run, sterilization cannot sustain a money supply that differs from the equilibrium level of money demand. Under a flexible exchange rate, a government regains long-run control over the nominal money supply. However, international capital mobility still limits the effectiveness of monetary policy. Any increase in aggregate demand induced by lower domestic interest rates is partially dissipated in increased expenditures on imported goods, financed by international capital flows. Moreover, exchange rate adjustments that occur rapidly in response to perceived changes in monetary policy are likely to lead to rapid adjustments of domestic prices and wage rates, thereby limiting the effect of monetary policy on output and employment.[3]

The implication of capital mobility on the efficiency of policies is illustrated in figure 5–4, which highlights the role of portfolio balance and describes the effects of open market operations under alternative exchange rate regimes.[4] Consider a portfolio composed of real cash balances M/P (where P denotes the price level) and common stocks K. Let the price of a security in terms of goods be p_k. It is assumed that the economy is small and fully integrated in world capital markets. As a result, since the foreign rate of interest is assumed to be given, the relative price of securities in terms of goods, p_k, is also assumed to be fixed for the small open economy. The price level P for the small open economy is assumed to equal SP^* where S denotes the exchange rate and P^* denotes the given foreign price. Thus, under fixed exchange rates the price level is given. The value of wealth W is thus

$$W = \frac{M}{SP^*} + p_k K \qquad (5.29)$$

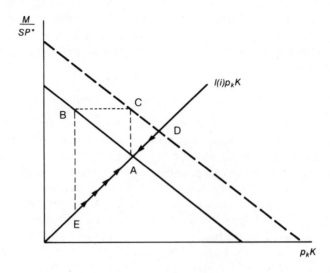

Figure 5–4. Portfolio Equilibrium and the Effects of Monetary Policy under Fixed and Flexible Exchange Rate Regimes

Suppose that the desired ratio of money to securities depends negatively on the rate of interest as in equation 5.30.

$$\frac{M}{SP^*} = l(i)p_kK. \tag{5.30}$$

Portfolio equilibrium is described by point A in figure 5–4. The negatively sloped schedule describes the wealth constraint and the positively sloped schedule describes the desired composition of assets given the rate of interest. An open market purchase moves the economy from point A to point B at which the money supply has risen and the holdings of securities by the private sector have fallen. Since at point B the composition of the portfolio has been disturbed and since asset holders have access to world asset markets at the given rate of interest, they will restore portfolio equilibrium instantaneously by exchanging the increased stock of cash for foreign securities and thereby returning to point A. Thus, *the facts that world capital markets are integrated and that open market operations are conducted in assets traded internationally at a given price, enable the private sector to nullify the actions of the monetary authority.* In fact, in this case open market operations amount to an exchange of foreign exchange reserves for securities between the monetary authorities and foreign asset holders, and the entire process of adjustment is effected through the capital account of the balance of payments. The leverage of monetary policy can be somewhat enhanced if it operates in financial assets that are isolated from world capital markets since, in the short run, the link between the rates of return on such assets and the world rates of interest is not as tight.

The same figure can be used for the analysis of a once-and-for-all rise in the quantity of money that is brought about through an unanticipated transfer of cash balances that moves the economy from point A to point C. The impact of this policy is to raise the value of assets and to raise the relative share of money in wealth. Portfolio composition equilibrium is restored by an immediate exchange of part of the increased monetary stock for equities as individuals move to point D. This exchange is effected through the capital account of the balance of payments. Since at D the value of assets exceeds the equilibrium value at A, individuals will wish to run down their holdings of both equities and real cash balances by increasing expenditures relative to income. This part of the process will be gradual. The transition toward long-run equilibrium follows along the path from D to A and is characterized by a deficit in the current account, a surplus in the capital account, and a deficit in the monetary account of the balance of payments.

Under flexible exchange rates, adjustments of real balances occur through changes in the exchange rate. Using the same diagram the effects of monetary policies are very different. An open market operation bringing the economy from point A to point B in figure 5–4 cannot be nullified through the capital account since under flexible exchange rates money ceases to be an internationally traded commodity. Portfolio equilibrium is restored by an immediate rise in the exchange rate (a depreciation of the currency), which moves individuals from point B to point E. As may be seen, the percent rise in the exchange rate exceeds the percent rise in the money stock; this is the overshooting phenomenon. Since at E the value of assets fall short of the long-run equilibrium value, individuals will wish to accumulate both equities and real balances by reducing expenditures relative to income. This part of the process will be gradual, while the transition from E to A is characterized by a surplus in the current account, a deficit in the capital account, and an appreciation of the currency.[5]

In contrast, when the rise in the quantity of money is brought about through a transfer moving the economy from point A to point C, the new equilibrium will be restored instantaneously through an equiproportionate depreciation of the currency, which restores equilibrium at A.

The previous analysis of open market operations assumed implicitly that the returns on government holdings of securities are rebated to the private sector (in a lump sum fashion) but that the private sector does not capitalize the expected future flow of transfers. As a result the open market operations did not change the wealth position of individuals who moved from point A to point B along the given wealth constraint. Under the alternative assumption that asset holders anticipate and capitalize the flow of transfers and treat them as any other marketable asset, they effectively conceive of the equities that are held by the government as their own. In that case the open market purchase only raises the supply of real cash balances and moves the economy from point A to point C. The effects of this policy are identical to the effects of the pure monetary expansion that is brought about through the governmental transfer.

The analysis of these two extreme cases implies that when international capital markets are highly integrated, *the effectiveness of the constraints on monetary policy under fixed and flexible exchange rate regimes depends on the degree to which the private sector capitalizes future streams of taxes and transfers as well as on the marketability of claims to such streams.*[6] When such claims are not fully perceived by individuals or by the capital market, the effects of open market operations are nullified rapidly under fixed exchange rates while the adjustment is gradual under flexible exchange rates. In contrast, when individuals and capital markets do fully perceive these claims, the adjustment to open market operations is only gradual when the exchange rate is fixed, while it is rapid when the exchange rate is flexible. These cases illustrate that the ranking of alternative exchange rate regimes according to the speed of adjustments to monetary policies and the division of the adjustment process between the current and capital accounts, are not unambiguous since they depend on the mechanism of monetary policy and on the public's perception of such policies.

Domestic Capital Mobility

A high degree of capital mobility also implies a low degree of effectiveness of fiscal policy. Under a flexible exchange rate, a fixed domestic money supply and a domestic interest rate fixed by conditions in world markets (and by exchange rate expectations that affect the forward discount or premium on foreign exchange) impose a strict constraint on the level of domestic income that is consistent with monetary equilibrium. Fiscal policy actions do not affect this constraint (except possibly by altering exchange rate expectations) and, hence, cannot affect the equilibrium level of domestic income. Under a fixed exchange rate, the money supply is not fixed because the capital inflow induced by an expansionary fiscal policy will increase the foreign exchange reserves of the monetary authority. The initial expansionary effect of any fiscal stimulus, however, is limited by the extent to which it falls on domestically produced goods that are not close substitutes for imports; and the subsequent multiplier effects of any fiscal stimulus are limited by the high marginal propensity to spend on internationally traded goods.

To achieve the maximum effect from fiscal and monetary policy in open economies, it follows that such policies should be directed toward goods and assets that are isolated from world trade, that is, toward goods and assets for which the home country is "large" relative to the size of the market. Changes in government expenditures on nontradable goods are likely to be more effective in influencing domestic output and employment than are changes in government expenditure on internationally traded goods. Similarly, open market operations involving financial assets that are not close substitutes for international financial assets are more likely to influence interest rates and thus other macroeconomic variables. This does not imply, however, that it is desirable to artificially restrict trade and capital movements in order to enhance the effectiveness of macroeconomic policy. Such restrictions have an important cost in terms of reducing the benefits that a country derives from integration of markets. Moreover, substitution possibilities among goods and among financial assets limit the effectiveness of restrictions on trade and capital movements.

International Exchange and Monetary Equilibrium Requirements

The international exchange of national monies and the requirement of monetary equilibrium also impose a severe limitation on the effectiveness of monetary policy. As stated before, under a fixed exchange rate regime the authorities lose control over the nominal money stock, while under a flexible rate regime the requirements of monetary equilibrium ensures that in the long run, changes in the nominal money stock lead to a proportionate change in all nominal prices and wages. Because of the rapid change in the exchange rate, *the constraint on monetary policy that is implied by the homogeneity postulate is likely to be manifested much more promptly in an open economy with flexible exchange rates than in a closed economy.*

An additional consideration constraining the conduct of macroeconomic policy follows from the dynamic linkage between current exchange rates and expectations of future exchange rates (see Mussa, 1976, 1984). This dynamic linkage implies that the effect of a given policy on the exchange rate, and thereby on other economic variables, depends on its effect on expectations concerning future policies. These expectations, in turn, are influenced by the past and by the current course of policy, and it is likely that the mere recognition of this dynamic linkage will influence the conduct of policy. *Being aware that the effectiveness of any particular policy measure depends on the way by which it influences the public's perception of the implications of the measure for the future conduct of policy may constrain the government in employing its policy instruments.* This mechanism, which is likely to be especially operative under a flexible exchange rate regime, imposes an additional constraint on the conduct of macroeconomic policy in the open economy.

The foregoing discussion focused on the implications of capital market linkages on the conduct of macroeconomic policy in an open economy. An additional linkage operates through international trade in goods and services. Such trade, which links the prices of goods produced and consumed in different national economies, has at least three implications for the conduct of policy. First, according to the principle of purchasing power parity, the price level in one country (in terms of domestic money) should equal the price level in a foreign country (in terms of foreign money) multiplied by the exchange rate between domestic money and foreign money. Because of transport costs, trade barriers, different weighting schemes for price indexes, and changes in relative prices of nontraded goods, this link is not rigid; but the evidence indicates that this principle holds fairly well over long periods (though it has weakened during the 1970s). The key implication of purchasing power parity is that *a country cannot chose its long-run inflation rate independently of its long-run monetary policy and the long-run behavior of its exchange rate.* A country, particularly a small country, that fixes the exchange rate between its domestic money and the money of some foreign country will experience a domestic inflation rate and a domestic rate of monetary expansion that are strongly influenced by the monetary policy of that foreign country. This is so even if changes in real economic conditions (which are largely independent of domestic monetary policy) induce divergences from strict purchasing power parity.

Second, the world monetary system and the conduct of national monetary policies must allow for changes in equilibrium relationships between national price levels induced by changes in relative prices of internationally traded goods and nontradable goods. To maintain a system of fixed exchange rates, changes in equilibrium relationships among national price levels must be accommodated by differentials among national inflation rates, supported by appropriate national economic policies. Under a system of controlled or managed floating, it is essential that countries either allow their inflation rates or the rates of change of exchange rates to accommodate equilibrium changes in relative national price levels. *A rule that rigidly links changes in the exchange rates to changes in domestic and foreign prices, in accord with relative purchasing power parity, is not consistent with this requirement.*

Third, macroeconomic policy can do little to offset changes in equilibrium levels of real income resulting from changes in relative prices of internationally traded goods. A case in point is the 1970s increase in the relative price of oil. Monetary policy can influence the extent to which the change in the relative price of oil affects general price levels and perhaps short-run levels of employment in oil-exporting and oil-importing countries. Tax and expenditure policies can affect the extent to which gains and losses of real income are translated into changes in real expenditure, or are financed by changes in foreign lending and borrowing. By influencing the level and distribution of real expenditure, fiscal policy can also affect the relative prices of non-tradable commodities and the distribution of the change in real national income among individuals within the economy. However, *neither monetary nor fiscal policy can alter to any appreciable extent the average change in the long-run level of real expenditure resulting from a change in the relative prices of internationally traded commodities that are beyond the control of national economic policies.*

In summary, the openness of the economy imposes constraints on the conduct of macroeconomic policy. These constraints may be reflected either in a reduced ability to influence the *instruments* of monetary policy (such as the nominal money supply under fixed exchange rates), in a reduced ability to influence the targets of monetary and fiscal policy (such as the levels of output and employment), or in an increased prudence in the use of policy because of the potentially undesirable effects on expectations. Similar considerations apply to both fiscal and monetary policies under fixed as well as flexible exchange rate regimes. In fact, the overall government budget constraint provides the link among monetary policy, budgetary policy, and other manifestations of macro policies; this interdependence makes the distinction among the various policy instruments less sharp.

This discussion suggests that while the exchange rate regime affects the nature of the constraints on policy, the constraints themselves stem from the openness of the economy. Furthermore, *the choice of the exchange rate regime does not alleviate the fundamental constraints even though it influences the manifestation of these constraints.* With this perspective one may rationalize the empirical findings that countries' behavior with respect to international reserve holdings has been more stable than what would have been predicted on the basis of the large changes in the legal arrangement.

Policymakers seem to have recognized that a move to a regime of clean float, which could have reduced the need for reserves, would have imposed significant costs associated with prompt translation of monetary changes into exchange rate changes as well as with large changes in real exchange rates. In view of these costs, policymakers have chosen to enjoy fully the "degree of freedom" that would have been granted to them by a move to clean float. Rather, the key finding reported in Frenkel (1983b) is that in spite of the large change in the legal framework associated with the breakdown of the Bretton Woods agreement and formalized by the various amendments to the Articles of Agreements of the International Monetary Fund, countries have continued to use international reserves and have continued to intervene in the markets for foreign exchange. As a matter of fact, an observer of the patterns of countries' holdings and usages of international reserves would be hard pressed to detect a drastic change in the patterns of holdings of international reserves corresponding to the drastic changes in the legal commitment concerning exhange market intervention. The change in economic behavior has been much less pronounced than expected on the basis of the theory concerning the benefits from the additional degree of freedom granted by the flexible exchange rate regime.

The constraints on the conduct of economic policy depend on the exchange rate regime. Therefore, the question of the country's *choice* of the optimal set of constraints on its policy instruments can be answered in terms of the analysis of the choice of the optimal exchange rate regime. Such analysis reveals that in analogy with Poole's (1970) analysis for the closed economy, the optimal exchange rate regime depends on the nature and the origin of the stochastic shocks that affect the economy as well as on the indexation rules that govern labor markets. (For details see Frenkel and Aizenman, 1982, and Aizenman and Frenkel 1985).

Finally, in concluding the discussion of the interactions between macroeconomic policies and the choice of optimal exchange rate regime as well as interactions between the exchange rate regime and the choice of optimal macroeconomic policies, it is relevant to recall one of the popular arguments put forward in favor of a pegged exchange rate. The argument is based on the *"discipline of the exchange."* Accordingly, it is argued that the obligation to peg the rate or to follow a predetermined intervention rule would alter fundamentally the conduct of policy by introducing discipline.

In evaluating this argument two points are noteworthy. First, it is not obvious at all that a flexible exchange rate regime exerts less discipline than a fixed rate regime. In fact, since changes in exchange rates are highly visible and are transmitted promptly into domestic prices, the consequences of undisciplined policies are readily apparent. In contrast, undisciplined policies under fixed exchange rates show up only in reserve changes, and then only after a significant delay. It stands to reason, therefore, that in principle a flexible exchange rate regime may also introduce discipline.

The second point is somewhat more general as it sheds doubts on the basic logic underlying the discipline argument. Accordingly, it is argued that national governments are unlikely to adjust the conduct of domestic policies and be disciplined by the exchange rate regime. Rather, it may be more reasonable to assume that the exchange rate regime is more likely to adjust to whatever discipline national governments choose to have. Accordingly, it is not the exchange rate regime that constrains economic policy, but rather the prevailing policy that constrains the choice of the exchange rate regime. It may be noted in passing that this is indeed one of the more potent arguments against the restoration of the gold standard. If governments were willing to follow policies consistent with the maintenance of a gold standard, then the standard itself would not be necessary; if however, governments are not willing to follow such policies, then the introduction of the gold standard per se will not restore stability since, before long, the standard will have to be abandoned. In short, no exchange rate system can protect us from bad policies.

Can Exchange Market Intervention Alleviate the Constraints on Monetary Policy?

The analysis of the international constraints on monetary policy is closely related to the analysis of the questions of whether the authorities can sterilize the monetary implications of the balance of payments and the monetary implications of interventions in the market for foreign exchange. It is the need for occasional interventions in the market for foreign exchange that provides some of the rationale for the continued stable holdings of international reserves documented in Frenkel (1983b). In this context, however, the difficulties in analyzing that question start with definitions since exchange market intervention means different things to different people (see Wallich, 1982). Some, especially in the United States, interpret foreign exchange intervention to mean *sterilized* intervention, that is, intervention that is not allowed to affect the monetary base and thus amounts to an exchange of domestic bonds for foreign bonds. Others, especially in Europe, interpret foreign intervention to mean nonsterilized intervention. Thus, for the Europeans an intervention alters the course of monetary policy, while for the Americans it does not.

The distinction between the two concepts of intervention is fundamental, and the exchange rate effects of the two forms of intervention may be very different depending on the relative degree of substitution among assets. In principle, sterilized intervention may affect the exchange rate by portfolio-balance effects (see Allen and Kenen, 1980, Branson 1979, and Henderson, 1977), and by signaling to the public the government's intentions concerning future policies, thereby changing expectations (see Mussa 1981). To the extent that sterilized intervention is effective in managing exchange rates, the constraint on the conduct of monetary policy would not be severe since the undesirable exchange rate effects of monetary policy could be offset by policies that alter appropriately the composition of assets.

In practice, however, the evidence suggests that nonsterilized intervention which alters the monetary base has a strong effect on the exchange rate while an equivalent sterilized intervention has very little effect (see Obstfeld, 1983), as well as the various intervention studies conducted by the board of governors of the U.S. Federal Reserve System and other central banks). These findings are relevant for both the theory of exchange rate determination and the practice of exchange rate and monetary policies. As to the theory, they shed doubts on the usefulness of the portfolio-balance model. As to the practice, they demonstrate that the distinction between the two forms of intervention is critical if the authorities mean to intervene effectively, and that it is inappropriate to assume that the open economy constraints on monetary policy can be easily overcome by sterilization policies. A more reasonable inference is that it is very difficult to conduct effectively independent monetary and exchange rate policies.

The preceding discussion defined interventions in terms of transactions involving specific pairs of assets. In evaluating these transactions it might be useful to explore the broader spectrum of possible policies. Figure 5–5 summarizes the various patterns of domestic and foreign monetary policies and foreign exchange interventions. These policies are divided into three groups as follows:

I : domestic nonsterilized foreign exchange intervention

I*: foreign nonsterilized foreign exchange intervention

II : domestic monetary policy

II*: foreign monetary policy

III : domestic sterilized foreign exchange intervention

III*: foreign sterilized foreign exchange intervention

This classification is based on the types of assets that are being exchanged. Thus, when the authorities exchange domestic money (M) for domestic bonds (B), the transaction is referred to as domestic monetary policy (as in II), while when the authorities exchange domestic bonds (B) for foreign bonds (B^*), the transaction is referred to as domestic sterilized foreign exchange intervention (as in III). Some have characterized pure foreign exchange intervention as an exchange of domestic money (M) for foreign money (M^*) rather than the exchange of domestic money for foreign bonds. To complete the spectrum, this type of exchange is indicated in figure 5–5 by I' and I'*, respectively.

This general classification highlights two principles. First, it shows that the differences between the various policies depend on the different characteristics of the various assets that are being exchanged. These different characteristics are at the foundation of the portfolio-balance model. Second, it shows that domestic and foreign variables enter symmetrically into the picture. Thus, for example, a given exchange between M and B^* can be effected through the policies of the home country or through a combination of policies of the foreign country. This symmetry suggests that there is room (and possibly a role) for international coordination of exchange rate policies. It also illustrates the "(n-1) problem" of the international monetary system: in a world of n currencies there are (n-1) exchange rates and only (n-1) monetary authorities need to intervene in order to attain a set of exchange rates. To ensure consistency, the international monetary system needs to

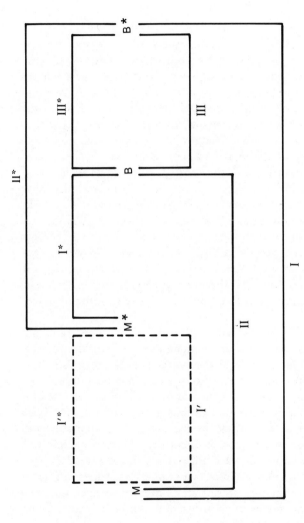

I   = domestic nonsterilized foreign exchange intervention
I* = foreign nonsterilized foreign exchange intervention
II = domestic monetary policy
II* = foreign monetary policy
III = domestic sterilized foreign exchange intervention
III* = foreign sterilized foreign exchange intervention
M   = domestic money
M* = foreign money
B   = domestic bond
B* = foreign bonds

Figure 5–5. Patterns of Domestic and Foreign Monetary Policies and Foreign Exchange Interventions

specify the allocation of the remaining degree of freedom (see Mundell, 1968). Thus, the (n-1) problem imposes an additional constraint on the conduct of macroeconomic policy in the interdependent world economy.[7]

Some Policy Implications

The foregoing analysis emphasized the constraints that are imposed on economic policy in the open economy. Under fixed exchange rates these constraints may be somewhat alleviated through sterilization policies, but the evidence sheds some doubts on the effectiveness of such attempts. As was also indicated, under flexible exchange rates the rapid changes in exchange rates also impose a constraint on the effectiveness of monetary policy in that they speed up the translation of monetary changes into changes in prices and wages. The recent volatility of nominal and real exchange rates, the slow pace of world economic recovery, and the strong dollar have been costly, have dangerously increased the popularity of protectionism, and also have resulted in an increased perception that exchange rate changes reduce the leverage of macro policy. Attempts to alleviate some of these constraints have given rise to various proposals concerning rules for intervention in the foreign exchange market. Some of these proposals are variants of a PPP rule according to which the authorities are expected to intervene so as to ensure that the path of the exchange rate conforms to the path of the relative price levels. These proposals, if effective, amount to guidelines for the conduct of monetary policy.

There are at least four difficulties with a PPP rule. First, there are intrinsic differences between the characteristics of exchange rates and the price of national outputs. These differences, which result from the much stronger dependence of exchange rates (and other asset prices) on expectations, suggest that the fact that exchange rates have moved more than the price level is not, in and of itself, sufficient evidence that exchange rate volatility has been excessive. Exchange rate volatility should be assessed by comparison with variability of prices of other assets such as securities. Viewed against this yardstick the evidence shows that the variability of exchange rates has been about half that of the stock market indexes. This, of course, does not mean that the volatility of either exchange rates or stock market indexes has been acceptable but rather that the degree of volatility may not be judged as being excessive just by pointing at the fact that exchange.rates have moved more than national price levels.

Second, the prices of national outputs do not adjust fully to shocks in the short run. Thus intervention in the foreign exchange market to ensure purchasing power parity would be a mistake. When commodity prices are slow to adjust to current and expected economic conditions, it may be desirable to allow for "excessive adjustment in some other prices.

Third, there are continuous changes in real economic conditions that require adjustment in the equilibrium relative prices of different national outputs. Under these circumstances what seem to be divergences from purchasing power parities may really reflect equilibrating changes.

Fourth, if there is short-run stickiness of prices of domestic goods in terms of national monies, then rapid exchange rate adjustments, which are capable of changing the relative prices of different national outputs, are a desirable response to changing real economic conditions. An intervention rule rigidly linking changes in exchange rates to changes in domestic and foreign prices in accord with purchasing power parity ignores the occasional need for equilibrating changes in relative prices.

Now that I have outlined the key limitations of a policy that adopts a rigid PPP rule, what is left of the usefulness of the PPP doctrine? Its main usefulness is in providing a guide to the general trend of exchange rates, particularly in circumstances where the main shocks underlying the trend are of a monetary origin. As for the conduct of macroeconomic policy, it serves as an important reminder that the exchange rate and the price level cannot be divorced from each other and that policies affecting the trend of domestic (relative to foreign) prices are likely to affect the exchange rate in a similar manner.

Emphasis on the fact that exchange rates and prices are both endogenous variables is important in view of the recent allegations that flexible exchange rates were inflationary during the 1970s and have slowed down the recovery from the beginning of the 1980s up to the time of this writing. Both exchange rates and prices respond to the same set of shocks and can be influenced by a similar set of policies. The fact that exchange rates adjust faster than commodity prices reflects the known phenomenon that asset markets clear relatively quickly. This fact does not imply that as an economic matter the chain of causality runs from exchange rates to prices.

Monetary policy can make a positive contribution to reducing costly and unnecessary fluctuations of exchange rates by reducing the variability of monetary expansion. This is especially important because exchange rates are affected not only by current policy actions, but also by expectations about future policy actions. If these expectations are highly sensitive to current policy, then instability of policies can have a magnified effect on the variability of nominal and real exchange rates. This variability can be reduced by adopting a stable and predictable pattern of government policy.

What should be the role of the exchange rate in the design of monetary policy? Generally, given that monetary and exchange rate policies should not be viewed as two independent instruments, consideration of the external value of the currency should play a relatively minor role in the design of monetary policy. The major consideration that should guide the monetary authority is that of achieving price stability.

While this prescription may seem to represent a revival of the "benign neglect" attitude, the opposite is the case. In the past, one of the major arguments for the benign neglect attitude in the United States was that the U.S. economy was relatively closed and the foreign trade sector was relatively unimportant. The typical statistic used to justify this position was the low share of imports in GNP. This argument was inappropriate in the past and is even less appropriate under present circumstances. The United States has always been an open economy. The relevant measure of openness to international trade in goods and services is not the share of actual trade in GNP but rather the share of tradable commodities in GNP (that is, potential trade), which is far larger than that of actual trade. Furthermore, as stated in the section **Capital Mobility and the Constraints on Macroeconomic Policies,** one of the main linkages of the United States to the world economy is operating through world capital markets into which the United States is clearly well integrated. The same principle applies to the measures of openness of most countries.

The prescription is based on the notions that the economy *is* open, that the external value of the currency *is* important, that the maintenance of price stability is an important policy goals, and that policy viewing the exchange rate as an independent target (or, even worse, as an independent instrument) is likely to result in unstable prices. Furthermore, if monetary policy succeeds in achieving price stability, it might be useful to allow for fluctuations of the exchange rate that provide for a partial insulation from misguided foreign monetary policies.

Even when monetary policy is not guided by exchange rate targets, it might attempt to offset disturbances arising from shifts in the demand for money. Such shifts in demand may be especially pronounced under a regime of flexible exchange rates. A policy that accommodates such demand shifts by offsetting supply shifts would reduce the need for costly adjustments of exchange rates and national price levels. The difficulty with implementing this policy is in identifying when a shift in money demand has occurred. Obviously, the nominal rate of interest is not a reliable indicator of money market conditions. The more relevant indicators are the components of the nominal rate of interest—the real rate of interest and the expected rate of inflation—but these components are unobservable.

Here the exchange rate may be useful as an indicator for monetary policy, especially when frequent changes in inflationary expectations make nominal interest rates an unreliable indicator of fluctuations in money demand. For example, as argued in Frenkel and Mussa (1980, 1981), a combination of a high nominal interest rate differential and a depreciation of the currency (a situation that prevailed in the United States during most of the 1970s) indicates a rise in inflationary expectations that should not be fueled by an accommodative monetary policy. On the other hand, a combination of a high nominal interest rate differential and an appreciation of the currency (a situation that seems to have prevailed in the United States since the latter part of 1979) indicates a rise in the demand for money. Under such circumstances accommodation by an expansionary monetary policy may be desirable.

The foregoing discussion of the implications of policies on the exchange rate dealt with exchange rate volatility. But it is important to emphasize that the chief complaint against the operation of the present system of managed float is that exchange rates of major currencies have been subject to large and persistent misalignments. Such misalignments (especially an overvaluation of the real effective exchange rate of the U.S. dollar and an undervaluation of the Japanese yen) have been costly because they impact adversely on resource allocation, induce adjustment costs (including unemployment), distort optimal levels of capital formation, and encourage protectionism.

The apparent misalignment of the U.S. dollar resulted from a combination of macroeconomic policies in the United States and abroad. The tight stance of monetary policy during the disinflationary period of the early 1980s, the loose fiscal stance in the United States, the contractionary fiscal positions in the United Kingdom, West Germany, and Japan, and the slow pace of economic recovery in Europe (relative to the United States) have all contributed to the drastic real appreciation of the U.S. dollar. It is important to identify these factors since unless they are dealt with seriously, it might be difficult to put a halt to the growing pressures for protectionism.

It is hard to recall another period in which sentiments for protection have been so widespread in the United States as they are at the present. An excessive emphasis on the U.S. budget deficit as the sole cause for the dollar's strength and the growing frustration with the efforts to reduce the U.S. fiscal deficit by conventional measures have brought about new desperate arguments for the adoption of protectionist measures like import surcharges. The danger with such recommendations is that they might receive the political support of two otherwise unrelated groups. They are likely to gain the support of the traditional advocates of protectionism who claim to defend local industry and workers from foreign unfair competition. But, more dangerously, they may gain the support of those whose exclusive concern with the budget deficit leads them to support almost any policy that raises fiscal revenue. Once in place, import surcharges (even those adopted as "temporary measures") are hard to remove since, as George Stigler once remarked, "a sustained policy that has real effects has many good friends." At the present there are very few measures whose long-term costs to the interdependent world economy may be as high as protectionist measures. Taxes on trade will hurt exports, and will restore inward-looking economic isolationism instead of outward-looking economic coordination. Protectionist measures will transmit the wrong signals to those developing countries that are still attempting to resist domestically popular pressures to default on their debt, and, further, they may ignite trade war. Therefore, one needs to resist the temptation to "solve" budgetary difficulties by means of import tariffs.

In view of the disruptive effects exerted by the strong and highly volatile dollar, and in view of the mounting pressures for protectionism and the apparent failure to restore fiscal soundness, various proposals for reform of the international monetary system have been put forward. Is this the time for reform? I believe not! If indeed an important cause for the current strength of the dollar lies in the fiscal positions of the United States, Europe, and Japan, then the solution for the problems does not call for a monetary reform. Nor does it call for tariffs and protectionism, for taxes on capital flows (or other measures that throw sand in the wheels), or for the adoption of mechanistic intervention rules. Rather, it calls for a restoration of fiscal order in which the United States adopts a more contractionary fiscal stance while Europe and Japan adopt a more expansionary stance. The central difficulties with the current regime do not rest with the exchange rate system per se or with the existing exchange rate policies; rather, they rest with the overall mix of the uncoordinated macroeconomic policies. It is unlikely, therefore, that the introduction of exchange rate targets or other superficial measures dealing only with the symptoms of the disease can do any good unless they are accompanied by drastic changes in the way in which macroeconomic policies are designed. Put differently, it makes no sense to agree just on real exchange rate targets without accompanying such an arrangement with a similar agreement about other targets for macroeconomic policies including, of course, fiscal policies. In fact, the adoption of policies that deal with anything but the ultimate root cause may do more harm than good. Indeed, placing excessive weight on the management of exchange rates may divert attention from the more central role that global macroeconomic policies play in the interdependent world economy.

Notes

1. Due to space limitation the chapter pays more attention to the role of monetary policy than to the role of fiscal policy. This should not be interpreted to argue that the open economy constraints on fiscal policy and the implications of international fiscal interdependence are of a lesser importance. For a discussion of the constraints on fiscal policies, see Frenkel and Mussa (1981). For an analysis of fiscal interdependence, see Frenkel and Razin (1986).

2. The analysis draws on Frenkel (1981).

3. This paragraph draws on Frenkel and Mussa (1981).

4. This analysis is based on Frenkel (1983b).

5. While these are the general characteristics of the adjustment process, the details of the precise path are somewhat more complicated since the expected transitional changes in the exchange rates will alter transitorily the rate of interest. Along

the path between E and D, the domestic currency appreciates and, if this appreciation is expected, the domestic rate of interest is below the world rate due to interest arbitrage. Therefore, during the transition period the desired ratio of money to equities will exceed the one described in figure 5–4, and the initial depreciation will be somewhat smaller than the one indicated by point E. The new equilibrium is reached at point A when the exchange rate reaches its new level, and when the domestic and foreign rates of interest are equalized.

6. The importance of the degree of capitalization and marketability of claims to future income streams was analyzed in the context of a closed economy by Metzler (1951) and Mundell (1960). For an application to an economy under fixed exchange rates see Obstfeld (1982).

7. For an analysis of the various dimensions of interdependencies, see Cooper (1968).

References

Aizenman, Joshua, and Jacob A. Frenkel. "Optimal Wage Indexation, Foreign Exchange Intervention and Monetary Policy," *American Economic Review* 75, no. 3 (June 1985): 402–23.

Alexander, Sidney S. "Effects of a Devaluation on a Trade Balance." *IMF Staff Papers* 2 (April 1952): 263–78.

Allen, Polly R., and Peter B. Kenen. *Asset Markets, Exchange Rates and Economic Integration.* Cambridge, England: Cambridge University Press, 1980.

Branson, William H. "Assets Markets and Relative Prices in Exchange Rate Determination," *Sozialwissenschaftliche Annalen* 1 (1979): 69–89.

Cooper, Richard N. *The Economy of Interdependence.* New York: McGraw-Hill, 1968.

Dornbusch, Rudiger. "Real and Monetary Apsects of the Effects of Exchange Rate Changes" in R.Z. Aliber (ed.), *National Monetary Policies and the International Financial System.* Chicago: University of Chicago Press, 1974, pp. 64–81.

———. *Open Economy Macroeconomics.* New York: Basic Books, 1980.

Fleming, J. Marcus. "Domestic Financial Policies under Fixed and under Flexible Exchange Rates." *IMF Staff Papers* 9 (1962): 369–79.

Frenkel, Jacob A. "Macroeconomic Policy in an Open Economy," *Estudios Monetarios VII: Alternatives de Politicas Financieras en Economias Pequenas y Avientas al Exterior.* Santiago: Director de Politica Financiera, Banco Central de Chile, 1981, pp. 53–97.

———. "Monetary Policy: Domestic Targets and International Constraints," *American Economic Review* 73, no. 2 (May 1983a): 48–53.

———. "International Liquidity and Monetary Control" in George M. von Furstenberg (ed.), *International Money and Credit: The Policy Roles.* Washington, D.C.: International Monetary Fund, 1983b, pp. 65–109.

Frenkel, Jacob A., and Joshua Aizenman. "Aspects of the Optimal Management of Exchange Rates," *Journal of International Economics* 13 (November 1982): 231–56.

Frenkel, Jacob A., and Michael L. Mussa. "The Efficiency of Foreign Exchange Markets and Measures of Turbulence," *American Economic Review* 70, no. 2 (May 1980): 374–81.

———. "Monetary and Fiscal Policies in an Open Economy," *American Economic Review* 71, no. 2 (May 1981): 253–58.

———. "Asset Markets, Exchange Rates and the Balance of Payments" in Ronald W. Jones and Peter B. Kenen (eds.), *Handbook of International Economics,* vol. II. Amsterdam: North-Holland and New York: Elsevier Science, 1985, pp. 679–747.

Frenkel, Jacob A., and Assaf Razin. "Fiscal Policies in the World Economy," *Journal of Political Economy,* forthcoming, 1986.

Henderson, Dale. "Modeling the Interdependence of National Money and Capital Markets," *American Economic Review* 67, no. 2 (May 1977): 190–99.

Johnson, Harry G. "Towards a General Theory of the Balance of Payments" in *International Trade and Economic Growth.* Cambridge, Mass.: Harvard University Press, 1958, pp. 153–68.

McKinnon, Ronald I., and W.E. Oates. "The Implications of International Economic Integration for Monetary, Fiscal and Exchange Rate Policy." *Princeton Studies in International Finance,* no. 16. Princeton, N.J.: Princeton University, 1966.

Meade, James E. *The Theory of International Economic Policy, Vol. I: The Balance of Payments.* London: Oxford University Press, 1951.

Metzler, Lloyd A. "Wealth, Savings and the Rate of Interest," *Journal of Political Economy* 59, no. 2 (April 1951): 93–166.

Mundell, Robert A. "The Public Debt, Corporate Income Taxes and the Rate of Interest," *Journal of Political Economy* 68, no. 2 (December 1960): 622–26.

———. "The International Disequilibrium System," *Kyklos* 14, no. 2 (1961): 154–72.

———. "The Appropriate Use of Monetary and Fiscal Policy under Fixed Exchange Rates." *IMF Staff Papers* 9 (March 1962): 70–79.

———. "Capital Mobility and Stabilization Policy under Fixed and Flexible Exchange Rates," *Canadian Journal of Economic and Political Science* 29 (November 1963): 475–85.

———. *International Economics.* New York: Macmillan, 1968.

Mussa, Michael L. "The Exchange Rate, the Balance of Payments and Monetary and Fiscal Policy under a Regime of Controlled Floating," *Scandinavian Journal of Economics* 78, no. 2 (May 1976): 229–48.

———. "Macroeconomic Interdependence and the Exchange Rate Regime" in Rudiger Dornbusch and Jacob A. Frenkel (eds.) *International Economic Policy: Theory and Evidence.* Baltimore: Johns Hopkins University Press, 1979, pp. 160–204.

———. "The Role of Official Intervention." Occasional papers, no. 6. New York: Group of Thirty, 1981.

———. "The Theory of Exchange Rate Determination," in *John F.O. Bilson and Richard Marston (eds.), Exchange Rate Theory and Policy.* Chicago: University of Chicago Press, 1984, pp. 13–78.

Obstfeld, Maurice. "The Capitalization of Income Streams and the Effects of Open-Market Policy under Fixed Exchange Rates," *Journal of Monetary Economics* 9, no. 1 (January 1982): 87–98.

────. "Exchange Rates, Inflation and the Sterilization Problem: Germany, 1975–1981," *European Economic Review* 21, no. 1/2 (March–April 1983): 161–89.

Poole, William. "Optimal Choice of Monetary Instruments in a Simple Stochastic Macro-Model," *Quarterly Journal of Economics* 84 (May 1970): 197–216.

Swoboda, Alexander K. "Equilibrium, Quasi-Equilibrium, and Macroeconomic Policy under Fixed Exchange Rates," *Quarterly Journal of Econmics* 86, no. 1 (February 1972): 162–71.

Tinbergen, Jan. *On the Theory of Economic Policy:* Amsterdam: North-Holland, 1952.

Wallich, Henry C. "Exchange-Market Intervention: Issues and Views," *Journal of Commerce* (August 12–13, 1982).

Comments

William Poole

J acob Frenkel has provided an extensive survey of the literature relevant to his title, and an illuminating analysis. I agree with most of Frenkel's commentary, and will add some of my own.

Frenkel begins with an assessment of the assignment problem and Mundell's solution to it. The Mundell solution seems to me to be very artificial. If separate monetary and fiscal authorities agreed on the economic model and on policy objectives, it would not make sense for them to accept separate assignments for achieving policy objectives. It would make more sense to assume that each authority sets its own policy instruments at the levels required for internal and external balance under the assumption that the other policy authority behaves in the same manner. The two policy authorities, sharing the same model and same objectives, would act as if they were departments of a single policy authority.

The problem is different if one authority—Authority F, say—is unable or unwilling to act to achieve equilibrium. In such a case the other authority—Authority M—would no longer act under the assumption that Authority F would set its policy instruments appropriately. Authority M would instead optimize subject to the policies followed by Authority F. It would not be sensible for Authority M to blindly pursue the assignment given to it knowing that the other authority was not going to act appropriately.

This reasoning might be applied to today's conditions by asking what the Federal Reserve should do given that the fiscal authority—the Congress and administration taken together—is unable to reduce the budget deficit. Put another way, the question is how the Federal Reserve might act differently if the budget deficit were smaller. Defining monetary policy in terms of money growth, it does not seem to me that the Federal Reserve should permit monetary policy to be determined by the level of the budget deficit. There is no significant trade-off between monetary and fiscal policy, so changing money growth as the budget deficit changes only risks compounding one set of policy errors with another. Using money growth to finance the large budget deficit risks accelerating inflation and rising interest rates. Inflation may reduce the real value of the dollar, but benefits flowing to U.S. export industries and import-competing industries hardly seem worth the cost that generalized inflation will bring. One of these costs is that rising nominal interest rates are likely to bankrupt many of our weakened financial intermediaries.

Leakages and Competitive Opportunities

Let me turn to a more general discussion of the constraints that openness imposes on adjustments in U.S. economic policies. These constraints are sometimes analyzed in terms of "leakages" abroad of the effects of changes in domestic policies. The very term suggests the usual central planner's complaint that the competitive marketplace is inhibiting the effectiveness of the planner's policies.

Openness, however, offers opportunities as well as constraints. Let me illustrate with two regional examples from within the United States. The first example is the New Hampshire liquor monopoly. This state liquor monopoly is highly aggressive. Its prices are low, its stores large, well-stocked, and conveniently located on major highways near the state borders. The state monopoly profits mightily from drawing customers from other states with higher prices. In the absence of "foreign" customers, the optimal policy of the state monopoly would have been quite different. With closed borders the profit-maximizing price would be high instead of low, and the New Hampshire taxpayer-consumer worse off.

A second example concerns the industrial development policies of the Sunbelt states. These states pursue local fiscal policies that maintain attractive tax and regulatory environments for the purpose of luring industry from other states. Many of these policies have been successful in promoting economic development.

In both of these examples, openness provides an opportunity to aggressively competitive states but a constraint to states attempting to pursue policies injurious to the interests of mobile resources. I conclude that the literature on macro policy contraints imposed by openness must come primarily from economists from the Snowbelt states, or at least economists with Snowbelt mentalities.

These examples, when transferred from the interregional to the international realm, seem to have more to do with microeconomic than macroeconomic policies. Perhaps the problem is less a matter of constraints introduced by openness than it is of a general conflict between microeconomic efficiency and macroeconomic policy. Many of the leakages in the open economy models are nothing more than manifestations of incentive effects so long ignored in Keynesian approaches to macroeconomic policy. The Keynesian planner finds it very inconvenient when investment flows to less-taxed opportunities such as consumer durables domestically or capital assets abroad.

Competitive Monetary Policies

With respect to monetary policy, the constraint involves the possibility of flows out of a country's currency, and assets denominated in its currency, into assets denominated in foreign currencies. This possibility, though, is the other side of an opportunity to attract foreign capital. A country can profit greatly from net foreign investment and from serving as an international financial intermediary.

To maintain a demand for its currency, a country must maintain price stability, political stability, and markets free of capital controls and regulatory impediments. These conditions are all desirable on domestic grounds. If maintaining these conditions attracts capital from abroad, it is because financial stability is an economic good in short supply around the world.

Most economists favor free trade on the grounds of both static efficiency and the dynamic effects competition has in breaking down the entrenched positions of lazy monopolies. Competition is good for both the "invader" and the "defender" firms. The same principle applies to "invader" countries that are successful in creating financial stability at the "expense" of capital flows out of "defender" countries.

Some observers argue that the international role of the dollar relaxes a constraint on U.S. monetary policy. That view does not seem to me correct. The United States profits from financial intermediation, but U.S. monetary policy is subject to competition from monetary policies abroad. Other countries also produce financial stability, and the funds that have come to the United States can readily leave for foreign shores should U.S. economic conditions deteriorate. Many countries have tried to avoid becoming reserve currency countries because of perceived constraints from capital "sloshing" around internationally.

Effect of the Exchange Rate System on Policy Constraints

Frenkel argues, and I am inclined to agree, that policy constraints and opportunities are not greatly affected by the exchange rate system. The fixed exchange rate system tends to constrain money creation, but there is always the opportunity to respond by imposing capital and trade controls as the United States did in the 1960s. The fixed rate system itself cannot impose discipline that the political system refuses to accept.

But the irrelevance of the exchange rate system is primarily a long-run proposition. In the long run, countries must adjust one way or another to changes in relative prices. The exchange rate system affects the characteristics of the short-run adjustment process. Frenkel spends little time speculating on what these characteristics might be.

I suspect that the difference between fixed and flexible exchange rate dynamics in the short run may have something to do with the distinction drawn by Arthur Okun between the "fix-price" and the "flex-price" sectors of the economy. Flex-price sectors are characterized by auction markets and atomistic traders. Fix-price sectors are characterized by relatively discrete price adjustments in markets with relatively few traders.

The flexible exchange rate market is itself a superb example of a flex-price sector. But this flex-price sector may turn certain other sectors that would otherwise operate on fix-price principles into sectors that must operate on flex-price principles. Because people do not understand why some markets function as auction markets, or a close approximation, while others are organized very differently, one should be slow to jump to any conclusions as to whether broadening the flex-price part of the economy is or is not a favorable development.

Finally, Frenkel's chapter and my comments have both concentrated on policy constraints and opportunities from openness under the assumption that the objective function contains only U.S. objectives. But foreign objectives belong in the objective function of the United States. The United States has an intense practical interest, not just an altruistic one, in political stability and economic progress abroad. The real constraint on U.S. economic policy has nothing to do with the ratios of imports and exports to GNP, but rather with the fact that the world is in many respects a nasty and brutish place. The United States is in a deadly serious competition that it will not win if all it does is maximize an objective function containing as arguments U.S. per capita real income and the inflation rate.

6

The Dollar Exchange Rate and International Monetary Cooperation

Ronald I. McKinnon

Since the early 1970s, floating exchange rates have been associated with international cycles of inflation and deflation with the United States as the epicenter. Random and essentially arbitrary exchange fluctuations have continually misaligned national price levels—culminating in extreme dollar overvaluation throughout most of the 1980s. In order to seal off domestic markets from these precipitate changes in foreign competitive pressure, a worldwide upsurge in protectionism has occurred—particularly in the United States.

But the international business cycle can be tamed with a better alignment of exchange rates if the principal industrial countries agree to coordinate their monetary policies. A set of rules is suggested for having the United States, Germany (representing the European bloc), and Japan symmetrically adjust their internal money growth rates so as to keep their exchange rates within officially announced target zones. The common price level would be stabilized through smoother growth in their joint money supply.

Only for the United States need such an agreement require a major change in the way in which monetary policy is currently conducted. By taking this more "open-economy" approach, however, the U.S. Federal Reserve System can do a better job of stabilizing the U.S. economy and the purchasing power of the dollar.

Dollar Overvaluation from 1981 to Mid-1985

Nobody can deny the great protectionist pressure that developed in the United States in the early 1980s. Nor is there doubt that from 1981 through

Additional empirical and theoretical support for the proposals advanced in this chapter can be found in the author's recent book, *An International Standard for Monetary Stabilization,* published by the Institute for International Economics (Washington, D.C.) and the MIT Press (Cambridge, Mass.), 1984. I would like to thank Kenichi Ohno for his great help in preparing this chapter.

mid-1985, the extraordinary appreciation of the dollar against European cur-rencies—and to a lesser extent against the Japanese yen—was the major force behind the protectionist momentum. From the overvalued dollar, the United States developed symptoms of a dual economy: buoyant output in the non-tradable sectors such as services of all kinds and military procurement, with depression in agriculture, mining, and most of civilian manufacturing open to foreign competition.

However increased protectionism would have been no solution at all. Reneging on the long-standing U.S. commitment to maintain free interna-tional trade would invite foreign retaliation, while undermining the economic basis for the postwar prosperity of the industrial world. In addition, restrict-ing imports entering the United States—while international financial pressure in favor of the dollar remained unchanged—would reduce U.S. demand for foreign currency and drive the dollar up further. U.S. exporters would then be doubly hurt through the higher dollar on the one hand and because of higher dollar prices of importable inputs on the other.

But to thwart protectionism, the continual tendency toward financial imbalance between the United States and the industrial countries of Western Europe and Japan must be righted. The large U.S. fiscal deficit is commonly (and correctly) blamed for much of the trade deficit—but it cannot explain why the dollar exchange rate got so far out of line. I hypothesize that mone-tary coordination among the United States, the European bloc, and Japan is the only practical way of first correcting dollar overvaluation (or undervalua-tion) and the preserving longer-run price and exchange rate stability.

The Fiscal Conundrum

However, the most common explanation of why the dollar became overval-ued points to fiscal policy rather than misplaced monetary policy.

Huge budget deficits, which the Federal Reserve refused to monetize, increased interest rates on dollar assets in real terms—after future U.S. price inflation is discounted. As capital was attracted from abroad in the early 1980s, the dollar was bid up in the foreign exchanges and overshot its long-run equilibrium until expected dollar depreciation offset the relatively high yields on U.S. government bonds and corporate securities. In the meantime, the unduly appreciated dollar depressed U.S. exports and stimulated imports.

This conventional argument sees a monotonic chain of causation: from budget deficits to interest rates to the dollar exchange rate to the trade deficit. It originated in 1981, when U.S. interest rates rose sharply—in response to the projected Reagan budget deficits and monetary tightness by the Federal Reserve—and the dollar also rose strongly in the foreign exchanges. The implication is that the U.S. fiscal deficit must be largely eliminated before the dollar's overvaluation can be overcome.

The alternative view, to be developed here, suggests that monetary policy may be assigned to stabilize the exchange rate in the face of substantial shifts in fiscal policy. Trade deficits would still develop to match budget deficits even if the nominal exchange rate did not jump and overshoot. One must distinguish the investment–savings imbalance (which determines the trade deficit) from whatever the exchange rate regime happens to be.

For example, suppose the United States had been on a fixed nominal exchange rate when the large budgetary deficits began to develop. Then a deficit in U.S. trade, of the same order of magnitude currently observable, would still have evolved — perhaps it would have evolved even earlier. The U.S. business downturn of 1982 would have been less severe if the Federal Reserve System had been obligated to have less tight money in order to prevent the dollar from appreciating so precipitately. With better maintained domestic income, U.S. imports would have been higher in the 1982–83 period.

The fundamental point is that, when capital is internationally mobile, nations will readily develop deficits or surpluses in the current account of the balance of payments under fixed exchange rates — as, say, under the late nineteenth century gold standard. At the present time, for example, the U.S. trade deficit will remain very large as long as the government fiscal deficit continues to force expenditures above income by creating a deficiency in saving throughout the U.S. economy. A better aligned (lower-valued) dollar would, however, ameliorate the depression in U.S. tradable goods industries even if it would not do much to correct the trade deficit per se.

That there is no necessary relationship between fiscal deficits and movements in nominal exchange rates can be seen from another angle. After all, few would claim that the large dollar depreciations of the 1970s were caused by U.S. budgetary surpluses. Indeed, the United States ran fiscal deficits — albeit much smaller ones — in those years. The large fiscal deficits in France after Mitterrand came into power in 1981 seemed to weaken the franc rather than strengthen it.

Furthermore, no monotonic or otherwise stable relationships seem to exist between nominal interest rates and a currency's strength in the foreign exchanges. Indeed much of the extraordinary rise in the dollar exchange rate from mid-1984 to the first quarter of 1985 was associated with *falling* U.S. interest rates. Specifically, from August 1984 to February 1985, U.S. interest rates fell 2 to 3 percentage points relative to those in Germany while the dollar was rising from 2.88 to 3.25 marks.

Although interest rates remain important, expectations of future political safety, price inflation, and other sources of future exchange rate movements often dominate the portfolio preferences of international investors. The gnomes of Zurich, Luxembourg, and Singapore continually look for the safest haven (currency) in which to place their internationally liquid assets.

Suppose the U.S. government moved seriously toward cutting expenditures. U.S. interest rates would fall immediately in anticipation of lower future fiscal deficits, and this effect by itself would tend to depress the dollar in the foreign exchanges. Against this, people might expect that the resulting reduction in the projected national debt would lessen the chances of price inflation in the distant future. Similarly, other taxes on the holders of dollar assets become less likely. The United States could then seem like an even safer haven for international capital.

Because of these opposing considerations, even resolute action by the U.S. government to eliminate its unsustainable fiscal deficit need not bring the dollar down in the foreign exchange markets—although it probably would. (The one dramatic exception is a general withholding tax on interest and dividend income, including that from all those U.S. securities owned by foreigners. That certainly would bring the dollar down.) At best, fiscal policy is a blunt instrument, subject to long delays and uncertainties, for influencing the exchange rate.

Enter Monetary Policy

In contrast, monetary policy is immediately flexible and can be made to influence the exchange rate unambiguously. From the nineteenth century gold standard to the fixed exchange rates of the 1950s and 1960s under the old Bretton Woods agreement, examples abound of countries successfully subordinating their monetary policies to maintaining a fixed exchange rate with some other stable money. Central banks can react quickly to international shifts in the demand for the money they issue.

In the asymmetrical Bretton Woods system, countries other than the United States were directly responsible for maintaining their exchange rates within 1 percent of either side of their formal dollar parities. For example, from 1950 to 1970, the Bank of Japan kept the yen within three-quarters of 1 percent of 360 yen to the dollar by raising yen interest rates and contracting them when international payments were in deficit, and expanding the yen money supply when the Japanese currency tended to appreciate. Japanese monetary policy, based on this fixed exchange rate rule, led to stable yen prices for the broad range of internationally traded goods and contributed to Japan's extraordinary postwar recovery.

Similarly, in these same two prosperous decades, European governments generally subordinated their monetary policies to preserve stable exchange rates for long periods—with small, infrequent adjustments in their dollar parities. Only Britain continually resisted the necessary internationalization of its domestic monetary policy with consequent balance of payments deficits and numerous sterling crises throughout the 1950s and 1960s. And Britain had the least succesful domestic growth and foreign trade performances of any Western European economy.

The Flaw in Bretton Woods

But the Bretton Woods system had an inherent weakness. The monetary policy of the center country, the United States, was insufficiently guided by any exchange rate or other international obligation of its own. Even the U.S. commitment to a weak form of gold convertibility, which was itself inadequate, had eroded by the late 1960s.

Consequently, in 1970–73, the international system of fixed exchange rates broke down when the United States increased U.S. money growth despite the fact that the dollar was under obvious downward pressure in the foreign exchanges, as shown in table 6–1. In 1971, President Nixon mistakenly forced the other governments to let the dollar be devalued rather than contract the U.S. money supply. Private investors took this as a signal to reduce their holding of dollar assets in favor of foreign currencies, forcing further depreciations of the dollar in 1972–73, as shown in figure 6–1.

The resulting great inflation in the dollar prices of goods and services in the 1970s (see table 6–2) was aggravated by another unwarranted depreciation of the dollar in 1977–79. Foreign governments became loathe to bend their monetary policies to reestablish fixed dollar parities with what they then saw to be a chronically depreciating international currency.

Responding firmly, albeit belatedly, to domestic price inflation, the U.S. Federal Reserve System tightened up its monetary control procedures in October 1979. But international confidence in the dollar was not restored until the election of a more conservative president in late 1980. The remarkable shift in portfolio preferences back into dollar assets, and the great dollar appreciation of 1981–82, surprised everyone. In response to this clear signal from the foreign exchanges that U.S. monetary policy was now too tight, the Fed did not loosen up soon enough. The result was the sharp deflation and depression of 1982.

That changes in the dollar exchange rate are an excellent leading indicator of inflation or deflation to come within the U.S. economy is clearly shown in figure 6–2. Although spread out for more than two years, the lagged impact of a change in the exchange rate on the U.S. Wholesale Price Index (WPI) seems to peak after five quarters. Thus figure 6–2 plots current changes in the WPI against changes in the dollar exchange rate five quarters earlier. Since floating exchange rates began in the early 1970s, the negative correlation is easily visible and quite remarkable: − 0.528 with the unsmoothed quarterly data and − 0.817 when smoothed with a five-quarter moving average.

Tradable goods are heavily represented in the WPI and that index is naturally more sensitive to exchange rate changes. But even the U.S. GNP deflator, with its large component of nontradable services, is sensitive with exchange rate effects peaking after eight quarters (McKinnon, 1985). Thus one can see that having the Fed key on the dollar exchange rate is quite consistent with its most basic objective: to stabilize the domestic U.S. price level.

Table 6-1
Money Growth in Domestic Currencies, Eleven Industrial Countries, 1956–84
(percentage change in annual averages of M-1)

	Belgium	Canada	France	Germany	Italy	Japan	Nether-lands	Sweden	Switzer-land	United Kingdom	United States	World Average	Rest of World[a]
Weights: GNP 1964	(.0132)	(.0394)	(.0778)	(.0892)	(.0494)	(.0681)	(.0144)	(.0167)	(.0113)	(.0796)	(.5408)		
1956	2.9	-1.2	10.3	7.2	8.5	16.4	-3.7	7.4	6.0	1.0	1.1	3.78	6.94
1957	-0.1	4.0	8.6	12.1	6.3	4.1	-2.0	3.4	1.8	2.7	-0.6	2.43	6.01
1958	5.8	12.8	6.4	13.1	9.9	12.8	11.9	1.6	9.2	3.0	4.3	6.47	9.04
1959	3.2	-3.2	11.4	11.8	14.0	16.5	4.5	18.0	6.1	4.6	0.1	4.53	9.74
1960	1.9	5.1	13.0	6.8	13.5	19.1	6.7	-1.2	10.2	-0.8	-0.4	3.72	8.58
1961	7.7	12.4	15.5	14.8	15.7	19.0	7.7	10.7	8.1	3.2	2.9	7.39	12.68
1962	7.2	3.3	18.1	6.6	18.6	17.1	7.5	5.6	16.6	4.4	2.1	6.18	10.99
1963	9.8	5.9	16.7	7.4	16.9	26.3	9.8	8.1	8.9	0.3	2.8	6.86	11.65
1964	5.6	5.1	10.3	8.3	6.7	16.8	8.5	7.7	0.2	5.0	4.1	6.16	8.59
1965	7.4	6.3	9.0	8.9	13.4	16.8	10.9	6.4	12.8	2.7	4.3	6.59	9.30
1966	6.7	7.0	8.9	4.5	15.1	16.3	7.2	9.9	3.1	2.6	4.6	6.31	8.33
1967	4.7	9.5	6.2	3.3	13.6	13.4	7.0	9.8	6.0	3.2	3.9	5.49	7.37
1968	6.8	4.4	5.5	7.6	13.4	14.6	8.8	-1.8	11.5	6.0	7.0	7.51	8.12
1969	2.3	6.9	6.1	8.2	15.0	18.4	9.4	2.0	9.5	0.4	5.9	7.00	8.30
1970	-2.5	2.4	-1.3	6.4	21.7	18.3	10.6	7.3	9.8	6.4	3.8	5.80	8.15

(Weights:

GNP 1977)	(.0172)	(.0487)	(.0885)	(.1122)	(.0471)	(.1404)	(.0228)	(.0195)	(.0148)	(.0572)	(.4316)		
1971	10.3	12.7	13.7	12.0	22.9	25.5	16.7	9.0	18.2	11.8	6.8	12.45	16.74
1972	15.0	14.3	13.0	13.6	18.0	22.0	17.7	11.8	13.4	13.1	7.1	12.21	16.10
1973	9.8	14.5	9.9	5.8	21.1	26.2	7.4	9.6	-1.0	8.6	7.3	11.06	13.91
1974	6.8	9.3	12.6	6.0	16.6	13.1	3.1	16.3	-1.7	4.8	5.0	7.78	9.88
1975	12.4	13.8	9.9	13.8	8.3	10.3	18.7	15.2	2.4	15.6	4.7	8.83	11.96
1976	9.6	8.0	15.0	10.4	20.5	14.2	11.8	14.0	7.3	13.8	5.7	9.91	13.10
1977	8.0	8.4	7.5	8.3	19.8	7.0	14.3	8.3	4.7	14.4	7.6	8.72	9.57
1978	6.7	10.0	11.2	13.4	23.7	10.8	5.3	13.6	12.7	20.1	8.2	10.99	13.11
1979	3.5	6.9	12.2	7.4	23.9	9.9	2.7	12.7	7.8	11.5	7.7	9.23	10.39
1980	-0.2	6.3	8.0	2.4	15.9	0.8	4.2	21.1	-5.4	4.9	6.2	5.53	5.01
1981	3.6	4.3	12.3	1.2	11.1	3.7	2.6	12.0	-0.9	10.0	7.2	6.50	5.96
1982	3.4	2.0	14.9	3.5	9.9	7.1	4.9	9.8	3.1	8.3	6.5	6.96	7.31
1983	5.0	10.2	12.1	10.3	17.3	3.0	10.6	11.4	7.6	13.4	11.1	10.10	9.48
1984	3.3	2.3	8.2[b]	3.3	8.4[b]	2.9	4.1	2.4[b]	2.5[b]	14.9[b]	6.9	6.08	5.45

Source: Federal Reserve Bank of St. Louis, *International Economic Conditions*, June and August 1985.

[a]United States excluded.

[b]Preliminary

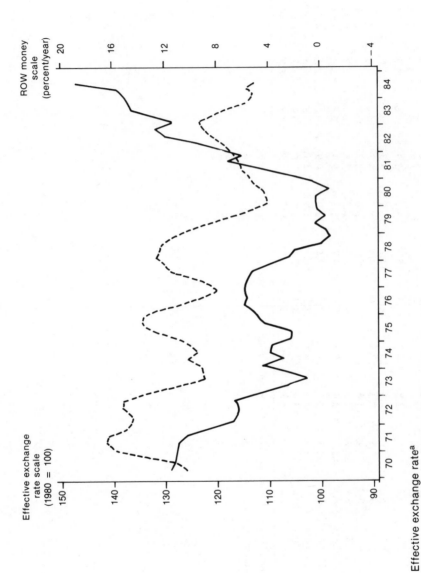

Effective exchange
rate scale
(1980 = 100)

ROW money
scale
(percent/year)

—————— Effective exchange rate[a]

– – – – – ROW money[b] (rate of change, smoothed)

[a]International Monetary Fund definition: MERM (trade) weighted nominal rate against seventeen countries.
[b]Percent growth in nominal money in ten industrial countries other than U.S. (see table 6–1).

Figure 6–1. U.S. Effective Exchange Rate and Money in the Rest of the World, Quarterly Observations, 1970–84

Although threatening to undermine the U.S. free trade ethic, the overvaluation of the dollar in the early 1980s had one significant advantage. The international concern over chronic U.S. inflation is now largely dissipated. Indeed, Japan has deflation while Germany and the United States have similarly low rates of price inflation, as shown in table 6–2. Thus 1985 is a good time to negotiate a new agreement for stabilizing exchange rates—at a much lower foreign exchange value for the dollar—while keeping international price inflation close to zero (see addendum).

For any new exchange rate agreement to be successful, however, the flaw in the old one must be corrected. In cooperation with other central banks, the U.S. Federal Reserve System must give exchange rate stability more weight in the future conduct of U.S. monetary policy. Speculative pressure is now too great for Japan or European countries to stabilize dollar exchange rates on their own; many have tried (and failed) to do so in recent years—particularly in the turbulent months of late 1984 and early 1985.

A New Monetary Order for the 1980s

Assume now that in making U.S. monetary policy, the Federal Reserve System abandons its traditional insular approach, which virtually ignores the foreign exchanges. By some miracle, suppose that the Bank of Japan, the Bundesbank (representing the European bloc), and the Fed all agree to coordinate their monetary policies to achieve exchange stability.

How could such a system be efficiently managed to nudge the dollar down in the foreign exchanges without significant inflationary consequences? Once this transition is completed, how can fixed exchange rates and stable prices be maintained?

Announcement effects are as important as the fact of monetary cooperation itself. To harness the market's expectations in favor of the new exchange rate regime, the three central banks must spell out what they intend to do in a consistent fashion. Only then will the required adjustments in national monetary policies turn out to be minimal.

So what should the triumvirate announce? The new monetary order would have four essential elements:

1. Explicit target zones for the yen–dollar and mark–dollar exchange rates;
2. A commitment to adjust domestic monetary policies symmetrically among the three countries to achieve these targets;
3. Rules for restrained, but decisive, direct interventions to correct "disorderly conditions" in the foreign exchanges;

Table 6–2
Price Inflation in Tradable Goods, Eleven Industrial Countries, 1958–84

(percentage change in annual averages of wholesale price indexes)

	Belgium	Canada	France	Germany	Italy	Japan	Nether-lands	Sweden	Switzer-land	United Kingdom	United States	World Average	Rest of World[a]
Weights: GNP 1964	(.0132)	(.0394)	(.0778)	(.0892)	(.0494)	(.0681)	(.0144)	(.0167)	(.0113)	(.0796)	(.5408)		
1958	−4.4	0.4	5.1	−0.5	−1.7	−6.5	−1.3	4.3	−3.2	0.8	1.5	0.68	−0.30
1959	−0.3	0.8	7.2	−0.8	−2.9	0.9	0.2	0.9	−1.6	0.3	0.2	0.57	1.00
1960	1.2	0.2	3.5	1.3	0.8	1.1	0.0	4.1	0.6	1.3	0.2	0.81	1.54
1961	−0.2	0.2	3.0	1.5	0.0	1.1	−0.2	2.2	0.2	2.6	−0.4	0.47	1.50
1962	0.8	1.1	0.6	0.9	3.2	−1.6	0.3	4.7	3.3	2.3	0.2	0.64	1.16
1963	2.5	1.3	2.9	0.5	5.3	1.6	2.4	2.9	3.9	1.0	−0.4	0.72	2.03
1964	4.7	0.9	3.5	1.0	3.0	0.4	6.1	3.4	1.3	3.1	0.2	1.15	2.27
1965	1.1	1.3	0.7	2.5	1.8	0.7	3.0	5.2	0.6	3.5	2.0	1.98	1.95
1966	2.1	2.9	2.8	1.7	1.5	2.4	5.0	6.4	1.9	2.9	3.4	3.02	2.57
1967	−0.9	1.9	−0.9	−1.0	−0.2	1.7	1.0	4.3	0.3	3.1	0.2	0.45	0.75
1968	0.2	2.2	−1.7	−0.7	0.6	1.0	1.9	2.0	0.1	4.1	2.4	1.68	0.83
1969	5.0	3.7	10.7	1.9	3.6	2.0	−2.5	3.5	2.8	3.7	3.9	3.99	4.09
1970	4.7	2.4	7.5	5.0	7.4	3.7	4.6	6.8	4.2	7.1	3.6	4.54	5.65

(Weights: GNP 1977)(.0172)	(.0487)	(.0885)	(.1122)	(.0471)	(.1404)	(.0228)	(.0195)	(.0148)	(.0572)	(.4316)		
1971	-0.5	2.0	2.1	4.3	3.3	-0.8	4.5	3.2	2.1	9.1	3.3	2.94	2.67
1972	4.0	4.3	4.7	2.5	4.1	0.8	5.1	4.6	3.6	5.3	4.4	3.74	3.24
1973	12.4	11.2	14.7	6.6	17.2	15.8	6.9	10.3	10.7	7.4	13.1	12.42	11.91
1974	16.8	19.1	29.1	13.5	40.8	31.4	9.6	25.3	16.2	22.6	18.8	22.00	24.43
1975	1.2	11.2	-5.7	4.6	8.5	3.0	6.7	6.4	-2.3	22.2	9.3	6.93	5.12
1976	7.1	5.1	7.4	3.7	23.8	5.0	7.8	9.0	-0.7	17.3	4.6	6.58	8.09
1977	2.4	7.9	5.6	2.7	16.6	1.9	5.8	9.2	0.3	19.8	6.1	6.35	6.55
1978	-1.9	9.3	4.3	1.2	8.4	-2.5	1.3	7.6	-3.4	9.1	7.8	4.99	2.86
1979	6.3	14.4	13.3	4.8	15.5	7.3	2.7	12.5	3.8	12.2	12.5	10.73	9.39
1980	5.8	13.5	8.8	7.5	20.1	17.8	8.2	13.9	5.1	16.3	14.0	13.33	12.82
1981	8.2	10.1	11.0	7.7	16.6	1.7	9.2	11.6	5.8	10.6	9.0	8.50	8.13
1982	7.7	6.0	11.1	5.8	13.9	1.8	6.6	12.6	2.6	8.6	2.1	4.80	6.85
1983	5.2	3.5	11.0	1.5	10.5	-2.2	1.8	11.2	0.5	5.5	1.3	2.73	3.82
1984	7.4	4.1	13.3	2.9	10.4	-0.2	4.2	7.9	3.3	6.2	2.4	3.98	5.18

Source: International Financial Statistics, 1984 Yearbook; July, 1985, line 63, wholesale price indexes including finished goods and primary products.

aUnited States excluded.

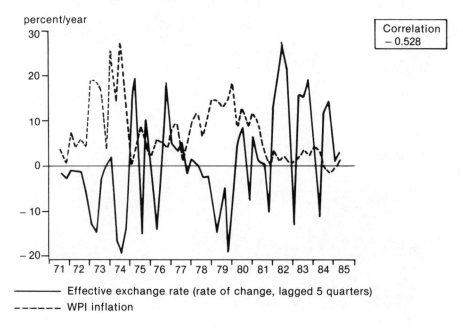

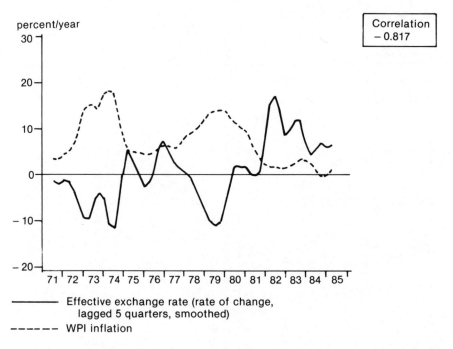

Figure 6–2. U.S. Effective Exchange Rate and the Wholesale Price Index, 1971–85

4. Joint management of aggregate money growth within the triumvirate in order to stabilize their common price level in the longer run.

I will now discuss each in turn.

Target Zones for Exchange Rates

Exchange rate targets would be designed and announced to achieve a rough purchasing power parity among the three countries, taking their current stable price levels as benchmarks. Illustrative calculations suggest that about 2.2 marks and 210 yen to the dollar—far under today's market quotations—approximate what the triumvirate should strive for.

(Warning: Economists have to understand that these exchange rate targets are designed to align national price levels, not to correct bilateral or multilateral trade deficits or surpluses. Even if the dollar were nudged down so that the U.S. price level became better aligned with those of Germany and Japan, the large U.S. fiscal deficit would still stimulate excessive consumption and leave a large U.S. trade deficit, albeit one that was somewhat smaller.)

Because of the current substantial difference in interest rates between the United States and the other two countries, a broad 10-percent band should be established around these two central rates. To illustrate, the dollar could be targeted to stay within a range of 2.10 and 2.30 marks, and within 200 to 220 yen.

In view of the present extreme misalignment of the dollar, these target zones are necessarily "soft" (Williamson, 1983). That is, the participating central banks are not committed to achieving them immediately. In particular, any massive official intervention in the foreign exchanges to push rates in the desired direction would be ruled out.

Nevertheless, the targets are real enough. The gnomes would clearly understand the direction in which the central banks were pushing. In view of the misinformation and confusion that now prevails in the exchange markets, a clear official declaration of exchange rate goals would allow private expectations to coalesce in support—provided that the accompanying program of monetary adjustment were credible.

Mutual Monetary Adjustment

Among the three countries, monetary adjustments would take place symmetrically for as long as the relevant exchange rate was outside its target zone—whether that be weeks, months, or years. When the dollar exchange rate was above its target zone(s), the Fed would expand the money supply and reduce interest rates while the Bundesbank and Bank of Japan contracted symmetrically (and act conversely if the dollar were ever to fall below its target range). In this way, the total "world" money supply would remain roughly constant, but relative amounts of constituent currencies would fluctuate to meet the demand for them.

For example, suppose that the current mark–dollar exchange rate were 2.80, that the Fed's normal long-term annual growth rate for *M-1* were between 4 and 6 percent, and that the Bundesbank's normal growth in what it calls "central bank" money were also between 4 and 6 percent. Then the Fed would be publicly committed to increasing its money growth above 6 percent (possibly reducing interest rates), while the Bundesbank would keep its money growth below 4 percent (possibly raising interest rates), until the mark–dollar rate fell below 2.3 marks and into its target zone.

To be successful in changing traders' expectations to push the mark–dollar exchange rate in the desired direction, this commitment to mutual monetary adjustment must be unambiguous. To avoid adverse expectations, other potentially conflicting rules need to be jettisoned.

For example, the surprisingly sharp rise of the dollar within two weeks in February 1985 from 3.2 to about 3.47 marks (DM) was due at least in part to an apparent conflict in the U.S. Federal Reserve System's immediate monetary objectives. In November and again in December 1984, the Fed cut the discount rate and embarked on much faster money growth; it correctly noted that such expansion was warranted because (among other factors) the dollar at 3.0 DM was grossly overvalued even then. And for November, December, and January, growth in U.S. *M-1* spurted to more than 11 percent measured on an annual basis.

However, in January the Fed then published — as required by the U.S. Congress — its money growth targets for all of 1985. A normal 4- to 7-percent growth range for *M-1* during 1985 was announced. Unfortunately, this published money growth target conflicted with the higher money growth actually taking place in early 1985. In February and March, actual *M-1* was far above the cone of "permissible" levels officially published.

The market came to expect that the Fed would have to contract to get *M-1* back on its "normal" path. In anticipation, U.S. interest rates rose sharply in February 1985, and drove the dollar up further in the foreign exchanges. This surge into dollar assets assumed panic proportions when Fed Chairman Paul Volcker, testifying before Congress on February 20, suggested that the Fed would end the progressively easier credit policy adopted in late 1984.

Clearly the Fed should have made clear that monetary ease would continue indefinitely, and that lower long-term growth in *M-1* would not be resumed until the dollar had fallen into its target zone. Fortunately, however, the Fed did persist with a higher rate of domestic monetary expansion — about 12 percent per year through mid-1985 — as if it were keying on the dollar exchange without admitting it. Finally, on July 16, 1985, in its midyear report to the U.S. Congress, the Fed officially abandoned its old 1985 target of 4- to 7-percent money and "rebased" the money supply at its new higher level. It then respecified domestic money growth to be 3 to 8 percent, from this now higher base, for the remainder of 1985.

Even without the dollar exchange rate as an official target, this massive additional monetary expansion undoubtedly helped prevent the dollar from increasing further. By mid-August 1985, it had fallen back to 2.8 marks — still considerably overvalued, and about where it was the year before. But the effect on the exchange rate was lessened because the Fed's stated intentions were (and are) somewhat ambiguous about how far it might like to push the dollar down.

The credibility of this unusual seeming attempt by the Fed to key on the exchange rate was further undermined by the absence of any agreement on how foreign central banks would react. Those countries with weak currencies — most particularly the European bloc — should have reduced their money growth below normal when the Fed undertook its unusual expansion in late 1984. Downward pressure on the dollar would then have come from both sides.

If, instead, the German and Japanese central banks behaved perversely by expanding in tandem with the Fed in 1985, the private markets would have no assurance that the dollar would be successfully pushed down. Not knowing what the other central banks were going to do, private speculators were less likely to support the Fed's actions by anticipating dollar depreciation.

Clearly, monetary adjustments by one central bank are much more likely to succeed in influencing the exchange rate if the market knows that the other two are supporting it. Thus one can see the great value of a formal, well-publicized international agreement on the format for monetary coordination.

Official Intervention in the Foreign Exchanges

The fact, or even the possibility, of direct official intervention in the foreign exchanges captures newspaper headlines. As the U.S. government agonizes over what to do about the exchange rate, the immediate focus is on whether or not the Federal Reserve Bank of New York — in consultation with the U.S. Treasury and the Federal Reserve System — should intervene as a buyer or seller of foreign exchange.

On March 8, 1985, the Federal Reserve Bank of New York announced that it had intervened to buy deutsche marks seven times between August and January in relatively modest amounts (for this huge market) of $100 or $200 million in each case. The European and Japanese central banks were known to have intervened more often and more heavily over the same period. As usual, the Fed refused to reveal the details of its more recent and substantially heavier interventions in February and early March 1985.

But this emphasis on direct intervention is misplaced, and so is some of the secrecy that veils the precise goals of these interventions.

With the integration of the U.S., European, and Japanese capital markets, gross stocks of private financial claims on — and liabilities to — foreigners tend to dwarf official exchange reserves. For example, by the end of 1983, private Japanese claims on foreigners were about ten times as high as official exchange reserves; and with the further Japanese financial liberalization in 1984, these gross private claims again increased. In financially open European economies such as Germany and Britain, the ratios of gross private claims on foreigners to official exchange reserves are even greater than in the Japanese case.

The upshot is that exchange reserves are too small for direct government intervention to have a significant impact on the huge internationally mobile private holdings of stocks and bonds. Indeed, ample evidence in 1984–85 suggests that official attempts to intervene in the absence of monetary coordination, and without influencing the (adverse) expectations of private traders, did wash out for all practical purposes. For stabilizing the exchange rate, official intervention will be ineffective *unless* it is accompanied by a supporting monetary policy. And these mutual monetary adjustments — as already described — need not require direct interventions in the foreign exchanges.

That said, there remains a limited role for direct official intervention to correct disorderly conditions in exchange markets over a short period — say, one trading day.

Having posted target zones for exchange rates (according to the hypothetical monetary agreement), the triumvirate of central banks could treat as "disorderly" any substantial exchange rate movement away from these official targets. For example, if the target is 2.1 to 2.3 DM per dollar, and the rate suddenly moves from 2.8 to 3.0 or more, then the market is disorderly: the movement is both large and in the wrong direction.

Indeed, such a perverse movement indicates either that private traders are not properly informed of official intentions or that the official exchange rate targets lack credibility. To reaffirm the central banks' objective of guiding exchange rates into their target zones, some stabilizing intervention is warranted.

To be both limited in magnitude and decisive in result, any such intervention should be reinforced by discrete monetary adjustments beyond previous measures. This is most easily accomplished by ensuring that interventions in the foreign exchanges are *symmetrically unsterilized* in their impact on each country's monetary base.

For example, to prevent the dollar from increasing further, suppose the

Bundesbank—in consultation with the Fed—purchases $200 million worth of marks in the open foreign exchange market. They could agree that the Bundesbank would retire those marks from circulation while the Fed expanded the U.S. monetary base by $200 million. Consequently, interest rates would likely rise in Germany and fall in the United States, thus helping to drive the dollar down.

This is powerful medicine. If the distribution of monetary base between the two countries is affected, even modest official exchange interventions have great leverage, as private traders will quickly realize.

Need Dollar Depreciation Be Inflationary?

Suppose the dollar exchange rate is pushed down into the target zones just suggested. Is it possible to avoid reigniting the kind of rapid price inflation associated with the depreciating dollar of the unhappy 1970s?

Yes, because of the inherent symmetry in the above proposal for monetary coordination. When the Fed expands, the other principal central banks contract below normal growth—and vice versa. The result is no unusual growth in the monetary base for the system as a whole, even as the dollar is pushed down to its purchasing power parity.

The great dollar depreciations of the 1970s were associated with increased monetary growth in the United States coupled with sometimes explosive monetary growth in Europe and Japan, as shown in table 6–1. The reason for this loss of monetary control abroad was foreign central banks' resisting (not very successfully) having their own currencies appreciate when international portfolio preferences had shifted sharply away from dollar assets. Through direct interventions to buy dollars and sell their own monies, or through equivalent domestic monetary expansions to reduce interest rates, they lost monetary control.[1]

This fundamental asymmetry in the world dollar standard, where other central banks react to the dollar exchange rate but the Fed usually does not, is seen in figure 6–3. For 1971 through 1985, one can see the strong negative correlation between percent changes in money growth in the rest of the industrial world (ROW) and percent changes in the dollar exchange rate. With unsmoothed individual quarterly observations, the simple correlation is − 0.305 as shown in the upper panel. The correlation becomes stronger at − 0.620 if a five-quarter moving average is used, as shown in the lower panel of figure 6–3.

The system went askew in the 1970s because the U.S. Federal Reserve System failed to contract when international demand unexpectedly shifted into foreign currencies at a time when the dollar was not overvalued, at least not overvalued by today's standards. Because the principal player, the Fed,

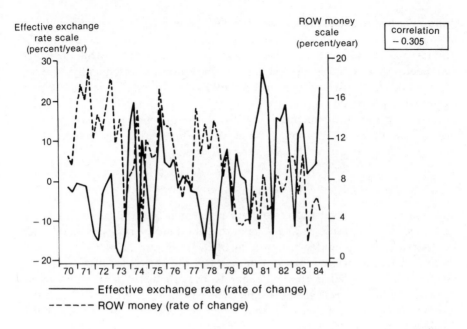

correlation
− 0.305

Effective exchange
rate scale
(percent/year)

ROW money
scale
(percent/year)

——— Effective exchange rate (rate of change)

- - - - - ROW money (rate of change)

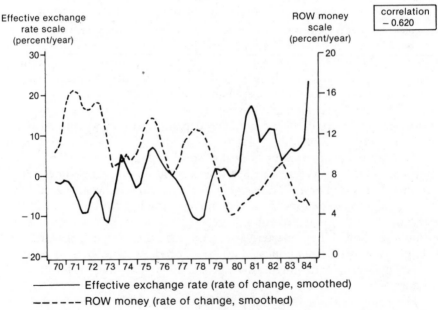

correlation
− 0.620

Effective exchange
rate scale
(percent/year)

ROW money
scale
(percent/year)

——— Effective exchange rate (rate of change, smoothed)

- - - - - ROW money (rate of change, smoothed)

Figure 6–3. U.S. Effective Exchange Rate and Money in the Rest of the World, 1970–84

was not playing the game correctly, the other central banks were simply overwhelmed.

Accidental or not, the great increase in "world" money growth in the 1970s had a strong inflationary impact on the prices of internationally tradable goods, whether manufactures or primary commodities. And all the major industrial economies experienced this price inflation (see table 6–2), particularly those such as the United States whose currencies had depreciated relative to the others. Undoubtedly, these foreign monetary repercussions help explain why fluctuations in the dollar exchange rate display the strong (lagged) effects on the U.S. price level shown in figure 6–2.[2]

Through mid-September 1985, however, the situation was quite different. The dollar was truly overvalued by any reasonable standard. The portfolio pressure in the foreign exchanges was strongly in favor of dollar assets — which increases the derived demand for U.S. base money. The situation was one of price stability — indeed, one of undue deflationary pressure in those sectors of the U.S. economy that must compete on world markets.

In these circumstances, it would be relatively safe to increase monetary expansion in the United States to drive the dollar down — and dangerous not to. But as long as the Fed remains expansionary, the other central banks must agree to maintain tight money during the transitional correction in the dollar exchange rate. Once exchange rates were aligned, the three central banks would, ideally, have also agreed to manage their joint money supply to stabilize the common price level into the indefinite future. Then private expectations would be favorable, and the unfortunate inflationary experience of the 1970s need not be repeated.

Of course, even if the dollar depreciates under these controlled circumstances, there will be a one-time increase in the dollar prices of tradable goods, and a simultaneous decrease in their prices when measured in marks or yen. But this change in relative prices is necessary to rescue unprotected American farmers, manufacturers, and miners from heavy taxation imposed on them by the dollar's overvaluation, and to prevent an outbreak of protectionism in the United States.

After this one-and-for-all correction in the dollar exchange rate, the principal central banks would begin their regular program of ongoing coordination. Nominal exchange rates would be kept within their preassigned bands and the common international price level would be better stabilized into the indefinite future. Governments could then more realistically negotiate new rounds of the General Agreement on Tariff and Trade (GATT) to remove nontariff barriers — many of which developed in the era of floating exchange rates — and the modest remaining tariff barriers. With a sufficiently stable international price level, even the difficult job of liberalizing trade in agricultural products would be more likely to succeed.

Addendum

After these comments were completed, on the weekend of September 21–22, 1985, a major exchange rate agreement was announced among the finance ministers and central bank heads of the five principal industrial countries: Britain, France, Germany, Japan, and the United States. Their stated intention was to undertake strong financial measures (measures not spelled out) to drive the dollar down. The announcement's effect was quite dramatic—the dollar fell by more than 10 percent over two trading days. That a better alignment for the dollar exchange rate has now become an objective of official policy is a major step forward in the preservation of free international trade.

On the other hand, it is far from clear that the officials involved have worked out a sufficiently coordinated program of mutual and symmetrical monetary adjustment, as sketched above, to sustain a better alignment of exchange rates and preserve price stability into the future. No details of a monetary program were released at the September meeting. Rather, the emphasis seemed to be on massive official interventions in the foreign exchange markets—which, however big, will tend to wash out unless the market views such interventions as harbingers of monetary adjustment to come.

Similarly, the agreement hinted that the Europeans and Japanese would cut taxes. But, as just suggested, the exchange rate effects of such fiscal adjustments by themselves are ambiguous.

Whether a coherent program of monetary coordination successfully evolves remains to be seen. However, the signs now, in January 1986, seem more favorable than I had previously dared hope.

Throughout 1985, the three principal central banks in fact supported the intentions of U.S., Japanese, and European officials to drive the dollar down. Growth in U.S. *M-1* was a relatively expansionary 12 percent, whereas German and Japanese *M-1* growth was much more restrained—about 5.5 percent. Equally important, the governor of the Bank of Japan formally announced on October 24, 1985, that, in order to keep the yen down in the foreign exchange markets, Japanese money growth would be restricted for the rest of the year.

The result of these several actions was an engineered fall in the dollar from as much as 3.4 DM and 260 yen in February 1985 to about 2.45 marks and 200 yen by December. These nominal rates are now (January 1986) much closer to any reasonable estimate of purchasing power parity.

However, the exchange system is not yet secured by a well-understood international agreement on future monetary coordination. If, for example, the dollar were to begin falling sharply to much below its present rough purchasing power parity, the three central banks should be prepared to quickly reverse roles: the Federal Reserve should tighten up as the Bundesbank and

Bank of Japan both undertook monetary ease. Then one could rest better assured that the principle of symmetrical monetary coordination had finally been accepted.

Notes

1. For a more complete description of how the international money multiplier works, see R. McKinnon (1982).

2. This chapter has not dealt with the precise definition of monetary targets for the three countries that would secure price stability in the longer run. This subject is treated in McKinnon, 1984, chap. 5. Such a monetary program would avoid sharp changes in the collective money supply while gearing its long-term growth to maintain a stable purchasing power over a common, broad basket of internationally tradable goods.

References

Frenkel, Jacob, and Michael Mussa. "The Efficiency of the Foreign Exchange Market and Measures of Turbulence." *American Economic Review* 70, no. 2 (May 1980).

———. "Asset Markets, Exchange Rates, and the Balance of Payments." In R. Jones and P. Kenen (eds.), *Handbook of International Economics,* vol. 2. Amsterdam: North-Holland, 1985.

McKinnon, Ronald I. "A New Tripartite Monetary Agreement or a Limping Dollar Standard?" *Essays in International Finance* no. 106. Princeton, N.J.: Princeton University, 1974.

———. "Currency Substitution and Instability in the World Dollar Standard." *American Economic Review* 72, no. 80 (June 1982).

———. *An International Standard for Monetary Stabilization.* Washington, D.C.: Institute for International Economics, 1984.

———. "The Dollar Exchange Rate as a Leading Indicator for American Monetary Policy." Palo Alto, Calif.: Stanford University, 1985 (unpublished).

Williamson, John. *The Exchange Rate System.* Washington, D.C.: Institute for International Economics, 1983.

Comments

Roger E. Brinner

T he chapter by Professor Ronald I. McKinnon presents arguments that the international business cycle can be tamed with a better alignment of exchange rates if the principal industrial countries agree to coordinate their monetary policies. The chapter itself, however, is devoted to defending narrower hypotheses: first, that nominal exchange rates can and should be stabilized through the collaboration of central banks, and second, that the U.S. price level would not be any higher had collaborative policies been pursued during the 1980s.

I can agree theoretically with the first of these hypotheses, but only with a number of reservations. I do agree that the exchange rate movements can be largely explained by monetary-financial parameters. I believe that the real exchange rate is primarily driven by real interest spreads. However, I have a great deal of both theoretical and practical trouble with the second hypothesis.

My major objection to the first is that fiscal policy coordination must also be far greater than admitted in the chapter if the McKinnon-requested monetary policy collaboration is to be feasible. McKinnon's law of macroeconomic policy is apparently: "The early bird gets the economic recovery." Specifically, the first nation to pursue expansionary fiscal policy must be given the right (indeed the obligation in the McKinnon regime) to pursue expansionary monetary policy *and* all other nations must pursue symmetrically contractionary monetary policies. I can agree that this scheme would possibly reduce the exchange rate reactions to fiscal policy initiatives by reducing the likely spreads in interest rates. However, I doubt if such a regime would reduce global business cycles, and I am fairly certain that it would augment the cross-country differences in growth rates and inflation rates.

Professor McKinnon's second proposition seems to be that U.S. inflation and the price level would not be appreciably different under alternative monetary regimes as long as global liquidity is similar. This does not seem likely to me. Taking the 1982–85 Reagan-Volcker era as a case study, had monetary policies been as requested by McKinnon, U.S. exports and credit-sensitive domestic spending would certainly have been stronger and imports weaker; the reverse would have been true for Europe and Japan. Would this not produce higher U.S. inflation and lower foreign inflation? I believe that the only conceivable way that inflation would not accelerate is if all of the extra demand produced by the fiscal stimulus were met by foreign production. This is an open economy, international version of the old crowding out hypothesis in its most extreme form, perhaps tied to the strictest possible interpretation of the so-called international "law of one price." Only such an extreme theoretical position could avoid inflation and business cycle repercussions in a McKinnon regime.

Moreover, is it conceivable that continental European parliamentary governments and their closely controlled central banks would have acceded to such a regime? Admittedly, since 1981, the U.S. unemployment rate has not fallen below 7 percent, but European unemployment has steadily risen in spite of the strong locomotive effects produced by extraordinary exports to the United States due to the overvalued dollar. I think the United States has been lucky that the European nations have been willing to be as conservative in their monetary policies as they have been in the face of strange U.S. fiscal policies. McKinnon's regime would have asked them to accept an even more intense and prolonged recession than they have faced.

In arguing against a fiscal policy explanation for today's international interest rate spreads and the resultant exchange rate misalignments, Professor McKinnon goes beyond simple devil's advocacy. Given the widespread acceptance in 1985 of the federal budget deficit as the prime source of financial market imbalances, a reminder of the role of monetary policy here and abroad is certainly useful, but his denial of fiscal impacts is extreme. This denial relies on contentions that either monetary policies could offset the fiscal impact or that changes in fiscal policy would induce offsetting shifts in currency demand curves through safe haven and inflation expectation effects.

The first argument certainly misses the point: *ceteris paribus,* fiscal stimulus by one nation requires it to draw a larger share of global savings. This should be expected to require a rise in this nation's real, expected borrowing costs relative to other nations. Technically, a movement along the private savings supply curve to that stimulating nation is required. Professor McKinnon would offset this by calling forth exactly matching increases in central bank supplies of funds. His claim that "there is no *necessary* [emphasis added] relationship between fiscal deficits and movements in nominal exchange rates" is therefore narrowly correct, but thoroughly misleading as a piece of policy advice. There is indeed a "necessary" relationship unless McKinnon's law is followed.

So much for theoretical considerations. What is the empirical evidence, at least as interpreted by the DRI model and associated research? One set of answers is provided by a set of counterfactual simulations of alternative monetary and fiscal policies during the period of McKinnon's exchange rate commentary, namely the Carter and Reagan presidencies. These simulations point to very important roles for both monetary and fiscal policy in the late 1970s drop in the dollar and its subsequent extreme rise. They confirm McKinnon's contention that the exchange rate has had a pronounced impact on domestic inflation, but they also make it very clear that his preferred match-up of stimulative U.S. fiscal and monetary policies would have produced significant added inflation in the United States. Such inflation would be unavoidable unless Europe and Japan had accepted extremely severe recessions. However, in that case, foreign prices would have fallen and McKinnon's nominal exchange rate stabilization program would have still left the United States with a pronounced *real* appreciation of the dollar and hence much the same protectionist pressure he mentions in his opening paragraph. The bottom line clearly is that there must be full consistency in both monetary and fiscal policies if real exchange rate stability is to be achieved.

Index

Abel, A., 137
Abrams, R.K., 90, *129*
"Absolute" interest parity, 47
Absorption approach to balance of payments, 185
Accounting, national income, 140, 184–186
Adjustment, mutual monetary, 223–225, 226
Age composition of population, private saving rate and, 39
Air travel, costs of, 10–13
Aizenman, J., 194, *203*
Alexander, S.S., 185, *203*
Alexander, W.E., 128n.25, *129*
Aliber, R., 48, *64*
Allen, P.R., *31, 31*, 195, *203*
Announcement effects, 219
Antitrust enforcement, international legal aspects of, 22, 23n.7
Arbitrage, 21, 48–49, 50, 54, 56
Argy, V., 62n.16, *64*
Articles of Agreements of the International Monetary Fund, 193
Assets, U.S.: foreign ownership of financial, 7–8; private ownership abroad, 6–7; valuation changes in, 145, 159n.5
Assignment problem, policy, 172–182, 207–208; capital mobility and, role of, 176–182; Mundell's solution to, 173–176
Atwood, J., 23, 23n.7
Autonomy, monetary, 16–18
Autoregression analysis. *See* Vector autoregression (VAR) analysis of economic interdependence

Balance of payments: absorption approach to, 185; credit expansion rate and, 182, 183, 184; demand for money and, 182, 183; deterioration in 1980s of, 138–144; determining current account of, 185; monetary approach to, 182, 183–186. *See also* Deficit, U.S. trade
Balance of trade, components of, 186
"Bandwagon" effects, 117
Bank of Canada, 117, 126
Bank of Japan, 214, 219, 223, 230, 231
Banks: foreign, in U.S., 7; IBFs, 21, 159n.7; U.S., foreign assets and liabilities of, 6, 7, 146; U.S., increased capital inflow going through, 165; central, international cooperation of, 219–229
Barriers: of distance, decline of, 10–14; to integration of financial markets, 63n.26; tariff, 10
Barro, R.J., 160n.23, *161*
Bartzak, T., 77n
Batten, D.S., 80, *129*, 129n.32
Baumgartner, U., *64*
Benign neglect attitude, 199–200
Bidirectional causality, 79, 107–108
Blinder, A.S., 160nn.19, 23, *161*
Blume, M., 63n.22, *66*
Blundell-Wignall, A., 127n.9, *130*
Bodie, Z., 160n.14, *161*
Boothe, P.M., 48, 61n.5, 63n.26, *64*, 128nn.21, 22, 29, *129, 130*
Bordo, M.D., 128n.26, *129*, 129n.32
Bosworth, B., 61n.4, *64*

Contributing Authors

Roger E. Brinner, group vice president and chief economist, Data Resources, Inc.

Richard N. Cooper, professor of economics, Harvard University

Jeffrey A. Frankel, professor of economics, University of California, Berkeley

Jacob A. Frenkel, professor of economics, University of Chicago

Benjamin M. Friedman, professor of economics, Harvard University

R.W. Hafer, research officer, Federal Reserve Bank of St. Louis

John Huizinga, professor, Graduate School of Business, University of Chicago

Peter B. Kenen, professor of economics, Harvard University

John Kuszczak, economist, Bank of Canada

Ronald I. McKinnon, professor of economics, Stanford University

Frederic S. Mishkin, professor, Graduate School of Business, Columbia University

John D. Murray, research adviser, Bank of Canada

William Poole, professor of economics, Brown University

Georg Rich, director, Swiss National Bank